D1715491

BEING AND EARTH

Paul Tillich's Theology of Nature

Michael F. Drummy

University Press of America
Lanham • New York • Oxford

Copyright © 2000 by
University Press of America,® Inc.

4720 Boston Way
Lanham, Maryland 20706

12 Hid's Copse Rd.
Cumnor Hill, Oxford OX2 9JJ

Library of Congress Cataloging-in-Publication Data

Drummy, Michael F.
Being and earth : Paul Tillich's theology of nature / Michael F. Drummy.
p. cm.
Includes bibliographical references and index.
1.   Tillich, Paul, 1886-1965—Contributions in doctrine of nature.
2. Nature—Religious aspects—Christianity. I. Title.
BT695.5.D78 2000   230'.092—dc21   00—056369 CIP

ISBN 0-7618-1791-3 (cloth: alk. ppr)

⊖™ The paper used in this publication meets the minimum
requirements of American National Standard for Information
Sciences—Permanence of Paper for Printed Library Materials,
ANSI Z39.48—1984

To my mother

Then God said to Noah and to his sons with him, "As for me, I am establishing my covenant with you and your descendants after you, and with every living creature that is with you, the birds, the domestic animals, and every animal of the earth with you, as many as came out of the ark..... This is the sign of the covenant that I make between me and you and every living creature that is with you, for all future generations: I have set my bow in the clouds, and it shall be a sign of the covenant between me and the earth."

Genesis 9:8-10, 12-13

'The earth and we' has...become a question of profound human concern and tormenting anxiety.... Our former naïve trust in the 'motherly' earth and her protective and preserving power has disappeared. It is possible that the earth may bear us no longer. We ourselves may prevent her from doing so. No heavenly sign, like the rainbow given to Noah as a promise that there would not be a second flood, has been given to us. We have no guarantee against man-made floods....

It may well be that we are living in such a moment...that man's relation to the earth and the universe will, for a long time, become the point of primary concern for sensitive and thoughtful people. Should this be the case, Christianity...will be compelled forward into the more daring inroads of the human spirit, risking new and unanswered questions,...but at the same time pointing to the direction of the eternal, the source and goal of man and his world.

Paul Tillich, from the sermon "Man and Earth" delivered on February 11, 1962 at Harvard University Memorial Church

Contents

Abbreviations of Works by Paul Tillich

BR	*Biblical Religion and the Search for Ultimate Reality.*
CB	*The Courage to Be.*
CEWR	*Christianity and the Encounter of the World Religions.*
DF	*Dynamics of Faith.*
EN	*The Eternal Now.*
FR	*The Future of Religions.*
GW	*Gesammelte Werke.*

HCT	*History of Christian Thought -- From Its Judaic and Hellenistic Origins to Existentialism.*
IH	*The Interpretation of History.*
IRCM	*The Irrelevance and Relevance of the Christian Message.*
LPJ	*Love, Power, and Justice.*
MB	*Morality and Beyond.*
MGS	*Mysticism and Guilt-Consciousness in Schelling's Philosophical Development.*
OTB	*On the Boundary: An Autobiographical Sketch.*
PE	*Political Expectation.*
PRE	*The Protestant Era.*
RS	*The Religious Situation.*
RV	*Religiöse Verwirklichung.*
SF	*The Shaking of the Foundations.*
SSTS	*The Spiritual Situation in Our Technical Society.*
ST	*Systematic Theology.*
TC	*Theology of Culture.*
WR	*What is Religion?*
WS	*The World Situation.*

Preface

Years ago, while vacationing in Vermont's remote Northeast Kingdom, I met a young man during a hike up Mount Pisgah. He was resting by the side of the trail near a precipice where the Department of Environmental Protection had instituted a program to re-introduce peregrine falcons. I sat down to join him. We munched on raisins and nuts, drank the water we had carried up with us, and watched the falcons soar and glide and dip. In the course of our conversation, he revealed that he had just recently moved to that area. I asked him what it was that prompted him to move to such an isolated region. I will never forget his response. In a very understated, matter-of-fact way he gestured toward the vista before us and said, simply, "For this." What was startling to me was that he mentioned neither career, nor family and friends, nor education, nor even financial security as reasons for his decision to move to this relatively unspoiled location. The *earth* itself was the cause of his relocation. His "this" signified both "earth" and "home". While there certainly existed a hint of escapism in his decision to move, I could not help but admire his passionate love for the earth and his willingness to act on it. We finally parted, went our separate ways, and have not seen each other since.

At the time, I lived, worked, and studied in the urban areas of southern New England and New York City that had for many years endured the ravages of mass industrialization, poor planning, and outright neglect. Air and water fouled; concrete and asphalt everywhere; major traffic congestion a daily occurrence; cities in crisis; the gap between rich and poor ever widening; native animal, insect, and plant species declining at an alarming rate. The quality of life was truly questionable. Here, the idea of "earth" was frequently suggestive of a commodity to be developed and subdivided, sold for a profit, or simply discarded or poisoned when it was of no further use. The experience of "earth" in this respect was regarded as anything but "home". A far cry from that which motivated my hiker friend to pick up and move to the mountains.

Also at that time I belonged (and still do) to a religious tradition that emphasized the notion that our true "home" lay beyond this world, that we are but pilgrims on this alien and hostile "earth". Despite the strong sacramental character of this tradition and its doctrine of the goodness of creation, I rarely recall ever hearing about the sacramentality of the earth *per se* as I sat in the pew, week after week (and, more often than not, day after day). I noticed that the elements used in the sacramental rites – water, wine, bread, oil – were largely appreciated for their instrumental and symbolic value only. The individual "sacraments" were administered by the church for the *spiritual* benefit of human beings alone. And while the Church certainly (and correctly) encouraged the pursuit of justice on behalf of the poor and the oppressed, it seldom included the plight of the earth under that rubric. The "earth" as a religious issue was simply not being discussed.

My hiker friend had stirred something deep within me that would not find full articulation for many years. How did I know then that I would discover in Paul Tillich (of all people!) a kindred spirit in my efforts to reconcile my religious faith with my innate reverence for the earth? And yet that is indeed what I found. Tillich's expansive vision of reality has helped me to understand the ecological crisis in terms of "ultimate concern". His analysis of the experience of finitude and anxiety as the way into the discussion of being and courage has enabled me to view the degradation of the planet as an issue of justice, requiring creative and responsible approaches to effectively deal with these problems.

Perhaps more than anything, however, I have been able to see through Tillich that there is nothing inconsistent with embracing the earth and remaining theologically authentic. Thanks to Tillich, today I can appreciate the earth as sacrament and recognize that as spiritual pilgrims we need not ignore this world. We can – and should – be both passionate lovers of the earth and religious seekers after God. It is my hope that this book conveys to others the hope and vision of a healthy planet and a vibrant faith that I encountered in the life, thought, and work of Paul Tillich.

It goes without saying that a project of this scope cannot be undertaken and brought to fulfillment without the help, advice, and support of many people. I would first of all like to thank Rick Grigg for introducing me many years ago to the richness and depth of Tillich's theological vision. His indefatigable support for this project – from its very precarious beginnings to its present form – was invaluable. As a second "mentor", Rick's direction and advice were always welcome and extremely helpful. Lest I forget, I must thank as well Christel Manning who, one evening in Walter Brooks' office, inadvertently suggested the topic for what would ultimately become the basis for this book – despite never having heard of Paul Tillich!

I also need to express my gratitude to Bob Cornelison, mentor and friend, whose encouragement, guidance, suggestions, editing, and insights are evident on every page of this book. Along with Bob, of course, I would like to thank Susan Simonaitis and Ewert Cousins, both of whom contributed by their comments and ideas to what is best in this book.

A special thanks is extended to Jane Owen and The Blaffer Trust, without whose financial support this project would never have seen the light of day. Moreover, Jane's sincere enthusiasm for seeing this work in print, and her genuine interest in "things Tillichean and natural", were most welcome and much appreciated. At the same time, the North American Paul Tillich Society deserves a "thank you" for allowing me the opportunity to meet Jane Owen, with a special thanks extended to Fred Parrella and Paul Carr. Beyond that, I would like to thank the Society for the important work it does in keeping alive the Tillich legacy and for encouraging the type of scholarship this book represents.

Without the many sacrifices and the loving commitment of my wife Joyce this book would have never been possible. Her tireless efforts to help me "stay on course" during times of doubt and indecision are too numerous to mention. It is no small task in an active family to keep distractions and interruptions to a minimum in order to ensure the success of a project like this. Her friendship, sense of humor, and wit were welcome oases in the lonely deserts one often finds oneself in during the writing of a book of this sort. I am grateful for her constancy, her unfailing dedication, and the tenderness of her forgiving heart.

I am of course indebted as well to many other family members and friends who assisted, facilitated, and tolerated my preoccupation with the preparation of this book. I would like to thank (in no particular order) my mother and father, Frank Seeburger, Carl Serbell, Roberta McKelvie, Jeremy Yunt, George Gordon, Tom O'Rourke, Susan Zucker, Kathi, Matt, Amy, Corky, Giacinta, Joyce Federlein, the guys from the Saturday Morning Meeting in Hamden, and, of course, Larissa and Dillon. If it were not for Jim Brownstein's generosity and willingness to let me work in a part-time capacity while the lion's share of this book was being researched and written, it would never have been completed. (Thank you, too, Howard.)

I owe a special measure of gratitude to Marla Kelley, whose assistance with the preparation of the final manuscript for publication was both timely and indispensable.

My daughter Erin was born during the latter stages of the writing of this book. While it is not formally dedicated to her, the presence of her precious little life in my own has made the subject of this book particularly poignant for me. It is my conviction that we must do everything we can to make the "earth" a more livable, more sustainable, and more meaningful "home" for future generations to inhabit. But even more than this, we must ensure the survival of the planet (to the extent that we can) not simply for the sake of our children and, hopefully, for their children as well, but for the sake of the planet itself – it deserves that much from us.

Finally, portions of Chapter Five of this book appeared in the April 2000 issue of *Worldviews: Environment, Culture, Religion* as an article entitled "Theonomy and Biology: Tillich's Ontology of Love as the Basis for an Environmental Ethic". The author gratefully acknowledges the consent of the editors of *Worldviews* to allow this material to be reproduced here in substantially the same form.

I would recommend that we give some sustained attention once again to the thought of the greatest – and sometimes least appreciated – modern American Reformation theologian, Paul Tillich. Tillich had a rich appreciation for nature and for the presence of God in nature.... Braaten...has called for a revival of interest in Tillich in the light of the new theology of hope. I would like to second the motion from the perspective of a yet-to-be produced Reformation theology of nature.[1]

Prolegomena

The Plight of the Planet

Over the last thirty years or so the worldwide ecological crisis has assumed a prominent place in our global consciousness. No longer is it possible to regard environmental problems as isolated, discrete events, aberrations of an otherwise healthy planet. Scarce a day passes now when we do not read about, hear of, or ourselves witness some environmental tragedy. Names and places like "Exxon Valdez," "Bhopal," and "Chernobyl" have become part of our collective vocabulary, giving rise to images of nearly incomprehensible suffering inflicted on both the human and non-human communities. In each of these disasters, what was often perceived as the most horrifying aspect of all was precisely the fact that they were not "isolated" or "containable" episodes but that, in fact, their occurrence produced an impact extending far beyond their immediate circumstances.[2]

Added to such headline-generating events as these are the less dramatic, though no less critical, continuous problems of "diminishing
natural resources; the increasing size of the human population;...losses of cultivable land through erosion and the growth of deserts; and the endangering of the life-support systems of the planet."[3]
If we also include such potential hazards as "global warming, holes in
the ozone layer, toxic wastes,...acid rain, drinking water contami-
nation, overflowing landfills, species extinction, destruction of the rain
forests, leakage of nuclear waste,...[and] lead poisoning," we are able
to construct a "litany of worry and woe"[4] that is truly alarming. In
fact, it can be said that problems such as these latter ones pose even
more of a threat than those of their more sensational counterparts
since they are much more numerous and their long-term effects are,
arguably, more devastating. The reason for this lies not merely in the
potential irreversible damage such problems may wreak on the planet
but, in their apparent benign progression, they are often overlooked
until it is, quite simply, too late.

Hence, whether the threat to the planet comes in the form of ex-
traordinary dramatic environmental catastrophes or by a gradual in-
sidious deterioration of natural ecosystems, what *is* indisputably evident is that the underlying fabric upon which all life on earth depends
appears to stand in the greatest peril.[5] This fabric consists of a complex network of interdependent relations in which the slightest alteration or abnormality in one part of the system can conceivably adversely
affect the entire web of life.

The Protestant Problematic and
The Tillichean Solution

The foregoing sobering diagnosis of the present health of the planet
raises questions concerning the causes of the current crisis. While it is
certainly outside the scope of this book to examine every factor that
has contributed to this crisis, I *will* argue that one of those factors is
the ambiguous attitude toward the non-human world that lies at the
heart of the Protestant theological tradition.[6] This ambiguity consists
in the fact that a significant emphasis on personal salvation through
grace alone can be observed within Protestantism which tends to severely limit the role of nature while, at the same time, there exists the

great Protestant "mystical-romantic" tradition which generally views the relationship between human beings and the earth more favorably. In its extreme forms, the former tradition (that which is most commonly associated with the Protestant Reform) has fostered attitudes of both indifference and outright hostility toward the material universe. In their devaluation of nature, these attitudes have provided (often unwittingly) a basis upon which to justify the wholesale neglect and devastation of the planet. This tradition in particular often suffers from what H. Paul Santmire has referred to as an "anthropocentric dynamics of grace."[7]

On the other hand, the latter tradition, that of the mystical-romantic, has occasionally taken its positive evaluation of the natural world to the point where the distinction between Creator and world becomes obscured; that is, it can tend toward a "deification" of nature. This tradition is often expressive of a revolt against the modern scientific and technological *Weltanschauung* associated with the Enlightenment. It will be argued, however, that this tradition has also contributed to the current ecocrisis insofar as it has sought, at times, to escape from the world into a form of "nature mysticism." While this mystical "flight from the world" seeks consolation and meaning in a communion with nature, it has nevertheless contributed, in turn, to a "back to nature" manner of thinking in the twentieth century that is characterized by a certain naïveté. It will be shown that this lack of realism on the part of the mystical-romantic tradition within Protestantism has thus, historically, encouraged (quite often unintentionally) the advance of the very phenomenon against which it has reacted, *viz.,* the ruin of the earth through unrestrained technological development.

It is the contention of this author that Paul Tillich's theological enterprise attempts to address and to resolve this ambiguity within Protestantism and, in so doing, recommends itself as a fertile and valuable resource for contemporary ecotheologians.[8] There can be found in Tillich a theology of nature that steered a middle course between a Barthian confessionalism, a sentimental romanticism, and a liberal Protestant technocratism. Accordingly, Tillich developed a complex understanding of the relationship among the divine, nature, history, science, and human beings.[9] This is because Tillich, rooted in an ontology tempered by what he referred to as the "Protestant principle,"[10] was able to formulate a genuine "theology of nature" that did not view Christianity as hostile or alien to nature. In acknowledging the need to unite this "Protestant principle" in his theological system with what he also characterized as the "Catholic substance,"[11] Tillich recognized the integrity of both the prophetic and the sacramental dimensions of the religious consciousness, and the problems that arise when they are considered as being in opposition to one another.

Moreover, Tillich "seems to share much of the Augustinian approach to nature and the Augustinian evaluation of nature. The question of the place and the validity of an exclusively technical or controlling knowledge of reality is one which Tillich frequently asks."[12] As early as 1945, for example, Tillich asks of the modern world if human mastery over nature through technological development has not deafened our ears to the "glory of the creation and its divine ground" of which the psalmist once sang:

> Are *we* able to perceive the hidden voice of nature? Does nature speak to us? Does it speak to you? Or has nature become silent to us...? Some of you may say, Never in any period of history was nature so open to man as it is today. The mysteries of the past have become the knowledge of children. Through every scientific book, through every laboratory, through every machine, nature speaks to us. The technical use of nature is the revelation of its mystery. Nature's voice *has* been heard by the scientific mind, and its answer is the conquest of nature. But is this all that nature says to us?
>
> Is...a communion between man and nature possible in our period of history? Is nature not completely subjected to the will and wilfulness of man? This technical civilization, the pride of mankind, has brought about a tremendous devastation of original nature, of landscape, of animals, of plants. It has kept genuine nature in small reservations and occupied everything for domination and ruthless exploitation.[13]

On the other hand, while Tillich throughout his life and work maintained a healthy skepticism toward the kind of unbridled technological progress that is generally associated with an Aristotelian inductive empiricism, he does not want to entirely deprecate technological or scientific achievement.[14] He is well aware that it is impossible to undo the centuries of scientific and technological development by going "back to nature" in some romanticized fashion.[15] Nor would he necessarily wish to, since he does acknowledge that science and technology, when utilized judiciously, can be of great benefit to us when dealing with problems related to the guardianship of the earth. Elsewhere, Tillich recognizes that technology too "must be liberated. Its mythos must also flow into the great mythos of the groaning of all living creatures and the yearning for a new being in which spirit and nature are reconciled."[16] In this respect Tillich's treatment of nature, in its attempt to bring technical reason into harmony with ontological reason,[17] will be shown to be consistent with what will be referred to as the Benedictine model of "creative stewardship."[18]

What will therefore be undertaken in this work is a critical retrieval of Paul Tillich's theology in an effort to ultimately provide the groundwork for an "ecology of being," or, more precisely, an "ecological ontology." The term "ecology of being" can be understood as a philosophical hermeneutic designed to maneuver a path through an analysis of the ontological structure of reality itself as it is made manifest in the current planetary crisis. In utilizing methodological elements borrowed from the biological science known as ecology, it seeks to uncover in the threat posed by this crisis the "saving power"[19] of Being. It is my contention that the appearance within the last generation of a degraded environment harbors within itself, at least potentially, the very means whereby such degradation can be overcome. In this way, I hope to substantiate Langdon Gilkey's claim that

> [a] Tillichean philosopher/theologian has much that is relevant to say about the spiritual origins of the present ecological crisis and a good number of categories to offer that may be helpful in the rethinking of the relation of the human being to nature. An ontological and a religious understanding of the unity of the natural and human world..., long scorned by the empirical sciences as representing the dying vestiges of a primitive, animistic view of nature, may well in our day provide the best opportunity in the West for the retrieval of that lost unity.[20]

Methods and Definitions

The primary method of theological inquiry to be used in the following study is that of an "ecological hermeneutic of history."[21] Such an approach "is predicated on the assumption of a divine and human concomitance with nature, rather than a divine and human disjunction from nature."[22] The basis of this method lies in what H. Paul Santmire calls "the ecological motif"[23] that can be found within the Judeo-Christian theological tradition. More specifically, this motif combines two metaphorical themes that can be observed in that tradition. The first is "the metaphor of migration to a good land", the second that of "the metaphor of fecundity." Santmire maintains that "since both are essentially nature-affirming metaphors,...when they are given together existentially"[24] they provide us with a hermeneutical lens capable of critically evaluating its subject in terms of ecological sensitivity. This method will be utilized at different places throughout the book, since it is the intention of this author to regard Tillich primarily from an historical point of view. By utilizing this method of inquiry, Tillich's works will be critically examined for their merit and substantive usefulness in support of the main thesis of this project, namely, that his theological vision is a valuable resource that can, and should be, recovered and reinterpreted in the light of the contemporary situation.

The other method to be employed is that of a "mutually critical correlation."[25] This term describes what David Tracy claims is "in fact nothing other than a hermeneutically self-conscious clarification and correction of traditional theology."[26] One of the "poles" constituting the hermeneutical conversation in this particular method will therefore consist of the question properly raised by creation itself and the threat posed to it by human interference and neglect. The other "pole" will be composed of those elements of Tillich's theological vision as critically retrieved in the apologetic or "answering" mode. By the terms "mutual" and "critical" is meant that each "pole" described above mutually appraises and scrutinizes the other in light of the other's constitutive merit. Use of the term "correlation" in this context conveys the understanding and assumption that there exists a fundamental ontological unity between both "poles" that renders dialogue between them meaningful and, hopefully, fruitful. This particular method will be most self-consciously utilized in Chapter Five where the primary constructive work will be carried out.

For purposes of definition, the term "theology of nature" itself should be examined at this point since it will be used widely throughout the book. The question of how, from a Protestant perspective, a "theology of nature" is distinguishable from "natural theology" is of great significance for the present work. Furthermore, it may be asked, how does such an enterprise understand the relationship between revealed religion and the natural world? To these concerns H. Paul Santmire offers six criteria which he deems necessary for a *"critical theology of nature."*[27] First, such a critical theology of nature must take into account the way in which contemporary biblical scholarship understands the foundational sources of the Christian tradition. That is, a theology of nature must acknowledge that the primary concern of the normative scriptures upon which the edifice of Christian theology rests is that of history, not nature. Second, human historicity (*i.e.*, the human capacity for self-transcendence) must also be taken seriously by a theologically critical approach to nature. Third, the question of special revelation or of "positive religion" will need to be addressed. Fourth, while the immanence of the divine in the material world would seem to be of primary significance for a critical theology of nature, the matter of divine alterity, or of transcendence, must be affirmed as well in order to remain faithful to the Judeo-Christian tradition. Fifth, a thoroughgoing familiarity with developments in the natural sciences must be accompanied by a humble acknowledgment of the limits of theology if a critical approach to nature expects to succeed. Finally, the social dimension that the question of nature raises for theology must also be included in any legitimate critical theology of nature. Accordingly, both the liabilities and the virtues of modern culture deserve attention in order to avoid an escapist "return to nature" mentality.

I would therefore define a Protestant theology of nature as the effort to interpret the God-world relationship in realistic and theocentric terms using the material universe, in concert with the biblical tradition, as a hermeneutical lens.[28] According to this definition, a traditional natural theology is rejected which emphasizes nature's value as a revelatory vehicle for human salvation alone and which accepts an understanding of nature as simply "a springboard, a place for crossing over" between humanity and God.[29] Moreover, the problematic Scholastic distinction between the supranatural and the natural is avoided. In this view, divine agency, the integrity of the non-human universe, the biblical testimony, and historical consciousness are all accorded appropriate and significant places within the theological vision.

Finally, the issue of inclusive language needs to be addressed at the outset. It almost goes without saying that if one wishes to do theology today one must employ a vocabulary that is both egalitarian and inclusive. These are principles that I have attempted to apply to my own writing throughout this book. I am also aware, however, that in a work such as this – involving a good deal of historical figures and ideas – one frequently encounters language which can often seem jarring to the modern ear sensitized to the problems of androcentric thought and language. Nevertheless, in an effort to preserve the integrity of quoted text and to maintain continuity within this work itself, I have opted neither to alter quoted material nor to indicate within quoted material the presence of language that some may find offensive.

The methods and definitions discussed above are by no means arbitrary.[30] The choice of these types of approaches and definitions arises out of their apparent compatibility with the material to be studied and evaluated, and the internal coherence afforded by the scope delineated thereby.

Notes

1.   H. Paul Santmire, "The Reformation Problematic and the Ecological Crisis," *Metanoia* 2 (June 1970), Special Supplement.
2.   For example, in the case of the Valdez oil spill, an entire section of the relatively unspoiled Alaskan coastline was contaminated; in Bhopal, India, the responsibility of the deaths of thousands lay with a chemical company (Union Carbide) whose corporate headquarters was in Danbury, Connecticut; and the radiation that was released into the atmosphere as the result of the meltdown of a core reactor at the Chernobyl nuclear power plant in the former Soviet Union affected dairy products worldwide.
3.   Robin Attfield, *The Ethics of Environmental Concern*, 2d ed. (Athens, GA and London: The University of Georgia Press, 1991), 1.
4.   Steven Bouma-Prediger, *The Greening of Theology: The Ecological Models of Rosemary Radford Ruether, Joseph Sittler, and Jürgen Moltmann* (Atlanta, GA: Scholars Press, 1995), 1.   Cf. also Elizabeth A. Johnson, *Women, Earth, and Creator Spirit* (New York and Mahwah, NJ: Paulist Press, 1993), 5-9 and Daniel P. Jones, "Warming Trend Sparks 1998 to Record," Longmont (Colorado) *Daily Times-Call*, 24 December 1998, A1.
5.   Even the most sympathetic experts in the field do not universally accept the assertion that the environmental situation of the present age is of a worse degree than that of its predecessors. See, for example, René Dubos' chronicling of ecological disasters in the ancient world in his essay "Franciscan Conservation vs. Benedictine Stewardship," in *The World of René Dubos: A Collection from His Writings*, ed. Gerard Piel and Osborn Segerberg, Jr. (New York: Henry Holt and Co., 1990), 378-381. See also Lewis Thomas' claim in support of the so-called "Gaia" hypothesis that the "earth is impermeable to

death" in his *The Lives of a Cell: Notes of a Biology Watcher* (New York: Viking Press, 1974), 3. Cf., however, Harold Coward's very recent conclusion following his insightful diagnosis of the present state of affairs: "Thus, the three-pronged problematic of population pressure, excessive consumption, and environmental degradation has emerged as perhaps *the* major challenge facing us today" ("New Theology on Population, Consumption, and Ecology," *Journal of the American Academy of Religion* 65/2 [Summer 1997]: 261).

6. In this regard, see Lynn White, Jr.'s provocative 1967 essay in which he alleges that "Christianity bears a huge burden of guilt" for the wedding of science and technology, a marriage of dubious value that has given "mankind powers which, to judge by many of the ecologic effects, are out of control" ("The Historical Roots of Our Ecologic Crisis," *Science* 155 [March 10, 1967]: 1206). Cf. as well Thomas Sieger Derr, "Religion's Responsibility for the Ecological Crisis: An Argument Run Amok," *Worldview* 15 (January 1975): 44: "In spite of [White's] comment about Christianity's 'burden of guilt' in the ecological crisis, he did not mean that it was the 'cause' of that crisis or of the technological society in which the troubles arose. Many times he warns readers that no historian can speak simply about 'causes,' that one must rather talk of multiple roots, of indirect action through cultural climates, of religious 'approval' of developments which may have other sources – and one must not neglect historical accidents, sheer chance, spontaneity." Finally, Elspeth Whitney questions White's "single-visioned reading of the past," with its emphasis on one value alone (*i.e.*, human domination of nature in the name of spiritual progress) "to the exclusion not only of other, non-religious values, but also of any consideration of how economic and political systems help create or reinforce values and provide the means for implementing those values" ("Lynn White, Ecotheology, and History," *Environmental Ethics* 15 [Summer 1993]: 169).

7. H. Paul Santmire, *The Travail of Nature: The Ambiguous Ecological Promise of Christian Theology* (Minneapolis: Fortress Press, 1985*)*, 122. Cf. Bernard E. Meland's discussion of the centrality of anthropocentrism in the Western philosophical tradition ("Grace: A Dimension within Nature?" *The Journal of Religion* 54 [April 1974]: 129).

8. In addition to the epigraph at the beginning of this chapter, H. Paul Santmire has long been suggesting that Tillich's theology should be re-examined and re-interpreted in the light of the contemporary ecocrisis. See, for example, his article "A New Theology of Nature?" *Lutheran Quarterly* 20 (August 1968): 290, n.4, and 291, and his *Travail,* 252, n.1. See also Gordon D. Kaufman, "A Problem for Theology: The Concept of Nature," *Harvard Theological Review* 65 (1972): 365-366, n. 21; Paul Lee, introduction to *The*

Meaning of Health by Paul Tillich (Richmond, CA: North Atlantic Books, 1981), 10; Theodore M. Green, "Paul Tillich and Our Secular Culture," in *The Theology of Paul Tillich,* ed. Charles W. Kegley (New York: Pilgrim Press, 1982), 97-98; James Carpenter, *Nature and Grace: Toward an Integral Perspective* (New York: Crossroad, 1988), 37-56; Langdon Gilkey, *Gilkey on Tillich* (New York: Crossroad, 1990), 183-185; Harold H. Oliver, "The Neglect and Recovery of Nature in Twentieth-Century Protestant Thought," *Journal of the American Academy of Religion* 60/3 (Autumn 1992): 383-384; Wolfhart Pannenberg, *Toward a Theology of Nature: Essays on Science and Faith,* ed. Ted Peters (Louisville, KY: Westminster/John Knox Press, 1993), 128-137; Sebastian Painadath, "Paul Tillich's Theology of Prayer," in *Paul Tillich: A New Catholic Assessment,* ed. Raymond F. Bulman and Frederick J. Parrella (Collegeville, MN: The Liturgical Press, 1994), 231; Andrew Linzey, *Animal Theology* (Urbana, IL and Chicago: University of Illinois Press, 1994), 199; Catherine Keller, "The Lost Fragrance: Protestantism and the Nature of What Matters," *Journal of the American Academy of Religion* 65/2 (Summer 1997): 358; Brennan R. Hill, *Christian Faith and the Environment: Making Vital Connections* (Maryknoll, NY: Orbis Books, 1998), 25-31; and Pan Chiu Lai, "Paul Tillich and Ecological Theology," *The Journal of Religion* 79/2 (April 1999): 233-249. Perhaps most salient of all in terms of re-evaluating Tillich's thought from an ecological perspective is the collection of essays appearing in Gert Hummel, ed., *Natürliche Theologie versus Theologie der Natur? Tillichs Denken als Anstoss zum Gespräch zwischen Theologie, Philosophie and Naturwissenschaft* (Berlin and New York: Walter de Gruyter, 1994).

9. See A. James Reimer, "Tillich, Hirsch and Barth: Three Different Paradigms of Theology and its Relation to the Sciences," in Hummel (ed.), *Natürliche,* 124.

10. This principle is a central one in Tillich's theology. He derives it from the Pauline-Lutheran tradition concerning the teaching on justification by grace alone, but he extends it to embrace all periods of history and religions: "Protestantism is understood as a special historical embodiment of a universally significant principle. This principle, in which one side of the divine-human relationship is expressed, is effective in all periods of history; it is indicated in the great religions of mankind; it has been powerfully pronounced by the Jewish prophets; it is manifest in the picture of Jesus as the Christ; it has been rediscovered time and again in the life of the church and was established as the sole foundation of the churches of the Reformation; and it will challenge these churches whenever they leave their foundation" ("Author's Introduction," in *PE,* vii-viii). Elsewhere, Tillich defines this important principle as "the restatement of the prophetic principle [of ancient Israel] as an attack against a self-absolutizing and, consequently, demonically distorted

church" (*ST* 1, 227); as "the critical element in the expression of the community of faith and consequently the element of doubt in the act of faith" (*DF,*
29); and as "the prophetic criticism...which judges all religious or quasi-
religious absolutism" (*CEWR,* 8).
11. By the term "Catholic substance" Tillich means "the concrete embodiment of the Spiritual Presence" or, in more conventional terms, the ecclesial
manifestation of the Third Principle of the Trinity (*ST* 3, 245). Cf. also *ST* 3,
6, and his essay "The Protestant Message and the Man of Today," in *PRE,*
194-195.
12. John P. Dourley, "Paul Tillich and Bonaventure: An Evaluation of Tillich's Claim to Stand in the Augustinian-Franciscan Tradition" (Ph.D. diss.,
Fordham University, 1971), 43.
13. Paul Tillich, "The Redemption of Nature," *Christendom* 10 (Summer
1945): 300. This article also appeared in substantially the same form under
the title "Nature, Also, Mourns for a Lost Good" in the first collection of Tillich's sermons, *The Shaking of the Foundations* (New York: Charles Scribner's Sons, 1946), 76-86.
14. On this point, see Paul Tillich, "The Decline and the Validity of the Idea
of Progress," in *FR,* 64-79. Albert J. Fritsch provides a similar perspective to
that of Tillich on the technology v. nature issue from a Roman Catholic point
of view in his insightful essay "Appropriate Technology and Healing the
Earth," in *Embracing Earth: Catholic Approaches to Ecology,* ed. Albert J.
LaChance and John E. Carroll (Maryknoll, NY: Orbis Books, 1994), 96-114.
15. See Gordon D. Kaufman, "A Problem for Theology: The Concept of
Nature," *Harvard Theological Review* 65 (1972): 364, and Alexandre Ganoczy, "Ecological Perspectives in the Christian Doctrine of Creation," *Concilium* 4 (April 1991): 50.
16. Paul Tillich, "The Logos and Mythos of Technology," in *SSTS,* 59-60.
17. Tillich, *ST* 1, 71-81.
18. The notion of a Benedictine model of "creative stewardship" was articulated by the medical scientist René Dubos in his essay "Franciscan Conservation vs. Benedictine Stewardship," op. cit.
19. Tillich, "Redemption," 305.
20. Gilkey, *Tillich,* 184.
21. Santmire, *Travail,* 189.
22. Ibid., 189-190.
23. Ibid., 25. For the discussion that follows, see 13-29.
24. Ibid., 28.
25. See Francis Schüssler Fiorenza, "Systematic Theology: Task and Methods," in *Systematic Theology: Roman Catholic Perspectives* 1, ed. Francis

Schüssler Fiorenza and John P. Galvin (Minneapolis: Fortress Press, 1991), 55-60.

26. Robert M. Grant with David Tracy, *A Short History of the Interpretation of the Bible,* rev. ed. (Philadelphia: Fortress Press, 1984), 170.

27. H. Paul Santmire, "A New Theology of Nature?" *Lutheran Quarterly* 20 (August 1968): 306. For the discussion that follows, see pp. 306-308.

28. I believe this definition is also consistent with the understanding of "eco-theology" as developed by Robert Booth Fowler in his *The Greening of Protestant Thought* (Chapel Hill, NC and London: University of North Carolina Press, 1995), 91-107. Cf. as well Jürgen Moltmann's understanding of the task of a theology of nature: "Every natural theology proceeds from the self-evidence of nature as God's creation. On the other hand, every theology of nature interprets nature in the light of the self-revelation of the creative God. So what is the relation between natural theology and the theology of nature? By asking this question we are turning the traditional interest in natural theology upside down: the aim of our investigation is not what nature can contribute to our knowledge of God, but what the concept of God contributes to our knowledge of nature" (*God in Creation: A New Theology of Creation and the Spirit of God,* tr. Margaret Kohl [San Francisco: HarperSanFrancisco, 1991], 53). Finally, Ian Barbour suggests that "a theology of nature does not start from science, as some versions of natural theology do. Instead, it starts from a religious tradition based on religious experience and historical revelation. But it holds that some traditional doctrines need to be reformulated in the light of current science" (*Religion and Science: Historical and Contemporary Issues* [San Francisco: HarperSanFrancisco, 1997], 100). Moreover, Barbour identifies four areas of investigation that are essential to any theology of nature: 1) Stewardship of Nature; 2) Celebration of Nature; 3) A Sacramental View of Nature; and 4) The Holy Spirit in Nature (ibid., 102-103).

29. Jean Claude Petit, "Von den Schwierigkeiten und Grenzen einer Theologie der Natur heute (Einige Bemerkungen im Blick auf Paul Tillich)," in *Natürliche Theologie versus Theologie der Natur? Tillichs Denken als Anstoss zum Gespräch zwischen Theologie, Philosophie und Naturwissenschaft,* ed. Gert Hummel (Berlin and New York: Walter de Gruyter, 1994), 4. Translation mine.

30. I am well aware of the pitfalls of "methodolatry" as pointed out by Mary Daly in her *Beyond God the Father: Toward a Philosophy of Women's Liberation* (Boston: Beacon Press, 1985), 10-11, and will make every effort to avoid them in this book.

The fountains mingle with the river,
And the rivers with the ocean;
The winds of heaven mix for ever
With a sweet emotion;
Nothing in the world is single;
All things, by a law divine,
In one another's being mingle....[1]

Chapter 1

The Protestant Problematic

In many ways, the equivocal attitude toward the natural world that would characterize the Protestant theological tradition was adumbrated in Augustine. The "patchwork"[2] character of his theological enterprise points to an essential ambiguity in his treatment of nature, an ambiguity that he would inadvertently bequeath to successive generations of the Christian West through the sheer force of his theological genius.[3]

Paul Tillich was well aware that Augustinian thought had profoundly shaped the recent tradition from which he spoke.[4] He was equally aware, however, of the problems associated with such an influence, such as the voluntaristic and intuitive character of Augustine's thinking. Tillich would seek in the sacramental notion of what he called the "Catholic substance" a complement to the relativizing corrective of the "Protestant principle," both of which are present to some degree in Augustine's theology. While Tillich certainly leaned toward

Augustine's intuitive, deductive approach to reality, particularly in his doctrine of God and in his existential analysis of modern life, he also recognized that the inductive, empirical, Aristotelian approach was equally important to the development of a full understanding of the world and of our place in it.[5]   Wary of the unrestrained growth of technology in the twentieth century with its deleterious effects on human beings and the natural world, Tillich nevertheless also warned of the dangers of retreating into a purely subjective inwardness in the form of personal religious piety or as an escape from the horrors of the modern world.   He was therefore appreciative of his own religious tradition for providing a framework in which the questions of truth and of faith could be meaningfully raised.   At the same time, he was critical of this same tradition for contributing, either directly or indirectly, deliberately or accidentally, to the neglect and devastation of the natural world.

It may be argued that the categories employed by Augustine in his theology of grace were applied almost exclusively to the question of *human* nature and, for that reason, should not be cited as in some way contributing to the modern "problem of nature."[6]   However, the narrow frame of reference provided by Augustine in his treatment of the question of nature and grace became *itself* part of the problem, for both theological and historical reasons.   Theologically, the idea that grace is operative solely in the human heart as "an internal and secret power, wonderful and ineffable,"[7] only begs the question of the relationship between grace and the non-human universe.   The power of grace, for Augustine, is in effect the presence of the Holy Spirit.   But nowhere do we find this power or this presence claimed by Augustine to so penetrate the non-human universe as to somehow transform, liberate, or otherwise redeem it.   Historically, Augustine's silence on this question was taken by subsequent figures to mean that the non-human universe was of little value for Christian theology, except as it related to issues of personal soteriology.   In the Protestant theological tradition (with some notable exceptions), this resulted in a profound stress being placed on individual salvation, leading ultimately to a de-emphasis on the sacramental character of the material world and its concomitant devaluation.   It is therefore this tension between grace and nature, spirit and matter, and creation and redemption that Tillich recognized as a forceful, yet problematic, element in both Augustine and the Protestant theological tradition, one which he would attempt to resolve through his own ontological approach.[8]

The Reformers

In large measure, it was in response to the treatment of the relationship between nature and grace by the Scholastics that the Protestant Reformers formulated their famous rallying cry of *sola gratiae.* "The natural theology of the Scholastics is roundly denounced" by Luther, Calvin, Zwingli, Melanchthon, et al., "and even its very limited denotation of the gracious element within nature is rejected."[9] We can find the roots of the eventual rise of modern secularism in Luther's nearly pathological obsession with personal grace as the only legitimate vehicle for justification. Despite his avowed humanism, in turning his attention to the inner life of the soul, Luther unwittingly paved the way for the perceived split between religion and science that eventually occurred in both consciousness and culture. For Luther, the operative realm of grace was strictly interior:

> When Luther turned catechist and found himself obliged to teach the doctrine of creation, he brought it all under the same *pro me* which he had found in the gospel of grace, and he reduced the whole world of nature to a repository of goods for the service of man.[10]

In response to the "Catholic system...of objective, quantitative, and relative relations between God and man," Luther asserted that "[t]he relation to God is personal. It is an I-thou relationship, mediated not by anybody or anything, but only by accepting the message of acceptance...."[11] In his search to find an answer to his famous query "How can *I* find a gracious God?" Luther admits, perhaps unknowingly, to his own anthropocentrism. When he states in his Small Catechism that "I believe that God has created me, together with all creatures,"[12] it is difficult to imagine that his understanding of creation was anything other than a human-centered one.

In contradistinction to the Roman "magical and legal elements" that were invoked at the time for the forgiveness of sins, for Luther grace was understood as "a personal communion of God with the sinner. There is no possibility of any merit; there is only the need to accept."[13] Grace, then, becomes the divine offer of forgiveness that will rescue us from our wretched situation, a situation in which the material world, while certainly created by God, nonetheless plays a relatively insignificant role in the dynamic interplay between human and Creator-Redeemer. The emphasis in such theology is on the human *response* to the divine offer. Since the non-human world is incapable of such a response, it does not assume a prominent place in Luther's theology of grace. He viewed nature as "the mask" of the *Deus absconditus,* through which God "acts with mankind in an irrational way,"[14] having "the effect of drawing the despairing soul to seek the humanity of Christ."[15] In this respect, Luther clearly accentuates the interior transformation of the human person under the influence of grace as contrasted with a relatively malevolent view of nature.

At the same time, however, "Luther said that God is nearer to everything than anything is to itself. He is fully in every grain of sand, but the whole world cannot comprehend him. He transcends everything finite, although being in it."[16] Moreover, Tillich states that "Luther himself...had the most positive relation to nature,"[17] expressed in the "Lutheran formula [of] *finitum capax infiniti* – the finite is capable of the infinite."[18] Tillich identifies a mystical element in Luther in which his "relationship to nature has much more the sense of the presence of the divine...in everything that is."[19] This is perhaps attributable to Luther's understanding of the God-world relationship implied in his idea of God, which Tillich describes as "one of the most powerful in the whole history of human and Christian thought. This is not a God who is a being beside others...."[20] Luther's doctrine of God combines the element of divine immanence with that of divine sovereignty, demonstrating "the greatness of God, the inescapability of his presence, and at the same time, his absolute transcendence."[21] Accordingly, Luther's God contains within the Godhead both the demonic and the divine, encompassing all of heaven and earth. In trying to hold these elements together in the unity that is God, Luther's mystical "side," in which the immediacy of the divine presence is felt and known in and through all creation, is counterbalanced by his more orthodox "side," that is, the one in which the experience of God as judge manifests "the distance of God from man."[22] The former "destroyed the traditional interpretation of God's omnipresence and expressed the doctrine...that God is in everything, in that which is central as well as in that which is peripheral."[23] The latter accentuates, in its paradoxical terminology contrasting the world with God, the constant need for personal repentance as the means for making the individual ready to personally receive the divine self-communication in the offer of grace.

Arising from this understanding of the God-world relationship is Luther's extremely incarnational christology in which he emphasizes the "real presence" in the sacrament of the Lord's Supper. It is expressed, according to Tillich, in Luther's "profound and fantastic doctrine of the ubiquity of the body of Christ":

> Christ is present in everything, in stone and fire and tree, but for us he is present only when he speaks to us. *But he can speak to us through everything.* This is the idea that God drives toward embodiment or corporeity, and that the omnipresence of Christ's body in the world is the form in which God's eternal power is present in the world.... [If this] is taken symbolically, it becomes a profound doctrine, because it says that God is present in anything on earth. He is always also present with his concrete historical manifestation in Christ. Luther meant this quite primitively, but his meaning is that in every natural object you can have the presence of Christ. In a Lutheran service during the Sundays in spring, you always find a tremendous amount of flowers and things of nature brought into the church, because of this symbol of the participation of the body of Christ in the world.[24]

As early as 1929, Tillich lamented the eventual loss of this type of sacramental appreciation for the natural universe in later Protestant traditions.[25] Actually, from the very beginning of the Protestant era, there was much disagreement concerning the relationship among symbol, sacrament, and nature. While the Reformers did reach accord in their common denial of the doctrine of transubstantiation, "they could not agree on the ubiquity of Christ's presence."[26] Tillich cites Luther's confrontation over this matter with Huldreich Zwingli in 1529 at Marburg as reflective of an unhealthy tension (from an ecological point of view) within the Protestant tradition that has remained unresolved to the present day.[27] For Zwingli, the body of Christ is not literally present in the sacrament of the Lord's Supper as it is for Luther. Following the humanists, Zwingli took the meaning of the word "is" in the statement "This is my body" to mean "signifies" or "means".[28] In other words, Zwingli does recognize the performative character of a sacrament insofar as it is able to awaken in the believer the "memory" of the events associated with the original Last Supper and to arouse him or her to "confession."[29] However, the transformation effected by participation in the sacred ritual of the Lord's Supper is, for him, "centered [wholly] on the subjective side."[30] That is, the eucharist "is present for the contemplation of faith, but not *per essentiam et realiter....* 'The body of Christ is eaten when we believe that he is killed for us.'"[31] In Zwingli's estimation, it is almost exclusively an intellectual enterprise that is involved when partaking of the sacraments.

For Zwingli, then, the sacraments were understood largely as "representational symbols" which acquired their efficacy only to the extent that the participant's faith would allow it.[32] While there may be discerned traces of the Scholastic sacramental doctrine of *ex opere operato* in Luther, Zwingli would have found quite objectionable any claim to sacramental efficacy beyond its subjective or psychological effects. According to Tillich, unlike Luther for whom "the presence of Christ is repeated in every act of the sacrament of the Lord's Supper,"[33] for Zwingli the sacrament of the eucharist

> is the representation of a past event, not in itself a present event. The present event is merely in the subject, in the mind of the believer. [Christ] is certainly with his Spirit present in the mind, *but he is not present in nature*. Mind can be fed only by mind, or spirit by spirit, and not by nature.[34]

Hence we see in Zwingli two dangerous elements appearing at the very outset of the Protestant tradition that would contribute greatly to the subsequent devaluation and neglect of the natural world. The first consists of a "humanistic intellectualism which separates the spirit from the body, a tendency which is ultimately rooted in Neo-Platonism."[35] In his subjectivist interpretation of the effects of the sacraments, particularly that of the eucharist, Zwingli "spiritualizes" the symbolic action of the sacraments to the point where their intrinsic value as bearers of salvific efficacy is rendered virtually non-existent. As Tillich observes, in contrast to Luther, whose interest in the spiritual significance of the sacraments is that of "incorporation," Zwingli's attitude is one of indifference to the actual substance which is at the center of the sacramental ritual itself (*i.e.*, water, bread, wine, etc.), since this has no direct bearing on the inward disposition of the participant.[36] The mystical element of indirect immediacy which is so prominent in Luther's thought, and which allows for a unified view of nature and spirit in the redemptive action of the sacraments, is wholly absent from Zwingli. The second, and related, unfortunate tendency that is present in Zwingli, and which has had particularly lamentable consequences in terms of the environment,

> has to do with the religious meaning of nature. In Zwinglian thought nature is controlled and calculable in terms of regular natural laws. By

contrast Luther's dynamic naturalism often goes into the demonic depths of nature, and is not interested in any laws of nature.[37]

The "spiritual differences"[38] between the early manifestations of Zwinglianism and Lutheranism can be found in the two Latin formulae used by each movement to express the relationship between, among other things, the natural world and the world of the spirit. Luther, with his insistence on *finitum capax infiniti,* claimed that mutual commerce was at least *possible* all along the entire spiritual/material spectrum. On the other hand, Zwingli, with Calvin, argues that *"finitum non capax infiniti* – the finite is not able to have the infinite within itself. This is a fundamental difference which shows up first in christology, then is extended to the whole sacramental life and the relationship to nature."[39] In sharply separating the two natures of Christ (*i.e.,* the bodily from the spiritual), Zwingli established a principle of discontinuity between the temporal and the eternal, the finite and the infinite, and the natural and the spiritual, that would, by theological extension, prove to have grave ecological consequences for later generations, at least in the Christian West. While I am by no means laying the blame for the current ecological crisis entirely on the shoulders of Huldreich Zwingli, the turn in his sacramental theology away from Luther's more mystical (albeit incomplete and inconsistent) theory of the sacraments exerted a profound influence on the whole of later Protestantism and, in consequent turn, on the world of nature. We can see elements of his thought reappearing in the radical inwardness of Kierkegaard and in the existential individualism of Bultmann and, certainly, in the "Ritschlian attitude of callously exploiting nature, turning everything into a mere thing to be used."[40] There is a metaphysical dualism operative in Zwingli's theology that, as we have seen, was present in Augustine and, as we shall later see, is developed along more philosophical lines by Descartes and Kant. While Tillich himself was – in line with his more Reformist predecessors and his own neo-orthodox contemporaries – critical of natural theology,[41] he nevertheless realized what the loss of a sacramental view of the universe signified for his own religious tradition:

The phenomenal growth of secularism in Protestant countries can be explained partly as a result of the weakening of the sacramental power within Protestantism. For this reason the solution of the problem of "nature and sacrament" is today a task on which the very destiny of Protestantism depends. But this problem can be solved only by an interpretation of nature which takes into account the intrinsic powers of nature. If nature loses its power, the sacrament becomes arbitrary and insignificant. Of course, the power of nature alone does not create a Christian sacrament. Nature must be brought into the unity of the history of salvation. It must be delivered from its demonic bondage. And just this happens when nature becomes a sacramental element.[42]

Calvin's perspective on nature shares an affinity with Zwinglianism in terms of its concept of natural law. As Tillich points out, both "Zwingli and Calvin accepted nature in terms of law.... The attitude towards nature in Zwinglianism and Calvinism is much more in accordance with the demands of bourgeois industrialized society to analyze and transform nature for human purposes."[43] While for Luther nature's "mask" hides a divine presence that is nevertheless "nearer to us than we are to ourselves," Calvin speaks in exalted terms of the world as being "the theater of divine glory" in which the drama of redemption is played out:

> Discriminately is this world called a mirror of divinity, not because there is sufficient clearness for a man to know God by looking at the world, but he has thus revealed himself to us by works, in these, too, we ought to seek him.... The faithful, however, to whom he has given eyes, see as it were, sparks of his glory shining in every created thing.[44]

Luther's accent on the transformation of the inner person, and the development of his theology of the Cross, together led him to a radically christocentric view. Calvin's universe, on the other hand, is a purely theocentric one. The question for Calvin was not where and how he could find a gracious God, but whether one's role in this unfolding drama matters at all. The almost fanatical stress he laid on the divine alterity led him to the conclusion that, as we have already observed, *finitum non capax infiniti* – the created order is separated from the Creator by an infinite gulf, a gulf that can *only* be traversed from the side of the Creator. In fact, this chasm consists not merely in separation but in *opposition:*

> It was the order of creation that the structure of the world should minister to us as a school in which we might learn the fear of God, and in consequence be transplanted to eternal life and consummate felicity; but after the Fall, wherever we turn our eyes there meets us above and below the curse of God, which, because on account of our sin it affects and en-

velops the innocent creatures, must inevitably plunge our hearts into despair.[45]

In a manner reminiscent of Bonaventure and Augustine, Calvin believed that there exist traces or "sparks" of divinity in both nature and history. However, our "vision" is so impossibly damaged by the Fall that only an act of divine providence can restore our sight. It is human sinfulness that has created this unfortunate state of affairs, not the design of God. "[T]he failure of God's self-disclosure in nature must be imputed to our guilt"[46] for, if Adam had never fallen, God's glory and goodness in nature would otherwise be fully manifest:

> This argument of Calvin only makes it plainer that he is fully serious in teaching that God wishes to disclose Himself in nature and history. If our rebellious attitude towards the signs of the Creator's glory were not to bring about our damnation as a consequence, then it would not be a question of a word of the living God uttered in the works of nature and the events of history. God is not mocked. His goodness cannot be despised with impunity.[47]

We see here in Calvin, as in Augustine and in many of those that followed him in the West, that the peculiar condition of fallenness that afflicts the entire created order leads human beings to fix their gaze on the things of this world rather than on the Creator. We seek, as it were, the right thing in the wrong places. Our innate desire to praise and worship the glory of the Creator becomes itself so twisted as a result of the Fall that we cannot even rely on this, humanly speaking, to bring us into right relationship with God: "We are not only blind and deaf with regard to the intimations of God in nature; we are crazy. Our deadness and perversity darkens everything, so that any insight which we gain becomes nothing more than a monstrous deception."[48] Consequently, the "light" of the created universe that pulsates with divine splendor is not visible to us apart from our undergoing a profound alteration in our fundamental orientation. "Thus in vain do so many lights shine in the universe; they cannot illuminate for us the honour of the Creator."[49]

The rationally deterministic character of Calvin's universe leads to an extremely negative view of the human condition. In emphasizing human corruption to the extent that he does, Calvin can, by contrast, bring to light the sublime glory of God. Tillich notes that Calvin's doctrine of divine preservation rests on a collaborative view of the cre-

ated universe. That is, "according to Calvin all things have instrumental character; they are instruments through which God works in
every moment."[50]   On this basis, Tillich asserts that Calvin's understanding of the God-world relationship can properly be classified as
"panentheism,...because this means that everything is in God.... This
is very close to Luther's idea."[51]   Moreover, according to Tillich, in
articulating his doctrine of divine preservation as a process of "continuous creativity, in that God out of eternity creates things and time
together," Calvin anticipated the deistic dangers that such a doctrine
potentially harbors.[52]   Like Tillich after him, Calvin understood God
not as a being beside the world but as the fundamental ground of being, that which makes being possible at all. "He knew that the doctrine of natural law could easily make God into something beside reality."[53] He therefore conflated the notions of originating and sustaining
creativity into his one doctrine of providence in an attempt to avoid the
deistic naturalism that would appear later primarily on English soil,
exerting such a profound influence on the Enlightenment and its cultural progeny, industrial society.

What *is* lacking, however, in Calvin's doctrine of preservation is an
adequate notion of the purpose for which creation has come into existence, that is, its inner *telos*. In other words, for Calvin creation does
not possess an intrinsic independence apart from God. It cannot, as it
were, "stand on its own." The question here is one not of *autonomy*,
but of *integrity*. According to Tillich, "[o]ne function of the divine
creativity is to drive every creature toward...a fulfilment...in actuality
[that] is beyond potentiality and actuality in the divine life."[54] This is
missing in Calvin. His strictly theo-mechanistic view of the universe
limits the created order to one of mere instrumentality. If, in Calvin's
terminology, the purpose of creation is for "the glory of God," such
glory must be understood in terms of a radical divine transcendence.
Therefore, despite the apparently panentheistic character of their respective theological enterprises, both Calvin and Luther reject the notion of interdependency between Creator and created:

> No Calvinist theologian will admit that God lacks something which he
> must secure from the creature he has created.... In creating the world,
> God is the sole cause of the glory he wishes to secure through his crea-
> tion. But if he is the sole cause of his glory, he does not need the world
> to give him glory. He possesses it eternally in himself. In Lutheran the-
> ologies God's purpose is to have a communion of love with his crea-
> tures.... Here again the implication is that God needs something he

could not have without creation. Reciprocal love is interdependent love. Yet, according to Lutheran theology, there is nothing which the created world can offer God. He is the only one who gives.[55]

There is a certain staticity and aloofness associated with such images of the divine. Therefore, by failing to relate the divine creativity to the future, Calvin, despite his desire to demonstrate otherwise, did in effect contribute to the later deistic view of the relationship between God and the world where "[n]ature was considered a system of measurable and calculable laws resting in themselves without beginning or end...[in which] one could speak of *deus siva natura,* a phrase which indicates that the name 'God' does not add anything to what is already in the name 'nature.'"[56] For this reason, Tillich insists that in any feasible doctrine of providence "directing creativity must be added to originating and sustaining creativity,"[57] something he himself tries to accomplish with his symbol of "eschatological pan-en-theism."[58]

Calvin's primary interest, therefore, when speaking of nature is "to assure *believers* that *their God* is the sovereign Lord over all things, not that the Creator is carrying out some purpose with the whole creation, with nature in particular, which is somehow independent of his will for human salvation."[59] Moreover, apart from the strictly theological problems associated with this perspective, it is Calvin's unique "ethical dynamism," arising out of his doctrine of divine election and attendant "inner-worldly asceticism"[60] that (in an inadvertent fashion similar to Luther) many claim to have influenced "later – secularized – developments in Western mercantile and industrial society and its ethic of domination over the earth."[61] According to Tillich, in this regard "[t]he idea of the kingdom of God, so important for Calvinistic thinking, took on the connotation of working for the transformation of nature for the sake of mankind."[62]

We are, at this point, quite a distance from the Scholastic doctrine of a Creator consubstantial with the creation. Calvin's virulent anti-naturalism was generated in response to the "natural theology" of the Scholastics, resulting in a dualistic view of the universe that is nearly Manichaeistic in design.[63] In an effort to preserve the integrity of Christ's redemptive sacrifice by emphasizing God's absolute transcendence, Calvin's doctrine of double predestination induced an anxiety about the status of one's personal "salvation" that led to an impossible *décretum horribile.* The material universe thus effectively becomes less a reflection of God's glory than some terrifying environment that must be overcome, mastered, and subdued *as a means of glorifying God.*

The "Turn to the Subject"

Harold Oliver sets the tone well for the present section when he briefly describes the transition from the sixteenth century to the modern period:

> Having abandoned – even derided – the Roman Catholic synergism of nature and grace, Protestant thought focused its energies wholly on the latter. This deplorable lacuna in the Reformation tradition had vast cultural and even ecological implications.... After the breakdown of the medieval synthesis and the rise of the Protestant religion of grace, the Roman Catholic interpretation of "nature and grace" became increasingly focused on soteriological and anthropological issues at the cost of neglecting the metaphysical and cosmological implications.... [T]he Roman Church lost credibility in the culture for its regressive stand against Copernicus and Galileo, just at the time Protestantism's *laissez-faire* attitude toward science would lend it an air of progressivism. Meanwhile, "nature" became the ward of science and technology, with little interference – and less wisdom – from the Church.[64]

According to Tillich, "world-consciousness" in the Middle Ages and even into the Renaissance was "still embedded in a mystical or ecstatic God-consciousness.... [Any] distinction between nature and the supernatural [was] abolished."[65] However, "[b]eginning with Galileo the mathematically-oriented natural sciences banished the supernatural. Nature becomes purely objective, rational, and technical; it becomes divested of the divine."[66] Augustine's residual dualism, as it was recovered in Calvin, found further expression in René Descartes' philosophical division of the world between "extended things or material bodies (*res extensa*) [and] thinking substances or the ego (soul) (*res cogitans*)."[67] That is, while Descartes was not specifically occupied with the traditional question of nature and grace, nonetheless "[t]he split between mind and matter which found 'clear and distinct' status in [his] thought was grounded in the split between nature and grace that dogged Western [Christianity] from the time of Augustine."[68] According to Descartes, matter of any sort, as an "extended" body, is dissimilar from "thinking substances," and is for that reason considered completely lacking in sensibility. With the declaration of his *cogito ergo sum,* Descartes established that human reason alone is of value; the material world, including non-human organisms, is turned into an object of precise mathematical investigation.[69] From this principle Descartes "derive[d]...his rational system of nature."[70]

For both Augustine and Descartes the human person was the focal point or "medium for the self-apprehension of the Unconditional."[71] An apprehension of the divine for both thinkers needed to be filtered through the lens of the individual's self-consciousness and could not occur through interaction with the natural world exclusively. Augustine's understanding of the individual's participation in unconditional certainty involved the "lived self," while for Descartes it involved the "thinking subject." In more philosophical language, Augustine expressed the principle of unconditional certainty "in terms of absolute life," whereas Descartes expressed it "in terms of absolute form."[72] While the distinction between the two views may appear subtle, it is significant. In the Augustinian notion of self-certainty, the "Unconditional element is extracted...in order through it to apprehend God."[73] However, in "the post-Cartesian outlook...the rational principle [is] extracted, in order from it to deduce God."[74] In other words, despite his dualistic tendencies, what Augustine tried to hold together in some sort of unity with his mystical-existential system is now completely severed by Descartes, never again to be reunited. What was once accepted as the *basis* of *immediate intuition* on the part of the human person is now understood as the *result* of *logical inference.* With Descartes, being is separated from thinking or, more precisely, is *subordinated* to it. Ontology becomes, in effect, the handmaiden of logic. According to Tillich,

[this] becomes fully apparent for the first time in the philosophy of the Enlightenment, which sought, with the aid of the technical-objective category of cause and effect, to infer God from the world. The certainty of God is made to rest upon the certainty of the world and the power of logical inference.[75]

Historically, the Cartesian "turn to the subject" is perhaps the philosophical development most responsible for the eventual desecration of the natural world in the West. Descartes' insistence on the bifurcation of mind and body, and his strict separation between subject and object, became the foundation for the modern scientific method of inquiry. It also served to reinforce a rupture in the Western religious consciousness that had its roots, as we have seen, in Augustine, and which had expanded under the influence of the Protestant Reformers. For the latter, the material world no longer figured prominently in theological discourse. The emphasis was almost exclusively devoted to personal soteriological issues.

With the development of the scientific method and the growing interiorization of religious faith, the non-human world gradually assumed a certain opaque, insensible quality to the modern observer. As a result of its "anthropocentric dynamics of grace," Protestantism during this period witnessed the gradual and relatively uninterrupted ascendancy of the modern scientific worldview. With some noteworthy exceptions (*e.g.*, Jonathan Edwards in the United States[76]), one could no longer hope to "discover the divine" in the non-human world nor appreciate it for anything other than raw material which needed to be examined, probed, and exploited in order to satisfy human curiosity and the desire for mastery and dominance over nature. Over the course of several centuries, the material world was thus slowly exhausted of any mystery or majesty it might have held for previous generations.

Rationalism and Nature

Kant's famous motto (*"sapere aude!"*) expresses well the Enlightenment's ubiquitous "attempt to build a world on...autonomous reason."[77] In its desire to resist all forms of heteronomy, whether political, religious, social, or even psychological, the Enlightenment sought to "throw off the shackles" of humankind's self-incurred tutelage through reliance on human autonomy and reason. It suggested in the concept of human autonomy that the universal law of reason lies within every person and, accordingly, when obeyed would provide freedom from the arbitrary institutions of church, state, and society:

> Autonomy is the natural law given by God, present in the human mind and in the structure of the world. Natural law usually means...the law of reason, and this is the divine law. Autonomy is following this law as we find it in ourselves.... The adherents of autonomy in the Enlightenment were opposed to anything so arbitrary as divine grace. They wanted to emphasize man's obedience to the law of his own nature and the nature of the world.[78]

This emphasis on autonomous reason was, therefore, consistent with the view of grace that had, for the most part, been put forth by Protestant theology. Since grace was understood as "an action which comes from outside man's autonomous activities,...it was [for Kant] an expression of something heteronomous."[79] Kant's attack on all forms of heteronomy, including religion, was based on human finiteness. In his first philosophical critique of the Enlightenment,[80] he showed that he was "the philosopher who saw most clearly and sharply the finitude of man and man's inability of breaking through the limits of his finitude to that which transcends it, namely, to the infinite."[81] This is what Kant borrows, and borrows in a profound manner, from the Protestant doctrine of grace. In rejecting the attempt on the part of the Enlightenment to develop a natural theology by interpreting the concepts of God, freedom, and immortality in terms of rational structure, he equally denies the claim of Protestant mysticism that there exists the possibility of subjective immediacy with the divine. According to Tillich, Kant's "humility before reality...goes much deeper existentially than in ordinary empirical philosophy":

> We are finite and must therefore accept our finitude. The Protestant idea that we can come to God only through God, that only grace can overcome guilt, sin, and our estrangement from God, and not we ourselves, and not good works can help us, this idea can be extended to the realm of thought. We cannot break through to God even in the realm of thought. He must come to us. This was a very fundamental change in contrast to the metaphysical arrogance of the Enlightenment which believed in the power of reason...to place man immediately in the presence of the Divine. Now men were in a prison, so to speak. Kant had placed man in the prison of finitude.... Certainly in this way Kant represents to a great extent the attitude of Protestantism.[82]

In practical terms, Kant's epistemology constitutes an intensification of the Cartesian subject-object dualism. With Kant, however, the whole of subjectivity resides in the human person; all else is treated as "object" or as the "in-itself", including both God and the non-human world. There is with Kant no notion of a "divine subject" interacting with the world. The Kantian categories of space and time obviate any type of unmediated relationship between God and the world. In Kant "[t]he mystical presence of the divine is radically denied."[83] Essentially, in his division of the world of knowledge from the world of values Kant drains the world of divinity.

The distance between God and the world that had been a controlling feature of Protestant theology thus found profound and far-reaching philosophical expression in Kant. No philosopher or theologian following him could avoid his epistemological criticism of the Enlightenment.[84] Moreover, Kant takes this radical break even further in his *Critique of Practical Reason* when he argues that "in our finite structure of [human] being there is a point of unconditional validity...[which] is the moral imperative and the experience of its unconditional character."[85] That is, in his attempt to break through the prison of finitude through the recognition of what he referred to as the "categorical imperative," Kant succeeded only in further delineating the boundaries of the finite world. The only aspect of existence which can give us dignity, concludes Kant, is morality.[86] Here he denies not only the efficacy of interior grace but contends, according to Tillich,

> that ecstasy in nature itself, for which we have the word miracle, is an encroachment upon the universal structure of reality. What remains is a philosophy of the kingdom of God. This kingdom is identical with the establishment of the moral man on earth.[87]

It was this identification of the Christian symbol of fulfillment with a Kantian ethical universe that would later exert such a profound influence on such nineteenth and early twentieth century liberal Protestant thinkers as Ritschl, Harnack, and Troeltsch, as well as on the Social Gospel movement in the United States. Such a radical emphasis on the universal moral imperative, particularly in the case of Ritschlianism, led to "a withdrawal from the ontological to the moral."[88] Kant's legitimate attempt at an epistemological "disenchantment" of the universe ultimately found extreme concrete expression when it was recovered by those of the "back to Kant" movement in the nineteenth century. "The whole religious message" of this movement, according to Tillich, "is a message which liberates the personality from the pressures of nature.... The function of salvation is the victory of spirit or mind over nature."[89] The reliance on an innerworldly morality accordingly allowed these neo-Kantian theologians to embrace many elements of the bourgeois ethic toward society and nature. Their belief in the progressive improvement of the human situation on earth relied on the bourgeois desire "to analyze and transform the whole of reality in order to control it. [T]he bourgeois had a calculating attitude, and to him nature and reality as a whole appeared to be made up of regular patterns on which he could rely."[90] In this way, according to Tillich, "the Ritschlian theology of retreat...could fortify the strong development of the bourgeois personality in the middle and end of the nineteenth century."[91]

This attitude of calculation and control toward the material world combined a Calvinist ethic with the Kantian epistemological interpretation of reality and a mechanistic Newtonian scientific worldview. The result was the elevation of the human moral realm at the expense of the non-human world. Kant's understanding of nature, set forth in his third critique,[92] was developed in accordance with the human capacity for judicious reasoning and remained consistent with his view that the noumenal world, or the "realm behind things," is incapable of being grasped by such reasoning. According to Tillich, it is here that Kant reveals that "[t]he purpose or goal of nature is the realization of the moral law."[93] In the realm of nature, then,

> Kant saw that judgments are possible, the judgment that nature is an organism as a whole and in the organic structures.... Kant did not say that nature is actually like this, but always added a qualification in terms of an "as if".... [H]e said that although the real nature with which we have to deal is the nature of Newtonian physics, we can nevertheless consider nature *as if* there were structures, meaningful structures, or organisms, and *as if* the whole universe had the character of an organic structure of this kind.[94]

Kant accordingly rejected the Enlightenment notion of a universal type of reason wherein a mutuality existed between the human mind and the whole of reality, similar to the *logos* concept of reason wherein both "word" and "world" can be equally grasped by each other. In Christian theology, the *logos* is a first principle that establishes order and structure in all realities.[95] It is the principle through which God created the world.[96] For this reason, "logos is...in the tree...as well as in the man who names the tree and describes the image of tree-ness which reappears in every individual tree."[97] Because of the presence of a universal structure of intelligibility in both tree and human being, according to this view there exists the possibility of a mutual "graspableness." Hence, while this concept of reason may not admit of an actual *interdependency* between the human and non-human spheres, it does provide the basis for a mutual *intelligibility* between both spheres by virtue of the very structure of reality itself. And while this "logos concept of reason was not the most important in the eighteenth century,...it was definitely a presupposition of that piety which praised the glory of creation."[98] In thus rejecting the *logos* conception of reason and reality, Kant effectively removed God from nature. And, according to Tillich, "if God is removed from nature, he gradually disappears altogether, because we are nature. We come from nature. If God has nothing to do with nature, he finally has nothing to do with our total being."[99]

Despite Kant's organic concept of nature, his severing of all connections between a metaphysical realm and the physical world merely reinforced the already growing scientific view that regarded the material world exclusively in objective, analytical terms. His "as if" of critical judgment was not sufficient enough to break out of the prison of finitude alone. He was unable to extend the principles of subjectivity and of the categorical imperative to the non-human world, thereby allowing for a genuine mutuality between the human and non-human realms. Nevertheless, the organic principle introduced by Kant concerning nature was subsequently "picked up by Romantic philosophy as a main principle for its philosophy of nature, only minus the 'as if.'"[100] This move constituted, for Tillich, "the watershed between critical philosophy and later ontological philosophy."[101] It would also become foundational for Tillich's own theological enterprise, providing him with a critical-ontological basis that was able to appropriate the integrity of the non-human world independent of Kantian epistemological claims to the contrary.

The "Great Synthesis"[102]

In addition to the Kantian *Gestalt* notion of nature, Tillich considers Nicholas of Cusa to be a formative, though indirect, influence on the nineteenth century romantic movement within Protestant theology. Claiming that Nicholas "represents the metaphysical foundations of the modern mind,"[103] Tillich finds in his main principle of *coincidentia oppositorum* an approach to reality that, in complementing Cartesianism, accords well with the romanticist reaction to Kant and the Enlightenment.[104] That is, in contrast to Descartes' basically methodological approach to reality (which influenced both empiricism and rationalism), Nicholas' ontological approach pursues a panentheistic direction which asserts that the finite is capable of the infinite:

In the world the divine is developed; in God the world is enveloped. The finite is in the infinite potentially; the infinite is in the finite actually. *They are within each other.* [Nicholas] expresses this in geometrical terms by saying that God, or better, the divine, is the center and periphery of everything. He is in everything as the center, although he transcends everything; but he is also the periphery because he embraces everything. They are removed from him and at the same he is in them.[105]

While it is unlikely that Luther ever heard of Nicholas of Cusa, his mystical understanding of the God-world relationship is, as we have seen, similar to Nicholas' idea of the *coincidentia oppositorum*. Accordingly, Tillich finds in Luther and Nicholas "a common development [that] underlies the modern mind in its ultimate concern,...in the fundamental principles of interpreting God and the world."[106] For Tillich, it is significant that the metaphysical character of such a view sees "[t]he divine...not in some place alongside of the world or above the world, but...present in everything human and natural."[107] Behind the mystical idea of the coincidence of opposites "was an experience that nature is not outside of creative reality, but is potentially before the creation in God...and then after the creation the divine is within it."[108] According to this view, nature and grace are understood in terms of interpenetration and interdependence. They are not seen as being mutually exclusive of one another or as being of a higher or lower order than the other. Tillich understands this principle to mean "that the finite is not only finite, but in some dimension it is also infinite and has the divine as its center and ground."[109]

It was therefore the Renaissance idea of *coincidentia oppositorum* as formulated in the Lutheran principle of *finitum capax infiniti* that, according to Tillich, became "the first principle of Romanticism on which everything else is dependent."[110] In particular, in Germany romanticism found religious voice in the work of, among others, Friedrich Schleiermacher. Raised in the traditions of the pietist Moravian Brotherhood, Schleiermacher sought to develop a theory of religion on the principle of identity that, in an attempt to circumvent the epistemological dualism of Kant, understood religion as an independently grounded way of experiencing the world that is sustained by the processes of history and nature. His first book, completed in 1799, holds that nature is the expression of the infinite and that religion is "the sensibility and taste for the infinite":[111]

Religion's essence is neither thinking nor acting, but intuition and feeling. It wishes to intuit the universe, wishes devoutly to overhear the universe's own manifestations and actions, longs to be grasped and filled by the universe's immediate influences in childlike passivity.... [It] also lives its whole life in nature, but in the infinite nature of totality, the one and all.... Religion breathes there where freedom itself has once more become nature....[112]

Later, in his major systematic work *The Christian Faith,* Schleiermacher sets forth his famous definition of religion as "the feeling of absolute dependence" or of "immediate self-consciousness."[113] This type of consciousness, according to Schleiermacher, arises not from an interaction with one's external environment or even with oneself as such, but instead constitutes an ongoing and continuous awareness of the fundamental givenness of life: "it is the consciousness that the whole of our spontaneous activity comes from a source outside of us...."[114] Tillich, while acknowledging that the term "feeling" here has unfortunately often been misunderstood and misinterpreted, understands the phrase "feeling of absolute dependence" to refer to "the impact of the universe upon us in the depths of our being which transcends subject and object."[115]

In his earlier work, Schleiermacher's initial romantic tendencies came very close at times to offering a pantheistic interpretation of Christian doctrine, wherein the distinction between the divine and the created orders is blurred. Here, in his mature work, the inclination towards identifying God with the world is severely curtailed, assuming in his skilled dogmatics more of a psychological consistency.[116] Schleiermacher's particular form of neo-Platonism allows for a flexibility that finds both God and the world linked through the stimulation of the religious consciousness:

[I]t must be directly evident...as a general principle of experience that the feeling of absolute dependence can be aroused through stimulations of our sensuous self-consciousness. For that feeling is most complete when we identify ourselves in our self-consciousness with the whole world and feel ourselves in the same way as not less dependent. This identification can only succeed in so far as in thought we unite everything that in appearance is scattered and isolated, and by means of this unifying association conceive of everything as one. For the most complete and universal interdependence of nature is posited in this 'All-One' of finite being, and if we also feel ourselves to be absolutely dependent, then there will be a complete coincidence of the two ideas – namely, the unqualified conviction that everything is grounded and established in the universality of the nature-system, and the inner certainty of the absolute dependence of all finite being on God.[117]

Schleiermacher's positivistic theological enterprise ultimately rests on a distinctive type of subjectivism that utilizes the phenomenon of the religious self-consciousness as a sort of filter through which the entire texture of his theology materializes. While never completely denying the integrity of the non-human world, Schleiermacher nevertheless holds that the doctrine of creation is secondary and derivative to that of the doctrine of preservation.[118] His primary – or one could even say sole – concern is with the perfection of the religious self-consciousness among the fellowship of believers. The Redeemer, for Schleiermacher, is the one who, as the *Urbild* or archetype of the perfectly realized God-consciousness, communicates to us the grace necessary to evolve toward this ideal.[119] Grace and nature may not be at odds in Schleiermacher's system, but clearly it is grace, as personally and corporately experienced justification, that predominates.

Despite basing his system on the principle of identity, for Schleiermacher the attempt at synthesis in overcoming the duality between subject and object remains largely rooted in an anthropocentric notion of grace. Schleiermacher was one of the first Protestant thinkers who would create a theological system that (justifiably) relied to a great extent on historical theology and which utilized a positivistic method of interpretation. What is important for Schleiermacher are the vehicles through which the religious consciousness makes itself known. These vehicles can best be observed as historical phenomena, as products of human culture and expressions of the universal religious spirit. In this view human history fulfills an important teleological role, that is, it points beyond itself to the goal toward which it is moving, toward fulfillment. But nature is not necessarily part of this movement. Just as in Kant the traditional Protestant doctrine of grace influenced his epistemology of human finitude, likewise in Schleiermacher the same phenomenon is operative, but this time in terms of historical consciousness. As the expression of the universal *human* religious consciousness, history is now contrasted with nature.

In Schleiermacher "[t]he idea of the fall is swallowed up by the idea of the evolutionary necessity of estrangement or sin."[120] What is anticipated in the Christ event is the overcoming of this state of estrangement. However, this state of estrangement and of its anticipated

fulfillment does not extend to the material world. The state of estrangement, or sin, arises solely out of the gap created by "the great
speed of the evolutionary process in the biological development of
mankind and the slower pace of moral and spiritual development of
man."[121] Since in Schleiermacher the need for redemption is shaped
by an anthropocentric doctrine of sin, he does not adequately take into
account the non-human universe in his doctrine of redemption. Accordingly, the "finite" that is redeemed in Schleiermacher's system
refers exclusively to humankind and not to the rest of creation.

   Among many of the German idealists of the early nineteenth century
who followed in the wake of the Kantian revolution, the writing of a
critical philosophy of nature became almost *de rigueur*.[122] They
sought to establish on this basis a "transcendental science"[123] eschewing the scientific heteronomy of Kant on the one hand and, on the
other, the unquestioned assumptions of the romantics and the fideists
concerning reason's inability to justify itself on its own terms:

> Kant's difficulty derived from his adherence to an essentially *dogmatic*
> (in this case, Newtonian) metaphysics of nature in which the primacy of
> the heteronomous was never challenged. It was no wonder, then, that the
> notion of a truly autonomous rationality could not be found in such a
> thoroughly uncritical notion of reality. It would be the task of a *Natur-
> philosophie* to show that the concept of the *empirical* would have to be
> abandoned and along with it such other important scientific notions as
> induction and causality....[124]

   However, figures such as Fichte and Hegel, who both devoted a
great deal of speculative effort to the development of such a project,
soon "found themselves increasingly locked in the human realm, with
the natural realm as lifeless, valueless stuff for human control."[125]
Hegel in particular considered the *human* spirit the central locus for
his dialectical analysis of the Absolute achieving completion in history.[126] Human culture was, for him, the profound manifestation of the
divine "otherness" in history seeking a higher form of reintegration.
The absolute Spirit is present in nature, but in terms of estrangement.
According to Tillich, Hegel applies to nature "the existentialist concept for what in religious symbolism is called the fall.... Nature is
spirit, but estranged spirit, spirit not yet having achieved its true nature."[127] This may be a departure from Schleiermacher's largely anthropocentric understanding of the religious meaning of the fall, but it
is a departure in terms of logic; it does not correspond to the actual

relationship between nature and spirit. While "[f]or Hegel man is born out of nature," the absolute Spirit can only come to itself in a creature which is self-conscious.[128] The non-human world, on the other hand, particularly the strictly inorganic realm, was of use to Hegel only insofar as it was able to rouse itself to successful participation in his dialectic of the Absolute coming to self-realization: "[T]he Idea generates Nature in its operation on matter as its opposite.... [T]he destiny of matter as slumbering, disorganized Spirit is to bring itself toward the fullest realization of the Idea in the form of the Absolute."[129] This strictly instrumental view thus subordinates nature to history in a fashion that is not dissimilar to Schleiermacher, but it does so for different reasons.

Despite their appropriation of the principle of mutuality between the infinite and the finite, the attempt on the part of both Schleiermacher and Hegel to create, respectively, a theological and philosophical "great synthesis" ultimately failed. Schleiermacher could not escape the emphasis on personal grace in his pietistic Protestant heritage, however compelling, original, and influential his interpretation of this doctrine proved, in fact, to be. The infinite, for Schleiermacher, appears in the *human* thirst for transcendence and not in the natural world. What Tillich (and other liberal Protestant thinkers) would learn from Schleiermacher is that one cannot speak of the divine without speaking of the human. All theology had to begin "from below," that is, with human experience.[130] However, in cutting off the non-human world from the dynamics of grace, Schleiermacher's positivistic attitude would later be utilized by the Ritschlian school to justify its own devaluation of nature in its uncritical acceptance of the destructive social and technological forces of its time.

Likewise, Hegel's classical idealist approach to the dialectics of world history stresses the pantheistic features of the God-world relationship. That is, while the finite is capable of the infinite, it becomes so only at the expense of its own integrity. Here Tillich would borrow the notion that nature shares with humanity the fundamental experience of estrangement or, in mytho-poetic biblical terms, of "fallenness." Consequently, as we shall see in Chapter Three, the non-human world was able to assume a genuine place in Tillich's doctrine of redemption and in his eschatology.

Schelling's Philosophy of Nature

In his early period (prior to 1804), Schelling generally followed Fichte
in attacking "the Kantian picture...of a transcendental ego which employs the categories to synthesize and structure an atomistic manifold
given to it by the transcendental object."[131] However, in the second
edition of his *Ideas for a Philosophy of Nature,* published in 1804, he
entered upon a second phase of his philosophical development characterized by the understanding that "the first principle of a philosophical
doctrine of nature [is] to go in search of polarity and dualism throughout all nature."[132] Here, Schelling is one of the first critics of post-
Kantian German idealism, no longer developing a conception of nature based on the Fichtean dialectic of subject and object, but rather
one founded on a neo-Platonic philosophy of the absolute. He attacked
that type of Fichtean moralism which regarded "[n]ature [as] only the
material which man must use in himself, in his body which is nature,
and outside of himself in his surroundings, in order to actualize the
moral imperative."[133] According to such a view, "[n]ature has no
meaning in itself."[134]

Between the first edition of the *Ideas,* published in 1797, and the
second, Schelling began to evolve a philosophy of identity that "now
encompassed the absolute, and duality was...understood as the division of a primordial neo-Platonic unity."[135] In the interim, having
"tired of [his earlier Fichtean] dialectic of logical necessity and its
pantheistic overtones,"[136] and also acquainting himself with Jakob
Böhme's theogonic principle of divine dynamism, Schelling began to
conceive of duality at this point as a "self-division of the undivided
absoluteness into subject and object,"[137] not merely as the transition of
one "moment" of the dialectic into its opposite. He felt that "[t]he
enormous sphere of the objective world must be thrown open to the
idea of truth...[because] [t]he unconditioned itself, freedom itself,
posits itself also in nature."[138] Consequently, nature's polarity consisted, for Schelling, not simply in an alternating dialectic of the forces
of repulsion and attraction but, rather, in the division of an original
unity:

> Matter, too, like everything that exists, streams out from the eternal es-
> sence, and represents in appearance an effect, albeit indirect and mediate
> only, of the eternal dichotomizing into subject and object, and of the
> fashioning of its infinite unity into finitude and multiplicity.[139]

Later, Schelling would take this principle of divine dynamism even further, claiming that God is not only the essence "behind things" but is also actually, truly present in the world of nature. For Schelling, the *logos* lives in nature as the living bond in the identity of real and ideal. According to Tillich, for Schelling "[n]ature is not the embodiment of emptiness, of the nonego to which the ego is exclusively opposed; rather, it is, in the deepest sense, spirit and will, creative identity."[140] In declaring that "nature and history throughout are the life of God,"[141] Schelling's philosophy of nature extends beyond the theoretical into the empirical, seeking to travel from the physical world to the metaphysical, where it is understood that "God is creative nature."[142] Schelling discovered in nature a vitality, an explosive dynamism that pointed to the very character of divine unity. In other words, for Schelling, *nature can tell us something about God's reality:*

> The divine unity is from eternity a living, actually existing unity; for the divine is just what cannot be otherwise than *actual.* But the unity is actual, real only in and with the form.... Since the one does not exist *as* such, but only in so far as it, as the one, *is* the many, hence neither the one as such, nor the many as such, *but only the living copula truly exists* [emphasis mine].... This conceptually eternal appearance in otherness of the essence and form is the realm of nature, or *the eternal birth of God in things and the equally eternal resumption of these things in God* [emphasis mine], so that, considered essentially, nature itself is only the entire divine presence....[143]

By locating, as it were, the divine subjectivity in nature itself, Schelling attempted to overcome the strict dualism of Fichte's "ethical mysticism" so strongly dependent on the human ego for its dialectical momentum.[144] With ethical mysticism, "the moralism of the Enlightenment [is brought] to its ultimate expression. The principle of the Enlightenment is the subjective, reflective, self-absolutizing ego, which sets itself in opposition to nature."[145] In ethical mysticism, the human individual's determination of nature stood in conflict to his or her moral task. But, according to Tillich, in Schelling, "there arises a completely new understanding of the relation of nature and spirit...[where] spirit [is joined] indissoluably to nature.... There is no spirit apart from nature any more than there is a nature apart from spirit."[146] That is, in this case Schelling's application of the principle of identity resulted in nature being conceived as a form of spirit in which the actualization of spirit "consists in the conquest of the opposition that spirit has within itself."[147] Spirit is seen here as a "higher kind of nature"[148] evident in the "powerful consciousness of mastery inspired by the unfolding process of life, which man rediscovers in nature because nature itself has found itself in him."[149] Hence, in Schelling's philosophy of nature

> spirit is actual only when it posits within itself the conflict of nature and spirit. Spirit is real only when it transcends itself as nature. Nature is nothing other than spirit in its immediacy, in its unconscious self-positing. Consequently, every idea of God is excluded from this point of view which, like the Fichtean idea of God, is founded upon the antithesis of nature and spirit. When it is said that God is spirit, this means that he *is the concrete spirit who comprehends spirit and nature within himself, and not the abstract spirit who remains beyond nature.*[150]

It is interesting to note that Schelling's neo-Platonic view of the essential relationship between the divine and the natural world is akin to that of the Augustinian-Franciscan tradition, especially as exemplified in Bonaventure. That is, Schelling

> felt that God is to be *seen* in nature, not merely grasped conceptually, that subjectivity is in nature itself and hence it can be known by man, that the appearance is but the result of a condition of guilt, a turning away of the individual will from God as the unity and blessedness of things. Then man must read aright "the book of nature itself," see in reality the living law of identity, the divine bond of things....[151]

For Bonaventure the material world is quickly left behind as soon as the individual soul begins to make the ascent toward God, thus emptying nature of any real value apart from its largely symbolic function as a "mirror" of the divine.[152] This is not the case, however, with Schelling. For him, nature possesses genuine intrinsic worth since it is an *actual* manifestation of the divine, albeit one that we cannot always perceive due to our "fallen" condition. Nevertheless, in identifying the divine as the "ground" or *prius* of being *("unvordenklich")*, that is, as being both transcendent to and containing within itself the eternal process of self-division into subject and object, the natural world in this view can never be "left behind": "This presentation of God's life, not outside of or above nature but in nature, as a truly real and present life, is certainly the final synthesis of the ideal with the real, of knowing with being...."[153] The integrity of nature, as the essential manifestation of the living presence of God in the totality of all things, can never be lost, nor is it of value only to the extent that it constitutes a narrow pathway to God beyond itself. The material universe here breathes with and belongs to the divine, while not being wholly identified with it. Schelling thus articulates a true "pan-en-theism" when he declares, following Proverbs 8:27, that

> the eternal can only be finite unto himself, only he himself can comprehend and circumscribe his own being. Therefore the finiteness of the world on the outside includes a perfect infinitude within.
> The whole spatially extended universe is nothing but the swelling heart of the godhead.[154]

According to Tillich, with Schelling "it had become impossible to base the opposition between God and man upon the opposition of spirit and nature, and consequently, the conception of sin as the unavoidable 'not yet' of the good will was overcome."[155] While Schelling never explicitly states it in terms of an ethic, the implication is clear that one cannot love God without embracing, or at least respecting, the natural world, including the human being. The religious nature mysticism arising from Schelling's application of the principles of identity and freedom to the question of the relationship of nature and spirit is seen by Tillich as constituting a successful "bridge" over the "gulf...that reflective thought has falsely fixed between God as spirit and nature, [and which] corresponds in every way with that which has been drawn between the ego and nature."[156] This "bridge" is constructed only "by a living contact with nature.... When I am one with nature, I am one with God, who is nature's quickening force."[157] Schelling's evolutionary view of nature and spirit "tried to show how slowly in all different forms of nature consciousness develops until it comes to man where it becomes self-consciousness."[158] Tillich himself would later incorporate this view to a great extent into his mature pneumatology in the fourth part of his system.[159]

For Tillich, "[t]he religious significance of this expansion of the sphere of identity and, thereby, of truth, lies in the fact that objective reality no longer contradicts the idea of God, but rather affirms it most powerfully."[160] He observes in Schelling's philosophy of nature a critical "turn toward the concept of grace over against the concept of law."[161] Schelling's ontological argument against the opposition of nature and spirit recovers for the Protestant tradition a sense of what Tillich refers to as "sacramental feeling."[162] The type of thinking associated with such feeling was, according to Tillich, "present in the whole sacramental experience of the early church, but to a great extent it was lost in the Reformation criticism, and then finally lost in the Enlightenment which based itself on the imperative."[163] Schelling's nature mysticism went a long way toward rediscovering this positive sensibility toward the natural world, where "[t]he true attitude toward nature is one of living empathy...."[164] Hence, for Tillich, Schelling's philosophy of nature is ultimately

> the science of nature in God. Nature is perfect; it forms a totality, a universe, but this totality is in God. Nature is the being of God, which develops by the power of contradiction, which stands in eternal identity with the divine self, with divine freedom.[165]

Tillich therefore considers Schelling's "philosophy or theology...very much a doctrine of grace, stressing the given divine reality before our merits and before our moral acts."[166] Over against the moralism of the Enlightenment, which deemed "nature not living, but dead," Schelling recognized "nature as a living force...[and] brought once more into light the innermost core of religion, communion with God through grace."[167] This was possible, according to Tillich, "because there was *perceived in nature something complete in itself, a totality of divine existence, which remained infinitely unattainable by moral progress."*[168] According to this view the natural universe enjoys an intrinsic integrity insofar as it shares in, and is expressive of, the divine life. Schelling is thus responsible, in Tillich's estimation, for taking the "decisive step toward the affirmation of divine grace...in [his] affirmation of nature."[169] He extends the principle of personal grace as a communication of the divine spirit as found in Augustine, Luther, and Calvin (and in modified form in Schleiermacher) to include the non-human world:

> If nature, which makes no conscious decision and has no moral imperative, has within itself the divine presence, then the divine presence is not only dependent on our moral action. It is prior in the development of reality, and it is also subsequent to our moral action. It is below and above the moral imperative.[170]

With Schelling we are therefore a far cry from Descartes' *res cogitans,* which found little importance in the material universe apart from the mathematical formulations that could be applied to it by the human mind, as well as from the Kantian and Fichtean moral imperative, which set itself over against the natural world in order to assert its uncompromising autonomy. Moreover, Schelling and later evolutionist and naturalist thinkers (*e.g.*, Darwin, Nietzsche, Bergson, Whitehead) challenged the mechanistic Newtonian view of the universe as being too static and deterministic. It is therefore of great significance that Tillich chose Schelling as the subject for both his philosophical and theological doctoral dissertations.[171] Schelling's reverence for the natural world as the expression of divinity would later be shared by Tillich.

Existentialism, Liberalism, and Neo-Orthodoxy

The fact remains, however, that Protestant theology, following the great romantic period of the early nineteenth century, remained anchored to its "anthropocentric dynamics of grace," choosing not to follow the Schellingian line of thought which offered the notion of a positive relationship among the divine, nature, and humanity. In fact, Tillich points to Schelling's lectures in Berlin near the end of his life as signalling the beginning of this return to a more traditional application of the concept of grace.[172] These lectures were attended by, among others, Søren Kierkegaard. Schelling's attack on the extreme essentialism of the left-wing Hegelians would be taken up later in the nineteenth century with even more intensity by Kierkegaard, for whom Hegel represented the worst of speculative German idealism.[173] The *Lebensphilosophie* articulated by Schelling in the Berlin lectures exerted a profound influence on Kierkegaard, whose emphasis on an extreme pietistic inwardness as the only place where God is to be encountered, involves an almost complete devaluation of nature:

> [God] is in the creation, and present everywhere in it, but directly He is not there; and only when the individual turns to his inner self, and hence only in the inwardness of self-activity, does he have his attention aroused, and is enabled to see God....
>
> The observer of nature does not have a result immediately set before him, but must by himself be at pains to find it, and thereby the direct relationship is broken. But this breach is precisely the act of self-activity, the irruption of inwardness, the first determination of the truth as inwardness....

Nature, the totality of created things, is the work of God. And yet God is not there; but within the individual man there is a potentiality (man is potentially spirit) which is awakened in inwardness to become a God-relationship, and then it becomes possible to see God everywhere.... [T]he astonishment over the vastness of nature and the countless forms of animal life, is not the true understanding.[174]

For Kierkegaard, of course, truth is to be found only in the experience of undiluted subjectivity.[175] What Kierkegaard is trying to defend against in such passages as that quoted above is the danger of identifying in any absolute sense the Creator with the created, viz., the sin of idolatry. In the tradition of the Hebrew prophets and of Calvin before him, he rails against the twin demons of natural theology and positivist science. He claims that what is needed to overcome "Lessing's ditch" is a "leap of faith" taken in "the decisiveness that inheres in subjectivity."[176] Kierkegaard was thus wholly preoccupied with the existential question, the question of "to be or not to be." According to Tillich, the asking of this question for Kierkegaard represents "the most significant thing in the world.... It is the ultimate concern about man's eternal destiny, the question of the meaning of life."[177] It is the question of being that is asked of each individual; it constitutes the ontological crisis that each person encounters in the darkness of his or her own existence. It does not, however, raise the question of the ultimate concern about the eternal destiny of the non-human world. It is solely occupied with human interiority and with the God-human relationship, and in that sense completely neglects the natural universe.

Kierkegaard's radical existentialist posture in the end obviates any type of constructive theology of nature, since for him the only content that is of any value is that of "paradox," represented in absolute fashion by the appearance of the Christ.[178] This is the only historical fact that matters for Kierkegaard. The "leap" he therefore suggests can be undertaken only in an irrational manner, that is, if one is willing to ignore nearly two millennia of human history. In the Kierkegaardian universe, history is not necessarily set against nature as it is in Hegel; both are equally irrelevant to the existential decision for or against faith. The radical existential diagnosis of the human condition offered by Kierkegaard and his insistence on an "infinite qualitative difference" between God and creation would be taken up in the twentieth century by such neo-orthodox figures as Rudolf Bultmann and Karl Barth.

Kierkegaard's wariness of a "retreat to idolatry"[179] assumes therefore the form of a deep skepticism toward anyone who cultivates what he terms a "sentimental...aesthetic"[180] sensibility. For this reason, Tillich sees Kierkegaard's role as that of a "prophetic voice. The prophet always speaks from the vertical dimension and does not care about what happens in the horizontal dimension."[181] What is also apparent, however, is that Kierkegaard's radical openness to the religious (or "spiritual") dimensions of an individual's life does, when viewed properly, seem to lend itself to a generally more sensitive appreciation for beauty and harmony in the natural world. At least it *acknowledges* that people can recognize this beauty and harmony even if, more often than not, they misconstrue the immediacy of the experience of natural beauty with that of an immediate experience of the divine. In other words, perhaps (as we shall see in Tillich) one can somehow preserve a "paradoxical" way of being passionate about the world while not losing oneself to it.[182]

The same cannot be said, as a rule, for the proponents of the "back to Kant" movement in the late nineteenth and early twentieth centuries. Ritschl, in surveying the devastation in the aftermath of the breakup of the universal synthesis attempted by Schleiermacher and Hegel, surrendered the claim to truth that such a synthesis sought to achieve. Instead, he and his followers (Troeltsch, Harnack, et al.) "withdrew to Kant's critique of practical reason and said: The divine appears through the moral imperative and nowhere else. The problem of truth was replaced by the moral answer."[183] Liberal Protestant theology consequently developed along two lines, that of "objective, scientific research and the moral principle or experience of the ethical personality."[184]

Because they were unable to develop a viable theology of nature, these "theologians of mediation" became like "an army retreating in the face of an advancing army."[185] The "advancing army" in this case was spearheaded by the "mechanistic naturalism" of Darwinism and its associated hybrids (Nietzsche, Bergson, Whitehead).[186] Without an adequate conception of the God-world relationship, the heavily moralistic theology following from Ritschl and his intellectual descendants devolved into a radically privatist doctrine of grace. For each advance made in the scientific world, liberal Protestant theology retreated further and further until all that was left was "an unworthy idea of God":

Evolution said that life has developed out of the inorganic realm. Then where is God? According to the traditional idea of creation God has created the organic forms; they have not developed out of the inorganic forms. Therefore, a particular work of God's creation must be postulated and on this thread the whole apologetic position was suspended. There was the lacuna in scientific knowledge, for science was not able to show how the organic developed out of the inorganic. Theologians enjoyed this lacuna, for they could place God in this gap left by science. Where science could not work any more, God was put to work, so to speak. God filled the gaps left by science.[187]

The antiscientific attitude of liberal Protestantism during this period had dire consequences for the natural world. By insisting that personal morality alone was the sphere of religion proper, it allowed for the virtual unrestrained growth of technology such as the world had never seen. At this point, the lack of an adequate Protestant theology of grace *and* nature becomes apparent insofar as Protestantism was unable to sufficiently raise the necessary opposition (on religious and moral grounds) to an increasing and uncritical dependence on science and technology. Claiming that "[t]heology does not need to put God to work to fill an empty space in our scientific knowledge,"[188] Tillich criticizes the type of apologetic theology that was practiced during this period for its irrelevancy in the face of such momentous cultural and social developments. The failure of theology to adequately assume its proper role as critic of culture, in this case, as critic of science and technology from the perspective of "ultimate concern," resulted not only in the unfortunate disregard for the natural world that has characterized the insatiable technological appetite of modern humanity but, also, in the loss of what it meant to be human at all:

> The safety which is guaranteed by well-functioning mechanisms for the technical control of nature, by the refined psychological control of the person, by the rapidly increasing organizational control of society – this safety is bought at a high price: man, for whom all this was invented as a means, becomes a means himself in the service of means.[189]

Tillich therefore sees a link between the modern phenomenon of dehumanization and that of ecological devastation. In part, he cites the hostile Ritschlian attitude toward nature and its bourgeois belief in the gradual perfectibility of the human person as functions of the same general problem. And that problem consisted in large measure in the "Ritschlian negation of ontology."[190] In its attempt to reduce Christianity to a form of communication which can only make value judgments (rather than ontological assertions), neo-Kantian theology argued on that basis that "we can evaluate Christianity as that religion which can overcome the forces of the natural and secure us as personalities of disciplined moral character."[191] This view was particularly distasteful to Tillich who, moreover, found in the "Ritschlian antiontological feeling" an inferior doctrine of God "in which the element of power...was denied or reduced almost to nothing."[192] For Tillich, therefore, the harmful effect of the theological split between nature and grace was never so evident as it was in Ritschlianism. And while he recognizes the greatness of liberal theology's courage in applying the historical method to questions of theological interest, including the biblical literature, he nevertheless criticizes such an approach for not taking sufficient account of nature:

> To tear apart nature and history and distribute them to two kinds of metaphysics would mean to disrupt genuine elements of reality....
> [H]istory is not a separate sphere of abstract freedom over or beside nature; rather it is one aspect of events, which at every moment also contain the other aspect: nature and the totality of its relationships. All history is also nature.... It is therefore impossible to combine a dynamic metaphysics of history with a static metaphysics of nature.... [N]ature at every moment holds something within itself which is not to be determined by static and immutable laws. That nature is, as it is, with these qualities...is not derivable; it is fate and therefore implies freedom. The meaning of this original quality of nature, of this underivable existence, finds its highest expression in history. In history, fate becomes visible as fate, implying freedom. In history, nature expresses its mystery: freedom and fate.[193]

For Tillich, the fate of humanity is inextricably linked with that of nature. If, as Tillich claims, the ambiguities of human history, both personally and collectively, will be conquered in the "vicarious fulfilment" of the essentialized Kingdom of God, then so too shall those of the non-human world.[194] Just as it is impossible from the point of view of the fundamentally polar structure of being to separate the "freedom and fate" of the mystery of nature in terms of temporal existence, so is it impossible to separate its "eternal destiny...from the destiny...of being in all its manifestations."[195]

The first half of the twentieth century witnessed a hostile reaction to the *Kulturprotestantismus* of liberal theology, with its reliance on historicism and morality as the keys to understanding Christianity. Such neo-orthodox thinkers as Karl Barth, Emil Brunner, and Rudolf Bultmann early on criticized nineteenth-century Protestantism for its radical "immanentism, cultural as well as philosophical."[196] Far from identifying humanity with nature, Bultmann criticized the romanticist tradition from the point of view of history: "Our relationship to history is wholly different from our relationship to nature. Man, if he rightly understands himself, differentiates himself from nature. When he observes nature, he perceives there something objective which is not himself."[197] Such a passage is a virtual definition of an anthropocentric understanding of nature. Tillich, in recognizing the importance of Bultmann's effort in the face of Barthian supernaturalism to save "the historical question from being banished from theology,"[198] nevertheless laments the fact that, in their "quest for the historical Jesus," Bultmann and his followers "demythologize" not only religious language but our religious understanding of the natural world as well.[199]

In his *Die Mystik und das Wort*, Brunner particularly singled out Schleiermacher as the villain who lent legitimacy to a history of religions approach to Christianity, and whose "mysticism" arose out of his easy uncritical reliance on romanticism with its virtual deification of nature,[200] "a case of his piety breaking through his systematic principles."[201] Tillich observes that in this regard "Brunner is right only insofar as one can say generally of all Schleiermacher's thinking that there is a tension between the purely philosophical and the more positivistic approaches to Christianity."[202]

And while Brunner insisted *contra* Barth that a *theologia naturalis* is possible by virtue of the "'general revelation' of God in nature, in the conscience and in history," the "point of contact" that has been established by God between Godself and the world (the *imago Dei*, as it were) is located exclusively in the human person, and not in nature.[203] The important element in the question of nature and grace for Brunner is not that of *nature*, as such, but of *sin*. That is, how can God's personal self-communication of grace through faith to the individual overcome the effects of sin? While not denying that God's self-revelation can appear in the natural world, for Brunner nature is here seen not in its own intrinsic dignity but *merely* as a vehicle for divine communication with the human person. Brunner's "natural theology," therefore, with its emphasis once again on the operation of grace within the human individual maintains, at least in principle, the split between nature and grace as it concerns the non-human world. This disparagement of nature at the expense of human salvation constitutes one of the primary differences between a "natural theology" and a "theology of nature."[204] Compare this to the comments of one observer concerning the relationship between the two forms of theology in Tillich:

> [Tillich] is certain that no natural theology is possible since for him nature in and of itself reveals nothing of God to human beings. There is revelation by God *through* nature but not *in* nature, rather like the idea that there is revelation through Jesus as the Christ rather than in him.... But how different is this view from the old natural theology? That theology posed a certain independence of nature from the divine, but as created it was in grace and therefore retained elements or vestiges of the gracious hand of its Creator.... Tillich is saying something similar but on different grounds. The relation between God and the world and so of God and humankind is conceived to be much more intimate and immediate. The *vestigia Dei* doctrine in the hands of some of its interpreters implied that God was remote from creation; Tillich's theory entails the constant impact of God upon all finite reality. The finite is never without its infinite ground, for the infinite is related to the finite in every aspect. The infinite is implicated in the finite even while infinitely transcending it....
>
> This fundamental perspective gives point to the view that [Tillich's] theology is first and last a theology of grace and along with this a theology of nature....[205]

Karl Barth acknowledges in his commentary on Romans 7:22-23 that it is "[i]n religion [that]...dualism makes its appearance."[206] By this he means that a distinction is made between the "inward" (or "spiritual") person and the "outward" (or "natural") person. Of course this is only an apparent dichotomy, Barth points out, a "contrast" that reveals only the actual tension that exists for everything that stands under the divine judgment. He rejects any attempt to synthesize the two in any fashion, since such syntheses are the work of arrogance and hence doomed to failure. He thus succeeds in maintaining the oppositional relationship between "Spirit" and "Nature" in his dialectical theology:

> But to which dost thou belong? Who are thou? Art thou 'spirit' or 'Nature'? Thou canst not deny 'spirit', and hold thee only to 'Nature'; for as a religious man, thou hast knowledge of God, and thy most particular perception is that 'Nature' desires to be altogether 'spirit'. Neither canst

thou deny 'Nature', and hold thee only to 'spirit'; for as a religious man, thou hast knowledge of God, and thou knowest only too well that 'spirit' desires to be altogether 'Nature'. Am I then both together?! Well, try: Art thou 'spirit-Nature' or 'Nature-Spirit'...?! Once attempt any such arrogant anticipation, and thou wilt soon perceive that the desired union cannot be manoevred merely by ranging the two alongside one another, or by amalgamating them, or be conglomerating them. The more thou dost madly endeavour to synthesize things which are directly opposed to one another, the more surely do they break apart and become manifestly antithetic.[207]

In opposing the two realms of "Spirit" and "Nature" in terms of a Kierkegaardian "infinite qualitative distinction,"[208] however, Barth only succeeds theologically in reinforcing the "dualism" he claims religion is responsible for creating. Once again, the Augustinian-Lutheran ambiguity concerning the relationship between nature and grace rears its head in an attempt to revive the Reformers' "anthropocentric dynamics of grace." For this reason Tillich, in his 1934-35 debate with Emanuel Hirsch, indirectly attacked Barth for his "tearing apart of" the divine and the created.[209] Tillich felt that, against Hirsch's "Chalcedonian" mixing of the two spheres and Barth's severing of them, that "only he, Tillich, remain[ed] faithful to the dialectical relationship between the two realms as intended by the fathers of Chalcedon."[210] Even in his later theological development, when he crafts his exalted christocentric incarnational theology culminating with the notion of the "Humanity of God," Barth never really extends his incarnationalism to the non-human universe.[211] It remains, in his words, "the-anthropological" and, therefore, relatively unconcerned with the role of nature, history, or culture in the divine drama of creation and redemption. Accordingly, among the three (*i.e.*, Hirsch, Barth, Tillich), it is Tillich whose

> theology of grace...is intrinsic to his theology of nature, without collapsing grace and nature. It could, therefore, be argued that...Tillich has the most viable model for a contemporary theology of nature; a model, with the most balanced view of the relation of the divine to the natural....[212]

This leads to the question: What form might such a "theology of nature" in Tillich actually assume? Before examining this question in specific detail in the third chapter, Chapter Two will next deal with Tillich's life-long personal and professional concern for the non-human world.

Notes

1. Percy Bysshe Shelley, "Love's Philosophy," in *A Reasonable Affliction: 1001 Love Poems to Read to Each Other,* ed. Sally Ann Berk and James Gordon Wakeman (New York: Black Dog and Leventhal Publishers, 1996), 314.
2. John H. Gay, "Four Medieval Views of Creation," *Harvard Theological Review* 56 (October 1963): 252.
3. James A. Carpenter speculates what Western theology might have looked like had Pelagius personally met with Augustine during Pelagius' trip to Hippo: "To the loss of both men (and perhaps to the church at large), Augustine was in Carthage. The two had great respect for each other's character, intelligence, and writings, and if they had met for extended conversation, they might have understood each other better even if not reaching fundamental agreement. The bitterness of the controversy might have been lessened, and perhaps their respective viewpoints would have been seen to have a certain complementarity. Imaginings such as these are not idle. They give further point to the claim that the split, or near split, between nature and grace in Western theology, developed so largely under the influence of Augustine, did not occur by reason of any imperious theological necessity but through circumstance and chance" (*Nature and Grace: Toward an Integral Perspective* [New York: Crossroad, 1988], 161-162).
4. Paul Tillich, *HCT,* 104: "We can trace a line of thought from Augustine...to the Reformers, to the philosophers of the seventeenth and eighteenth centuries, to the German classical philosophers,...to the present-day philosophy of religion...which is based on the immediacy of the truth in every human being."
5. Ibid., 111: "I am in basic agreement with Augustine with respect to the philosophy of religion, but not necessarily in other things. For example, as a *Gestalt* theologian or philosopher I am closer to Aristotle than to Augustine or Plato, because the idea of the living structure of an organism is Aristotelian, whereas the atomistic, mechanical, mathematical science is Augustinian and Platonic."
6. On this point, see Gordon D. Kaufman, "A Problem for Theology: The Concept of Nature," *The Harvard Theological Review* 65 (1972): 337-366.
7. Augustine *On the Grace of Christ, and On Original Sin* (in Philip Schaff, ed., *Nicene and Post-Nicene Fathers* 5 [Peabody, MA: Hendrickson Publishers, 1995]) 1.25.
8. Tillich, *HCT,* 104, 125-126.
9. Carpenter, *Nature,* 9.
10. George S. Hendry, *Theology of Nature* (Philadelphia: Westminster Press, 1980), 17.

11. Tillich, *HCT*, 228-229.
12. Martin Luther, *Small Catechism*, in *The Book of Concord*, trans. and ed. Theodore G. Tappert (Philadelphia: Fortress, 1959), 10.
13. Tillich, *HCT*, 230.
14. Ibid., 259.
15. Santmire, *Travail*, 125.
16. Tillich, *HCT*, 374. Cf. Paul Tillich, "Dimensions, Levels, and the Unity of Life," *Kenyon Alumni Bulletin* 17 (1959): 5.
17. Paul Tillich, *ST* 3, 356.
18. Tillich, *HCT*, 262.
19. Ibid., 259.
20. Ibid., 247.
21. Ibid., 248.
22. Ibid., 240.
23. Tillich, *ST* 1, 277.
24. Tillich, *HCT*, 261. Emphasis mine.
25. Paul Tillich, "Natur and Sakrament," in *GW* 7, 105-123. This important essay originally appeared in *RV* (published in 1929) and later appeared in English translation in *PRE*, 94-112.
26. Tillich, *HCT*, 261.
27. Tillich, "Nature and Sacrament," *PRE*, 94.
28. Tillich, *HCT*, 260.
29. Ibid., 261.
30. Ibid., 260.
31. Ibid.
32. For a discussion on the various distinctions to be made among representational symbols, presentational symbols, and sacraments, see James C. Livingston, *Anatomy of the Sacred: An Introduction to Religion*, 2nd ed. (New York: Macmillan, 1993), 74-76, 130-132.
33. Tillich, *HCT*, 261. Cf. also 373.
34. Ibid., 260. Emphasis mine.
35. Ibid., 262.
36. Ibid.
37. Ibid.
38. Ibid., 261.
39. Ibid., 262.
40. Durwood Foster, "Afterglows of Tillich," *Newsletter of the North American Paul Tillich Society* 23/1 (January 1997): 5. The statement quoted here is attributed to Tillich in his reproach of Foster and others for their uncritical willingness to go fishing. Cf. Tillich's discussion on the overcoming of the subject/object split of technical activity under the impact of the Spiritual Presence in *ST* 3, 258-260.

41. Tillich, *ST* 1, 30.
42. Tillich, "Nature and Sacrament," 112. Cf. Tillich, *ST* 1, 120: "Nature in special sections or nature as a whole can be a medium of revelation in an ecstatic experience. But nature cannot be an argumentative basis for conclusions about the mystery of being."
43. Tillich, *HCT,* 259.
44. Jean Calvin, *Commentary on Hebrews,* quoted in Edward A. Dowey, Jr., *The Knowledge of God in Calvin's Theology* (New York: Columbia University Press, 1952), 135-136.
45. Jean Calvin *Institutes of the Christian Religion* (trans. F. L. Battles [Grand Rapids, MI: William B. Eerdmans Publishing Co., 1986]) 2.6.1.
46. Wilhelm Niesel, *The Theology of Calvin,* trans. Harold Knight (Philadelphia: Westminster Press, 1956), 47.
47. Ibid., 48.
48. Ibid., 46.
49. Calvin *Institutes* 1.5.14.
50. Tillich, *HCT,* 265.
51. Ibid.
52. Tillich, *ST* 1, 262.
53. Tillich, *HCT,* 265.
54. Tillich, *ST* 1, 264.
55. Ibid.
56. Ibid., 262.
57. Ibid., 264.
58. Tillich, *ST* 3, 421. A full appraisal of this seminal notion in Tillich's system will be discussed in Chapter Three.
59. Santmire, *Travail,* 126.
60. Tillich, *HCT,* 347.
61. Santmire, *Travail,* 127. Cf. also of course Max Weber, *The Protestant Ethic and the Spirit of Capitalism,* trans. Talcott Parsons (New York: Charles Scribner's Sons, 1930).
62. Tillich, *HCT,* 347.
63. In this regard, Tillich observes that the Reformers' relatively positive view of nature was nevertheless influenced by a deeply pessimistic assessment of human freedom: "The Renaissance begins with the affirmation of the world, such as antiquity never knew, and in Protestantism the final remains of ascetic mysticism which Christianity had accepted are thrust off, and it is affirmed more and more clearly that things are created by God in perfect innocence. But with this new affirmation of nature is combined a deep realization of the discord in nature itself. Not matter, not the creature as such, but the freedom of the creature creates the dissension. The doctrine of original sin, which Protestantism carries through to the most radical consequences, and

which drives it to the boundary of Manichæan dualism, is the expression of the new view of the Demonic" (*IH*, 110).

64. Harold H. Oliver, "The Neglect and Recovery of Nature in Twentieth-Century Protestant Thought," *Journal of the American Academy of Religion* 60/3 (Autumn 1992): 379.

65. Paul Tillich, *WR*, 128.

66. Ibid.

67. Tillich, *HCT*, 337.

68. Carpenter, *Nature*, 9.

69. René Descartes, *Meditations* 6, 12th ed., ed. and trans. John Veitch (Edinburgh and London: W. Blackwood, 1899), 164, 238.

70. Tillich, *HCT*, 113.

71. Tillich, *WR*, 125.

72. Ibid.

73. Ibid., 129.

74. Ibid.

75. Ibid.

76. Paula M. Cooey's masterful study of Jonathan Edwards demonstrates the importance the natural world played in his theology of creation, foreshadowing in some respects an "ecology of being": "Edwards' doctrine of God characterizes God as dynamic being that communicates itself as origin, pattern, and destiny of all reality.... For [him] nature plays a dramatic role in this process of communication.... Under the proper conditions nature communicates or reveals divine consent to human being. This communication has implications for the relationship between God and nature and between human being and the rest of nature as well as human/divine relationships. Chief among them is that nature communicates daily the divine destiny and human participation in this destiny" (Paula M. Cooey, *Jonathan Edwards on Nature and Destiny: A Systematic Analysis*, Studies in American Religion 16 [Lewiston, NY and Queenston, ON: Edwin Mellen Press, 1985], 80.)

77. Tillich, *HCT*, 289.

78. Ibid.

79. Ibid., 344.

80. Immanuel Kant, *Critique of Pure Reason*, trans. J. M. D. Meiklejohn (London and Toronto: J. M. Dent and Sons, 1934).

81. Tillich, *HCT*, 362. See also Paul Tillich, *MGS*, 33-38.

82. Tillich, *HCT*, 362.

83. Ibid., 364.

84. Tillich makes the point that "[e]ven a man like Karl Barth who is so firmly rooted in the classical tradition has fully accepted the Kantian criticism of natural theology" (Ibid., 360). At the same time, Tillich sees his own method of correlation as an attempt to respond to the oft-repeated slogan of

his student years: "Understanding Kant means transcending Kant" (Ibid., 366).

85. Ibid., 362-363. Cf. Tillich, *MGS*, 38-42.
86. Tillich, *ST* 3, 46-47.
87. Tillich, *HCT*, 365.
88. Ibid., 514.
89. Ibid.
90. Ibid., 342.
91. Ibid., 514.
92. Immanuel Kant, *Critique of Judgment*, tr. Werner S. Pluhar (Indianapolis, IN: Hackett Publishing Co., 1987).
93. Tillich, *MGS*, 42.
94. Tillich, *HCT*, 365-366.
95. Tillich even goes so far as to maintain that "[a]ny theology which does not have an understanding of the universal character of the logos structure of the world, and that means of reason in the sense of logos, becomes barbaric and ceases to be theology" (*HCT*, 327). When this dominant trait is missing from Christian theology, according to Tillich, the doctrines of creation and redemption are liable to be set in opposition to one another. This in turn can lead to a division (at least in principle) within Godself and, consequently, to a dualistic view of the universe in which the "corrupted" creation needs to be redeemed by a "pure" savior. Tillich finds evidence of this type of heretical thinking throughout the history of Protestant thought, including the earlier period of neo-Orthodoxy. Ibid.
96. John 1:3.
97. Tillich, *HCT*, 326.
98. Ibid., 327.
99. Ibid., 422.
100. Ibid., 366.
101. Ibid.
102. Ibid., 371.
103. Ibid., 373.
104. See Tillich, *MGS*, 29.
105. Tillich, *HCT*, 373. Emphasis mine.
106. Ibid., 374.
107. Ibid.
108. Ibid.
109. Ibid.
110. Ibid.
111. Friedrich Schleiermacher, *On Religion: Speeches to Its Cultured Despisers*, trans. Richard Crouter (Cambridge and New York: Cambridge University Press, 1988), 103.
112. Ibid., 102.

113. Friedrich Schleiermacher, *The Christian Faith,* ed. H. R. Mackintosh and J. S. Stewart (Edinburgh: T and T Clark, 1956), 16.
114. Ibid.
115. Tillich, *HCT,* 392. Elsewhere Tillich observes of Schleiermacher's famous definition of religion that it "meant the immediate awareness of something unconditional in the sense of the Augustinian-Franciscan tradition.... 'Feeling'...referred not to a psychological function but to the awareness of that which transcends intellect and will, subject and object. 'Dependence'...was, on the Christian level, 'teleological' dependence – a dependence which has moral character, which includes freedom and excludes a pantheistic and deterministic interpretation of the experience of the unconditional. Schleiermacher's 'feeling of absolute dependence' was rather near to what is called [in my system] 'ultimate concern about the ground and meaning of our being'" (*ST* 1, 41-42).
116. Schleiermacher, *Christian Faith,* 174, 192.
117. Ibid., 173.
118. Ibid., 170-193.
119. Ibid., 262-264, 476-505.
120. Tillich, *HCT,* 409-410.
121. Ibid., 409.
122. See on this point Karl Löwith, *Nature, History and Existentialism,* ed. Arnold Levison (Evanston, IL: Northwestern University Press, 1966). Also see, for example, G. W. F. Hegel, *Philosophy of Nature,* trans. A. V. Miller (Oxford: Clarendon Press, 1970) and J. G. Fichte, *The Science of Knowledge, with the First and Second Introductions,* trans. P. Heath and J. Lachs (Cambridge: Cambridge University Press, 1982).
123. Joseph L. Esposito, *Schelling's Idealism and Philosophy of Nature* (Lewisburg, PA: Bucknell University Press and London: Associated University Presses, 1977), 24.
124. Ibid., 22.
125. Carpenter, *Nature,* 11.
126. G. W. F. Hegel, *Phenomenology of Spirit,* trans. A. V. Miller (Oxford: Clarendon Press, 1977).
127. Tillich, *HCT,* 419.
128. Ibid., 422.
129. Esposito, *Schelling's Idealism,* 26.
130. This type of approach is what prompted Feuerbach to argue that "theology is nothing else than an unconscious, esoteric pathology, anthropology, and psychology" (*The Essence of Christianity,* tr. George Eliot [New York: Harper and Row, 1957], 89), and Karl Barth to level his most aggressive attacks directly at Schleiermacher.

131. Robert Stern, introduction to *Ideas for a Philosophy of Nature as Introduction to the Study of This Science* by F. W. J. von Schelling, trans. Errol E. Harris and Peter Heath (Cambridge: Cambridge University Press, 1988), xvi.

132. F. W. J. von Schelling, *Sämmtliche Werke* 2, ed. K. F. A. Schelling (Stuttgart and Augsburg: J. G. Cotta, 1856-61), 459. Translation mine. Cf. Tillich, *MGS*, 53: "The philosophy of nature is the application of the principle of identity to nature. The synthesis of the many and the one, of subject and object, ought to be realized in nature just as it is in the ego."

133. Tillich, *HCT*, 442. Tillich describes Schelling's attack on Fichte as "a kind of holy wrath," even quoting from Schelling on this point: "'It is a blasphemy of the Creator to think that nature is only there in order to be the material for our moral glory; nature has the divine glory in itself'" (Ibid.).

134. Ibid.

135. Stern, Introduction, xx.

136. Frederick deWolfe Bolman, Jr., introduction to *The Ages of the World* by F. W. J. von Schelling, trans. idem (New York: AMS Press, 1967), 4.

137. Schelling, *Ideas*, 47.

138. Tillich, *MGS*, 53.

139. Schelling, *Ideas*, 179.

140. Tillich, *MGS*, 54.

141. Bolman, Introduction, 64.

142. Tillich, *MGS*, 54.

143. Schelling, *Sämmtliche Werke* 7, 59. Translation mine.

144. Tillich, *MGS*, 57.

145. Ibid., 58.

146. Ibid., 57.

147. Ibid.

148. Ibid.

149. Ibid., 55.

150. Ibid., 58. Emphasis mine.

151. Bolman, Introduction, 26-27. Cf. F. W. J. von Schelling, *The Night Watches of Bonaventura*, tr. Gerald Gillespie (Austin, TX: University of Texas Press, 1971).

152. See, for example, Bonaventure *The Soul's Journey Into God* (trans. Ewert Cousins [New York: Paulist Press, 1978]) 5. Cf. Santmire, *Travail*, 103.

153. Schelling, *Sämmtliche Werke* 7, 34. Translation mine.

154. Schelling, *Ages*, 215.

155. Tillich, *MGS*, 58. Cf. Ibid., 94: "The conquest of divine egoism by divine love is the process by which God becomes personal, he becomes nature and man; for divine egoism, made gentle by love, is nature in God."

156. Ibid., 55.

157. Ibid.

158. Tillich, *HCT*, 442.
159. See Tillich, *ST* 3, 11-294.
160. Tillich, *MGS*, 54.
161. Tillich, *HCT*, 442.
162. Ibid., 443.
163. Ibid.
164. Tillich, *MGS*, 122.
165. Ibid., 95-96. Emphasis mine.
166. Tillich, *HCT*, 443.
167. Tillich, *MGS*, 59.
168. Ibid. Emphasis mine.
169. Ibid.
170. Tillich, *HCT*, 442-443.
171. His dissertation for the doctorate in philosophy was *The Construction of the History of Religion in Schelling's Positive Philosophy*, tr. Victor Nuovo (Lewisburg, PA: Bucknell University Press, 1974) and, for the licentiate in theology, *MGS*.
172. Tillich, *HCT*, 447.
173. See, for example, Søren Kierkegaard, *Concluding Unscientific Post-script*, trans. David F. Swenson and Walter Lowrie (Princeton, NJ: Princeton University Press, 1941), esp. 99108. Cf. Paul Tillich, *CB*, 135-139 and "Existential Philosophy: Its Historical Meaning," in *TC*, 84.
174. Kierkegaard, *Concluding*, 218, 220-221.
175. Ibid., 169-224.
176. Ibid., 105. Cf. Tillich, *HCT*, 464-472.
177. Tillich, *HCT*, 470.
178. Ibid., 471.
179. Ibid., 221.
180. Søren Kierkegaard, *Fear and Trembling* and *The Sickness Unto Death*, trans. Walter Lowrie (Princeton, NJ: Princeton University Press, 1941, 1954), 95.
181. Tillich, *HCT*, 474.
182. In this regard, Catherine Keller has recently suggested that perhaps a modified version of Kierkegaardian inwardness may indeed prove favorable to a healthy contemporary ecological sensitivity: "The Creator for any Protestant will be unidentifiable with any piece or combination of pieces of the creation – especially construed as a closed totality of already done deeds.... Ecojustice Protestants may or may not find God 'there.' I would only want to ask where the Spirit is, if not animating the creation itself. To draw Protestants into care for that 'everywhere,' one will need to respect some version of Kierkegaardian indirectness, a certain non-Cartesian inwardness of spirit. But the trick will be to affirm that spirit-potential without surrendering to the dissociative lull of

the private pietism into which Protestantism, after its radical moments and its Kierkegaardian leaps of faith, so easily falls" ("The Lost Fragrance: Protestantism and the Nature of What Matters," *Journal of the American Academy of Religion* 65/2 [Summer 1997]: 365).

183. Tillich, *HCT*, 513.
184. Ibid.
185. Ibid., 454, 455.
186. Ibid.
187. Ibid., 456.
188. Ibid., 457. Cf. Tillich, *DF*, 80-85.
189. Tillich, *CB*, 138.
190. Tillich, *HCT*, 514.
191. Ibid., 515.
192. Ibid.
193. Tillich, *IH*, 163.
194. Tillich, *ST* 3, 409.
195. Ibid.
196. Oliver, "Nature," 382.
197. Rudolf Bultmann, *Jesus and the Word* (New York: Charles Scribner's Sons, 1934), 1.
198. Tillich, *HCT*, 538.
199. Ibid., 523.
200. Emil Brunner, *Die Mystik und das Wort: Der Gegensatz zwischen oderner Religionsfassung und christlichen Glauben dargestellt an der Theologie Schleiermachers* (Tübingen: Verlag von J. C. B. Mohr, 1924).
201. Tillich, *HCT*, 406.
202. Ibid., 407.
203. Emil Brunner and Karl Barth, *Natural Theology: Comprising "Nature and Grace" by Emil Brunner and the Reply "No!" by Karl Barth*, tr. Peter Fraenkel (London: Centenary Press, 1946), 22-35.
204. For further discussion of the differences between "natural theology" and "theology of nature," see Sigurd M. Daecke, "Theologie der Natur als 'natürliche Theologie?' Interdisziplinäre und ökologische Überlegungen mit Tillichs Hilfe," in *Natürliche Theologie versus Theologie der Natur? Tillichs Denken als Anstoss zum Gespräch zwischen Theologie, Philosophie und Naturwissenschaft*, ed. Gert Hummel (Berlin and New York: Walter de Gruyter, 1994), 249-270; and Sallie McFague, *The Body of God: An Ecological Theology* (Minneapolis: Fortress Press, 1993), 73-78.
205. Carpenter, *Nature*, 51-52. Emphasis mine.
206. Karl Barth, *The Epistle to the Romans*, 6th ed., trans. Edwyn C. Hoskins (London: Oxford University Press, 1968), 268.
207. Ibid., 268-269.

208. Ibid., 99.
209. Paul Tillich, "Um was es geht: Antwort an Emanuel Hirsch," *Theologische Blätter* 14 (May 1935): 119.
210. A. James Reimer, "Tillich, Hirsch and Barth: Three Different Paradigms of Theology and its Relation to the Sciences," in Hummel (ed.), *Natürliche Theologie*, 102. According to Reimer, it was Hirsch's involvement with National Socialism that led to his "mixing" of the Chalcedonian categories: "National Socialism, as the name denotes, allegedly was an attempt to combine a strong rootedness in nature (nationalism and the myth of origin) and a scientific, technological shaping of nature (socialism). In actual fact, it was caught in a contradiction: the romanticization of nature, on the one hand, and the technological exploitation of human and non-human nature, on the other. Hirsch...was, nevertheless, critical of any romanticization and deification of nature. He rejected the reduction of human existence to biological origins, by emphasizing our transcendence over the natural realm of necessity, and the breaking of ancient magic, myth and superstition through modern science. Yet, in his rather uncritical linking of humanness with national consciousness, with a strong biological-racial component, he falls prey to Tillich's charge that he has mixed the divine and the human-natural categories of Chalcedon" (Ibid., 116).
211. Karl Barth, *The Humanity of God*, tr. John N. Thomas (Richmond, VA: John Knox Press, 1960). Tillich was, however, encouraged by the publication of this book, feeling that to a certain extent Barth had bridged the yawning abyss between creation and Creator by putting a "face to God" (*HCT*, 538).
212. Reimer, "Tillich," 124.

Tillich points the way, as he tried to do in everything he thought and wrote, as one of the great fighters against the demonic 'structures of destruction' that would destroy life as we know it on this earth, whether through synthetic simulation or radiation and pollution.[1]

Chapter 2

Nature and Method
in Tillich's Life and Work

As we have seen from Chapter One, Paul Tillich was profoundly aware of the tensions and ambiguities inherent in the tradition from which he spoke concerning the relationship of nature and grace. While basically aligning his own philosophical and theological enterprise with that of the Augustinian line of thought, Tillich's inspiration was drawn from an eclectic range of intellectual, historical, and personal influences and sources. Perhaps the most brilliant quality Tillich possessed was his ability to bring together seemingly unrelated (and, at times, contradictory) impulses, ideas, movements, symbols, traditions, and images, and create out of this otherwise strange mélange a remarkably intelligible synthesis of thought and meaning. What is equally remarkable (for purposes of the present study) is that Tillich's treatment of the relationship between the human and non-human communities can appear, at times, right at home with the contemporary dialogue among ecotheologians.[2] Accordingly, while Tillich never fully developed a "theology of nature" to the extent that he did his "theology of culture," I will nevertheless attempt in the next chapter to formulate such a theology of nature out of those components of his work which address the question of the relationship obtaining among God, humankind, and the earth. The task of crafting a theology of nature out of Tillich's own work requires the addressing of some preliminary concerns first. Accordingly, this chapter will deal with the substantial influence the non-human world exerted on Paul Tillich's life and work as well as the question of the viability of Tillich's correlational method with respect to a theology of nature.

A Lifelong Concern

Paul Tillich's profound concern for, and rich appreciation of, the natural world was evident throughout his life, from his early childhood until his death. In one of his well-known autobiographical sketches Tillich relates that, as a young person, despite the strong attraction the "myth of the city" held for him, his "ties to the country...[were] even stronger":

> Nearly all the great memories and longings of my life are interwoven with landscapes, soil, weather, the fields of grain and the smell of the potato plant in autumn, the shapes of clouds, and with wind, flowers and woods. In all my later travels through Germany and southern and western Europe, the impression of the land remained strong. Schelling's philosophy of nature, which I read enthusiastically while surrounded by the beauty of nature, became the direct expression of my feeling for nature.
>
> The weeks and, later, months that I spent by the sea every year from the time I was eight were even more important for my life and work. The experience of the infinite bordering on the finite suited my inclination toward the boundary situation and supplied my imagination with a symbol that gave substance to my emotions and creativity to my thought. Without this experience it is likely that my theory of the human boundary situation, as expressed in *Religiöse Verwicklichung* [sic], might not have developed as it did.
>
> There is another element to be found in the contemplation of the sea: its dynamic assault on the serene firmness of the land and the ecstasy of its gales and waves. My theory of the "dynamic mass" in the essay "Masse und Geist"...was conceived under the immediate influence of the

turbulent sea. The sea also supplied the imaginative element necessary for the doctrines of the Absolute as both ground and abyss of dynamic truth, and of the substance of religions as the thrust of the eternal into finitude.... Many of my ideas were conceived in the open and much of my writing done among trees or by the sea.[3]

An example of this last statement is provided by Wilhelm and Marion Pauck in their biographical portrait of Tillich. During the writing of his dissertation for his Licentiate in Theology from the University of Halle, Tillich "sat on a veranda looking out upon green fields and surrounded by blooming linden trees which gave off a honeyed fragrance, endlessly writing out excerpts from Schelling...."[4] The Paucks observe that at that time "[n]ature intoxicated him as never before," and that "later, in America, he tried to duplicate the...experience in his...home on Long Island, where he grew trees, dined outdoors, and worked for hours in his garden."[5] During the last years of his life, which were spent at the Divinity School of the University of Chicago, Tillich would often walk from the campus to Lake Michigan where "even in sub-zero weather...he watched the forces of nature at work: he saw the abyss, sensed the depths, felt the dynamic forms in the pounding of the surf on the beach which made it seem like an ocean."[6] He even acknowledged at one point to being "a quasi-pagan lover of trees."[7]

It is evident from the foregoing that, by his own admission, nature played an enormous role in the development of some of Tillich's most important philosophical ideas and theological doctrines. He rarely conceived of his own theoretical work in abstract terms but was always concerned with the concrete existential implications of it. It is therefore important to realize that, for Tillich, the basic philosophical approach he would adopt, that of the ontological, arose not merely from the formative intellectual influences of a wide range of thinkers associated with quite disparate philosophical and theological ideas (among them, as we have seen, Plato, Aristotle, Augustine, Bonaventure, Nicholas of Cusa, Luther, Schleiermacher, Hegel, Schelling, and Kierkegaard), but was equally inspired by his own interaction with the non-human world. For Tillich, the world of nature was, above all, *vital and real.* He discovered in his encounter with the natural world, as he did in the experience of being human, both harmony and terror, both *logos* and abyss, both depth and form, both the divine and the demonic. These elements reflect the polar character of the structure of being for Tillich and, as such, are capable of revealing to us the true nature of the divine life.[8] Moreover, there was an unmistakable integrity about the natural universe that would help Tillich formulate a realistic sacramental theology and a theory of symbolics that rested on an *analogia entis*.[9]

Even in his later life, when Tillich's early "quasi-romantic" attitude toward nature had become tempered by a sort of prophetic or critical realism, it is obvious that the relationship between the human and non-human worlds was of great concern to him. In an address given in February 1963 at the Pacific School of Religion at Berkeley, California, Tillich shows himself to be one of nature's staunchest defenders in the face of what he perceived to be the assault on the earth by modern technology:

> Likewise must we resist abusing nature as a mere "thing" to be controlled. If we had a different feeling toward nature, we would have a different feeling for the wholeness and holiness of life. *Not* having this contributes to our loss of everything sacramental – because if the whole universe is not seen sacramentally, the partial sacraments die off.[10]

Here, Tillich combines a mystical-romantic appreciation for the sacramental quality of nature with a sobering chastisement of Western culture's incomprehensible zeal to bring the non-human world under its complete domination. As will be shown later, he was *able* to do this because, from the point of view of the ontological unity of all creation, he perceived in the violation of the natural world a diminishment not only of the integrity of that world but of the world of human meaning as well. In other words, for Tillich the assault on the non-human world, by its very nature, tears at the interdependent fabric that unifies all life, from the biological to the cultural. He was *willing* to take up the cause of the non-human world (even when it was hardly popular or fashionable) because, through his own experience of and appreciation for nature, he considered himself an advocate who was compelled to speak out on behalf of a community that could not defend itself. For Tillich, nature was a living, breathing expression of the divine which, in its own existential reality, was nevertheless distinguished from humanity by an "infinite, qualitative difference."[11]

Notwithstanding therefore the several well-known anecdotes concerning Tillich's "terror" of certain elements of the non-human world,[12] it is apparent that the natural universe was held in the highest regard by Tillich throughout his life. The earth and its creatures were in many ways sources of both inspiration and ballast for Tillich, help-ing to keep his philosophical theology grounded in the tangible reality of the material universe. It could be said that as nature informed and nurtured his own theological outlook, so too did Tillich, in accordance with the biblical mandate, consider himself a caretaker of the earth.[13] In this way, Tillich in a sense "existentialized" nature, treating it al-ways with reverence and defending it with the "passionate desire"[14] of a lover. There existed a very important mutuality for Tillich between addressing the question of one's own existence and that of the uni-verse: "Whoever has penetrated into the nature of his own finitude can find the traces of finitude in everything that exists."[15] This un-derstanding of the ontological interrelatedness of all creation under-cuts the anthropocentrism of many of Tillich's intellectual ancestors. He discovered that, by virtue of their common origin, human beings share a common destiny with the universe. What distinguishes human beings from other aspects of creation, however, is that *we are the only species that is aware of this* and, consequently, shoulder an enormous responsibility for the care of both the human and non-human commu-nities:

> Whenever man has looked at his world, he has found himself in it as a part of it. But he also has realized that he is a stranger in the world of objects, unable to penetrate it beyond a certain level of scientific analy-sis. And then he has become aware of the fact that he himself is the door to the deeper levels of reality, that in his own existence he has the only possible approach to existence itself. This does not mean that man is more approachable than other objects as material for scientific research. The opposite is the case! It does mean that the immediate experience of one's own existing reveals something of the nature of existence gener-ally.[16]

Hence, the fate of the earth was not a hypothetical doctrinal question for Tillich but was, rather, a matter of "ultimate concern," one which shaped his theological vision and resulted in a prophetic and coura-geous advocacy on behalf of the entire created universe. It could therefore be said of Tillich that, among many other projects in his life, he attempted to translate his own profound concern for God's creation into an intelligible theological framework, that is, into a theology of nature.

Methodological Considerations

Tillich's method of correlation has been compared to "an ellipse with two foci: One focus represents the existential question; and the other the theological answer."[17] This refers to Tillich's understanding of the fundamental ontological structure of reality in terms of mutual polarity. Tillich himself described his method thus: "it makes an analysis of the human situation out of which the existential questions arise, and it demonstrates that the symbols used in the Christian message are the answers to those questions."[18] In the present study, however, it will be shown that Tillich recognized that such an "answering" theology must also include the "non-human situation" in its analysis if it is to be complete and effective.[19] For by asking "the question implied in [our] finitude...[,] the question implied in finitude universally" is also asked.[20] Similarly, while he distinguishes between the philosophical "question" and the theological "answer" formally, Tillich sees each implied in the other:

> As a theologian he does not tell himself what is theologically true. As a philosopher he does not tell himself what is theologically true. But he cannot help seeing human existence and existence generally in such a way that the Christian symbols appear meaningful and understandable to him.[21]

For this reason, Tillich never saw himself as "saunter[ing] through a distraught cultural scene passing out theological answers at each corner...."[22] Tillich's theological method is therefore consistent with his conviction that "[t]he boundary is the best place for acquiring knowledge."[23] His concept of operating "on the boundary" always "implies more of a link than a separation."[24] Whether the two sides of the boundary consisted of philosophy and theology, church and society, city and country, religion and culture, or the human and non-human communities, Tillich's methodological principle of correlation always considered each side as possessing certain unique values that needed to be understood and appreciated accordingly.

One of the things Tillich was always at great pains to avoid in himself, and to warn others about, was the theologian who oversteps his or her boundaries by offering judgments about matters which are of preliminary concern.[25] His first formal criterion of theology, then, is that *"[t]he object of theology is what concerns us ultimately. Only those propositions are theological which deal with their object in so far as it can become a matter of ultimate concern for us.*"[26] Hence, for example,

> [p]ictures, poems,...music...[,] [p]hysical or historical or psychological insights...[,] [s]ocial ideas and actions, legal projects and procedures, political programs and decisions...[,] [p]ersonality problems and developments, educational aims and methods, bodily and mental healing, can [all] become objects of theology....[27]

They become such, however, only insofar as their power is able to express or mediate to us some aspect or aspects of that which concerns us ultimately. Theology, then, functions as a method of investigation within the human sciences that is concerned exclusively and solely with the question of ultimacy. Nevertheless, *"nothing is excluded from this function."*[28] All of culture, history, and, by implication, the natural universe can, at least in principle, become an object of theology by virtue of its role as "a medium, a vehicle, pointing beyond itself"[29] to the unconditioned.

The second formal criterion of theology relates to the content of our ultimate or unconditional concern. Tillich defines it thus: *"Our ultimate concern is that which determines our being or not-being. Only those statements are theological which deal with their object in so far as it can become a matter of being or not-being for us."*[30] It is significant, especially for purposes of this study, that Tillich does not specify "any special content, symbol, or doctrine"[31] that might fulfill this criterion, thereby limiting its ability to raise the existential question. It remains open, as human beings are open to the fundamental indeterminacy of existence. Hence no "god...or angel...or...man"[32] can become a legitimate object of theological inquiry if it does not possess "the power of threatening and saving our being."[33]

As can be seen from the foregoing discussion, the validity of objects of theological inquiry rests in their ability to adequately raise the existential question and thereby render themselves suitable as matters of ultimate concern for human beings. However, the ultimacy sensed therein resides not in the objects themselves, but in what they can reveal of the unconditioned or in how they can orient us toward the unconditioned. It is the "dimension of depth"[34] implicit in and underlying all of reality that is therefore of unique interest to theology. It is the proper "subject matter", so to speak, of theology. Our own experience of finitude can be the very means whereby we are opened up to and grasped by the infinite which permeates the universe and all that it contains. The vision of the universe as a prism through which the divine can be apprehended and encountered is not alien to Tillich:

> Religion can be defined as the encounter with the holy, and the holy can be defined as the manifestation of what concerns us ultimately and with unconditional seriousness. *The holy is a dimension of reality that shines through the bearers of the holy, be it stars and trees, ocean and earth, paintings and buildings, music and words, or persons and historical events.* Through all of them one can encounter the holy. Through all of them human beings have encountered the holy, although none of them is holy in itself. They are holy as bearers of the holy. They are holy *because in them something is encountered that is a matter of ultimate concern....*[35]

Hence, it is not the matter of utilizing the material and phenomena of the universe that is in question, but *the way in which* they are utilized. When the "trees, ocean and earth" are seen simply as ends in themselves or, worse still, as means to purely human ends, the dimension of depth that they could potentially reveal to us is lost. Their intrinsic "sanctity" as bearers of the holy becomes devalued and squandered. This situation is expressive of the ambiguity inherent in every existing thing since it consists in a "mixture" of both being and non-being, of the essential and the existential:[36]

> The holy is omnipresent in so far as the ground of being is not far from any being; the holy is demonized because of the separation of the infinite ground of being from every finite reality.... The danger...is that the "special places," the peculiar materials, the ritual performances, which are connected with a sacrament claim holiness for themselves. *But their holiness is a representation of what essentially is possible in everything and in every place.* The bread of the sacrament *stands for all bread and ultimately for all nature.*[37]

For Tillich, then, the created universe *can* be an appropriate object of theological investigation, *provided the question of ultimacy remains primary.* That is, the questions raised by the devastation and neglect of the natural world by human beings must always be stated in terms of what they ask, and what they can reveal to us, about the structure of being and meaning itself. Having thus answered affirmatively the question of whether the natural universe can be an appropriate object of theological investigation, we have now seen as well that Tillich included within his method of correlation the phenomenon of [38]global environmental destruction. The next chapter will therefore undertake an exposition of the theology of nature that can be found in Tillich's work.

Notes

1. Paul Lee, introduction to *The Meaning of Health* by Paul Tillich, ed. idem (Richmond, CA: North Atlantic Books, 1981), 10.
2. See Langdon Gilkey, *Gilkey on Tillich* (New York: Crossroad, 1990), 184.
3. Paul Tillich, *OTB*, 17-18.
4. Wilhelm and Marion Pauck, *Paul Tillich: His Life and Thought* 1 (San Francisco: Harper and Row, 1976), 31.
5. Ibid.
6. Ibid., 180.
7. Ibid., 278.
8. Paul Tillich, *ST* 1, 74-86.
9. Ibid., 239-240. Cf. Paul Tillich, *DF*, 41-54.
10. Paul Tillich, *IRCM*, 61-62.
11. Tillich, *DF*, 83.
12. For example, Langdon Gilkey relates the story of how Tillich, despite the reputation he enjoyed as "the one 'nature mystic' among the then great theologians," refused to take a walk in the Tennessee woods with Gilkey for fear of *"zerpents"* (*Tillich*, 199-201). Cf., however, the explanation of one biologist of humanity's collective fear of creatures reptilian: "To summarize the relation between man and snake: life gathers human meaning to become part of us. Culture transforms the snake into the serpent, a far more potent creation than the literal reptile. Culture in turn is a product of the mind, which can be interpreted as an image-making machine that recreates the outside world through symbols arranged into maps and stories. But the mind does not have an instant capacity to grasp reality in its full chaotic richness; nor does the body last long enough for the brain to process information piece by piece like an all-purpose computer. Rather, consciousness races ahead to master certain kinds of information with enough sufficiency to survive. It submits to a few biases easily while automatically avoiding others...

"The combined biases are what we call human nature. The central tendencies, exemplified so strikingly in fear and veneration of the serpent, are the wellsprings of culture. Hence simple perceptions yield an unending abundance of images with special meaning while remaining true to the forces of natural selection that created them" (Edward O. Wilson, *Biophilia* [Cambridge, MA and London: Harvard University Press, 1984], 100-101). In other words, Tillich's understandable aversion to snakes was a combination of both biological and cultural evolution: he couldn't *help* becoming immobilized at the sight of them.

13. Genesis 1:28.

14. Tillich, *DF,* 116.

15. Tillich, *ST* 1, 62-63.

16. Tillich, *ST* 1, 62.

17. Heinz Zahrnt, *The Question of God: Protestant Theology in the Twentieth Century,* trans. R. A. Wilson (New York: Harcourt, Brace and World, 1966), 307.

18. Tillich, *ST* 1, 62.

19. On this point, see Harold Coward, "New Theology on Population, Consumption, and Ecology," *Journal of the American Academy of Religion* 65/2 (Summer 1997): 261: "Paul Tillich proposed that theology proceeds by what he called 'a correlational method'.... In response to the challenges and questions posed by human existence, theology searches its sources of revelation and tradition for answers. It is only recently that the various religions have had to question their sources with regard to the interaction of humans with the environment – in response to the explosion in numbers of people and the consumption of the earth's resources at a rate that threatens to exhaust its life sustaining capacity." Cf. the discussion on the choice of a modified version of Tillich's correlational method by Stephen H. Webb in his *On God and Dogs: A Christian Theology of Compassion for Animals* (New York and Oxford: Oxford University Press, 1998), 18-20.

20. Tillich, *ST* 1, 63.

21. Ibid.

22. Gilkey, *Tillich,* 178.

23. Tillich, *RV,* 3. Translation mine.

24. Zahrnt, *Question,* 303.

25. In this regard, see Ibid., 8-28 and Tillich, *DF,* 80-85.

26. Tillich, *ST* 1, 12.

27. Ibid., 13-14.

28. Ibid., 13. Emphasis mine.

29. Ibid.

30. Ibid., 14.

31. Ibid.

32. Ibid., 14-15.
33. Ibid., 14.
34. Paul Tillich, "Religion as a Dimension in Man's Spiritual Life," in *TC*, 7; "Aspects of a Religious Analysis of Culture," in *TC*, 43-47; "The Lost Dimension in Religion," in *SSTS*, 43; *ST* 1, 218; *ST* 3, 113. Cf. Paul Tillich, "Depth," *Christendom* 9 (Summer 1944): 317-325.
35. Paul Tillich, "The Relationship Today between Science and Religion," *SSTS*, 152. Emphasis mine. Cf. Rudolf Otto, *The Idea of the Holy*, trans. J. Harvey (London: Penguin Books, 1959). Cf. Tillich, *DF*, 121: "Without symbols in which the holy is experienced as present, the experience of the holy vanishes."
36. Tillich, *ST* 3, 12.
37. Paul Tillich, "Nature and Sacrament," in *PRE*, 111. Emphasis mine. Cf. *BR*, 8: "[P]hilosophy tries to show the presence of being and its structures in the different realms of being, in nature and in man.... But in each case it is not the subject matter as such with which philosophy deals but the constitutive principles of being, that which is always present if a thing participates in the power to be and to resist nonbeing."

There is no plant in the ground
But tells of your beauty, O Christ.
There is no creature on the earth
There is no life in the sea
But proclaims your goodness.
There is no bird on the wing
There is no star in the sky
There is nothing beneath the sun
But is full of your blessing.
Lighten my understanding
of your presence all around, O Christ.
Kindle my will
  to be caring for Creation.[1]

Chapter 3

Paul Tillich's Theology of Nature

While the terms "theology of nature" and "ecological theology" did
not enter into usage among theologians except near the very end of
Paul Tillich's life, it is clear from the foregoing chapter that his concern for the non-human world as a matter of personal and theological
interest was of inestimable importance throughout his life. This
chapter will therefore take up those aspects of Tillich's thought that
specifically and intentionally include the non-human world in their
treatment of the traditional categories of systematic theology.[2] While
not a fully evolved theology of nature in the sense that we have come
to understand the term among contemporary eco-theologians, this
chapter will show that Tillich nevertheless addresses the very fundamental questions of the sacramentality of the universe; the relationship
between history and nature; the fall and redemption of nature; and the
relationship among the divine, human, and non-human dimensions.
Additionally, his notion of the "multidimensional unity of life" and his

attempt at a "theology of the inorganic" both help to provide the basis for a meaningful discussion concerning the role, purpose, and character of the non-human world in theological discourse. Finally, while Tillich's correlational method allows for much interplay between the philosophical question of being and the theological answers offered by revelation, the intent here clearly is to draw out from Tillich's systematic thought those elements that would prove most useful for further *theological* consideration.

A New Realism

Over the course of his life, Paul Tillich developed a theocentric vision of reality embracing a realistic, historical view of nature that is not set in opposition to grace. In rejecting other interpretations of nature as inadequate and problematic (*i.e.*, the magical-sacramental, the technical-quantitative, the vitalistic, the symbolic-romantic), Tillich formulates a novel interpretation – that of "new realism."[3] In this he is influenced by, among others, Schelling, Goethe, and Rilke, who in his estimation "have proposed this way of penetrating into the depth of nature."[4] According to one Tillich scholar, for Tillich

> [n]ature is realistically interpreted, first if its power and meaning is sought in and through its objective, physical structures themselves. There is no superimposed power or meaning. There is just the one reality in which power, matter-of-factness, meaning and objective structure are all of a piece. Secondly, nature is realistically interpreted if it remains historical, that is, related to history, not to a utopia that comes at the end of time and means precisely the *end* of time. Such a utopia is unhistorical. Nature must be imbedded within the historical process of time and space as we know them.[5]

As we shall see, Tillich likewise conceived of history as "imbedded" in nature. But not so with grace. Tillich's understanding of grace is that of the wholly gratuitous presence of God, that is, the Spiritual Presence.[6] Grace is prior to everything that is and, as such, transcends the subject-object split.[7] As both prius (creating grace) and power (saving grace) of being, grace confers on the entire created universe a certain "holiness of being," despite the continuous attempts of humanity to profanize and desecrate both itself and the non-human elements that share existence with it.[8]

It cannot be inferred, however, from the idea of the "holiness of being" that emerges from a realistic interpretation of nature that *sacramental* qualities should be attributed to all things. According to Tillich, "[t]he intrinsic power [or dignity] of nature as such does not create a sacrament.... It is only through a relation to the history of salvation that it is liberated from its demonic elements and thus made eligible for a sacrament."[9] The fact that something exists (*i.e.*, that it participates in being), does not qualify it for a sacrament. This is because all life is ambiguous and otherwise distorted, capable of bearing both demonic as well as divine power. But insofar as nature participates in the history of salvation and is liberated from the demonic (*i.e.*, its negative elements are eliminated in the unambiguous manifestation of its essential character), it can be made capable of becoming a sacrament. Nature in its estranged or existential state can only be understood as a *bearer* of sacramental power and therefore, as Tillich reminds us, Christianity must reject purely natural sacraments.[10]

Only when viewed in its relation to salvation history and grasped by faith can a natural object become a genuine sacrament. In this regard, Tillich's particular form of panentheism[11] informs his realistic assessment of the power and function of sacrament in actual existence:

> No finite object or event would be excluded as long as it was the bearer of a transcendent power and integrally related to the history of salvation. This is true in principle, but not in our actual existence. Our existence is determined not only by the omnipresence of the divine but also by our separation from it. If we could see the holy in every reality, we should be in the Kingdom of God. But this is not the case. The holy appears only in special places, in special contexts. The concentration of the sacramental in special places, in special rites, is the expression of man's ambiguous situation.[12]

For Tillich, then, "it is not the quality of the materials as such which makes them media of the Spiritual Presence; rather, it is their quality as brought into sacramental union."[13] The religious richness and power of the unity of being and meaning that can be known in the experience of a sacramental act that utilizes sacramental materials is lost when, as in some Protestant traditions, "only the word has retained a genuinely sacramental character."[14] While hardly denying that the "Word" remains a legitimate bearer of sacramental power, Tillich laments the loss of a more comprehensive sense of sacramentality among Protestants that included materials obtained from the natural world. The radical emphasis on a "theology of the Word" by neo-orthodox theologians during his career in Germany was continuously countered by Tillich with his insistence that a genuine sacramentality need not be considered a function of a dreaded "natural theology."[15]

Since both Word and sacrament are capable of communicating the Spiritual Presence they should not, according to Tillich, be seen as being contradictory but rather as complementary of the same phenomenon. He points out that, in fact, "the sacrament is 'older' than the Word" since, "[b]ecause of the sequence of the dimensions, the objective sign [*i.e.*, the sacrament] precedes the subjective [*i.e.*, the Word]."[16] Here he points out that all things are dependent on even the inorganic substratum of existence, including the Word itself: "We need also to realize that the word has its basis in nature, and hence that the usual opposition between word and sacrament is no longer tenable."[17] While "[t]he word appeals to our intellect and may move our will..., [t]he sacrament, if its meaning is alive, grasps our unconscious as well as our conscious being.... It is the symbol of nature and spirit, united in salvation."[18] Indeed, Tillich recognized that emphasis on the Word alone and the attendant weakening of the sacramental power within Protestantism was at least partially responsible for "[t]he phenomenal growth of secularism" that he witnessed in Europe during the first half of his life.[19]

Again, as we saw in Chapter One, it was the traditional Protestant teaching on nature and grace with its emphasis on the transformation of the inner person that, to a greater or lesser extent, set the stage, on the one hand, for the rapid development of technological progress in the modern era and, on the other, for an impoverished attitude toward the natural universe. It is for this reason that Tillich's concern for the non-human world and our relationship to it led him to conclude that "the solution of the problem 'nature and sacrament' is today a task on which the very destiny of Protestantism depends."[20] He realized even in the 1920s what the loss of a sacramental sense of the world had resulted in, and had come to signify, for his tradition *and* for the world itself. He was also realistic in his assessment of this situation when, in 1945, he asked the following question: "Are we still able to understand what a sacrament means? The more that we are estranged from nature, the less we can answer affirmatively."[21] He recognized in the Reformist tendency to use the Protestant principle in its biblicist form as *the* single, normative criterion for doing theology, that the richness of God's creation was, as a result, increasingly ignored or rejected as unsuitable for legitimate theological reflection. Without eliminating the prophetic element that makes Protestantism what it is, Tillich nevertheless sought to "re-sacramentalize" the universe with his emphasis on the participation of nature in the universal healing work of salvation:

> The formula "Protestant principle and Catholic substance" refers definitively to the sacrament as the medium of the Spiritual Presence. The concept of the multidimensional unity of life provides for this formula. Catholicism has always tried to include all dimensions of life in its system of life and thought; but it has sacrificed the unity, that is, the dependence of life in all dimensions, including the religious, on the divine judgment.[22]

Tillich's "new realist" assessment of the sacramentality of the natural world thus furnished the basis for another concept that proved central to his theology of nature, that of the multidimensional unity of all life. Such an understanding of the interdependent and interrelated character of the life processes of the universe and of the integrity of the non-human world was a remarkable position to maintain for a Protestant thinker in the middle years of the twentieth century. It would lead him ultimately to create as part of his theology of nature what he referred to as a "theology of the inorganic," something which had not as such been attempted prior to Tillich.

The Multidimensional Unity of Life and
A Theology of the Inorganic

In the Introduction to the third volume of his *Systematic Theology*, Tillich notes that, while he is "convinced by [Teilhard de Chardin's] description of the evolutionary processes in nature,...[he] cannot share his rather optimistic vision of the future."[23] Such an attitude is perhaps reflective of the principal difference between the Protestant and Roman Catholic approaches to the question of eschatology, or at least of Paul Tillich's particular version of Protestantism. That difference consists largely in the contrast between a fundamentally "sacramental" view of creation and the universe (the Roman Catholic position) and that of a more "paradoxical" one (the Protestant position). Tillich finds merit in both positions and, accordingly, attempts in his system to unite, as was observed earlier, the "Catholic substance" with the "Protestant principle." Nonetheless, it is apparent from passages as that quoted at the beginning of this section that his Lutheran heritage ultimately (and understandably) brings him down on the side of the latter.

Tillich was acutely aware (as we shall see) of the demonic "structures of destruction" which frustrate and disrupt life at every turn. While the power of being as redeeming or healing power is manifest throughout the universe, life as such is characteristically marked by a decided ambiguity. For Tillich, then, the evolutionary theory of the universe does not necessarily lend itself to an optimistic eschatological interpretation, especially with regards to the role of humanity.[24] In fact, the ultimate fate of the universe and of our place in it is left as an open question by Tillich. In part this is because of his insistence that "theology cannot rest on scientific theory,"[25] including evolutionary theory. For Tillich, all theories, whether scientific or theological, are at best partial expressions of the truth and need to be verified by how well they measure up to our experience and to the truth supplied by revelation. Every scientific or theological theory is subject to modification and in danger of being ultimately rejected. Nonetheless, it is the task of the theologian to ask the ultimate questions, including the question of the end and fulfilment of history and of time. Moreover, according to Tillich, for the theologian it is irresponsible and *un*theological to ignore the findings of science, for one is then in danger of lapsing into an unintelligible "traditional supranaturalism" or an "exclusive Christocentrism."[26] Tillich therefore refuses to avoid the questions of ultimacy that religion seeks to answer, risking in the process the loss of the Christian message[27] and insisting that

> [e]ven if the questions about the relation of man to nature and to the universe could be avoided by theologians, they would still be asked by people of every place and time – often with existential urgency and out of cognitive honesty. And the lack of an answer can become a stumbling block for a man's whole religious life.[28]

In speaking, therefore, of such relations, Tillich prefers to use the metaphor "dimensions" rather than "levels."[29] He recognizes the danger and difficulty of using such "levels" language since it rests on a hierarchical notion of reality that is no longer defensible in the modern world. More specifically, "levels" language supports what he refers to as "perhaps the most fundamental [dualism] in the interpretation of our world, that of the supranatural and the natural...[;] [r]eality is divided into a realm of supranatural-divine things and a realm of natural-human things."[30] In eschewing "levels" language to describe the relationship among all aspects of creation, Tillich seeks to develop a universal concept of life, which includes within it even the inorganic realm:

> [T]he genesis of stars and rocks, their growth as well as their decay, must be called a life process. The ontological concept of life liberates the word "life" from its bondage to the organic realm and elevates it to the level of a basic term that can be used within the theological system....[31]

This understanding of the immense diversity and vast interconnectedness of all life, including that which is normally not considered "living," enables Tillich to employ the notion of "the multidimensional unity of life" in describing life in its essential nature.[32] Life, understood ontologically, is for Tillich the "actuality of being," consisting in the essential qualities of life being actualized under the conditions of existence.[33] By considering the term "life" in this way, Tillich is, in the end, able to intelligibly and realistically include the inorganic, organic, and historical dimensions of reality in his comprehensive eschatological vision.

In discussing the relationship among the varied dimensions of life, Tillich acknowledges first and foremost that the "religious significance of the inorganic is immense, but...is rarely considered by theology.... A 'theology of the inorganic' is lacking."[34] He therefore undertakes the task of creating one, arguing that "the inorganic has a preferred position among the dimensions in so far as it is the first condition for the actualization of every dimension."[35] Not unlike the "preferential option for the poor" advocated by liberation theologians of recent years, Tillich's application of the principle of the multidimensional unity of life to a theological understanding of the inorganic accords the inorganic dimension a favored status among the various dimensions of life. It must always be considered in terms of its biochemical primacy among all the dimensions of life, for all "realms of being would dissolve were the basic condition provided by the constellation of inorganic structures to disappear."[36] In this sense, the inorganic dimension *actually* "participates" in every form of being, a claim that cannot categorically be made of the more intricate dimensions, such as that of spirit. These more complex dimensions are *potentially* present in the inorganic while relying on the inorganic for their form and substance.[37] Tillich does not view the realm of the inorganic in its essential nature in terms of "lifeless matter" forming the least important link in the great "Chain of Being," but sees it rather as containing the essential building blocks of all of life. For this reason, he is able to recognize in it a genuine integrity that exists independent of any estimation of value that may or may not be placed upon it by human beings.

The same, of course, can be said for the successive dimensions of life in their respective essential natures. That is, each possesses its own corresponding integrity by virtue of its ontological inclusion within the framework of the multidimensional unity of life. The difference between the inorganic and the organic is that "the dimension of the organic is essentially present in the inorganic; its actual appearance is dependent on conditions the description of which is the task of biology and biochemistry."[38] In the organic realm, Tillich distinguishes between the vegetative and animal dimensions because of the appearance within the animal of the psychological realm. Finally, evolving out of both the inorganic and organic dimensions is that of the personal-communal, or "spirit."[39] Tillich identifies spirit with the *power* of life and, as such, it "is not identical with the inorganic substratum which is animated by it; rather, spirit is the power of animation itself and not a part added to the organic system."[40] He therefore equally rejects the strict Cartesian dualism between the *res cogitans* and the *res extensa* as well as a psychologistic or biologistic monism, appealing instead to an organic, *Gestalt* notion of human life. For it is only in the human species that spirit makes its appearance and comes to full actualization as the historical dimension.[41]

While the theological interpretation of evolutionary theory must take into account the appearance of new dimensions of life, for Tillich it is not obliged to explain what the conditions for the appearance of such new dimensions actually are. Such explanations are the province of science, not of theology. What is important for theology to consider is precisely that something "new" *does* in fact occur that accounts for the appearance of each unique dimension of life. For this reason Tillich finds the terms "becoming" or "process" inadequate in attempting to explain what happens during the actualization of life. Seen from the point of view of the historical dimension, an understanding of the dynamics of life can only be developed with a comprehensive ontology:

> It is the universal character of actual being which, in the philosophies of life or process, has led to the elevation of the category of becoming to the highest ontological rank. But one cannot deny that the claim of the category of being to this rank is justified because, while becoming includes and overcomes relative non-being, being itself is the negation of absolute non-being; it is the affirmation that there is anything at all.... It is questionable, however, whether the words "becoming" and "process" are adequate for a view of the dynamics of life as a whole. They are lacking in a connotation which characterizes all life, and that is the creation of the new. This connotation is strongly present in references to the historical dimension, which is actual – even if subdued – in every realm of life, for history is the dimension under which the new is being created.[42]

The appearance of the "new" in each dimension of life depends therefore on the "interplay of freedom and destiny under the directing creativity of God."[43] It is neither a function of a fundamentally closed system of "becoming-within-itself" nor the product of a God who intervenes in the natural processes of life. Rather, the "new" is an expressive quality identifying the uniqueness of everything that is and which consists in the actualization of being under the dimension of the historical. The appearance of the "new" within history points to the immanental *and* transcendental character of the unconditional in its universal overcoming of non-being.

But the actualization of being, or life, is "at every moment...ambiguous."[44] In accordance with the fundamental ontological polarities, Tillich identifies three unifying functions shared by every dimension of life which, disrupted by existential estrangement, form the controlling features of its ambiguous character: "self-integration is countered by disintegration, self-creation is countered by destruction, self-transcendence is countered by profanization."[45] The basic structure of self-identity and self-alteration is effective in each function. Both the basic structure and the functions of life are analogically evident in every dimension of life, from the subatomic particle in the inorganic realm that struggles to preserve its "centeredness" against the forces of disintegration, to the attempt on the part of religion in the dimension of the spirit to resist profanization by asserting its greatness through moral and cultural transformation.[46] In analogous fashion,

Tillich even assigns an essential "dignity" and "inviolability" to all realms of life, including the inorganic and the organic:

> [O]ne element of dignity is inviolability, which is a valid element of all reality, giving dignity to the inorganic as well as to the personal.... The hypothesis that man first encountered reality as the totality of things and then elevated these things to divine dignity is more absurd than the absurdities it attributes to primitive man. Actually, mankind encountered the sublimity of life, its greatness and dignity, but...in ambiguous unity with profanization, smallness, and desecration.... Much of what has been said about greatness and dignity in the inorganic universe is immediately valid in the organic realm and its several dimensions.[47]

In this way, Tillich develops an extraordinarily comprehensive philosophy of life that is in general accordance with the scientific theories of evolution of his time. At the same time, he utilizes a transcendental phenomenological approach to the questions raised by the breaking open of life in its universally ambiguous character. That is, in his analysis and evaluation of the multidimensional unity of life, the question of ultimacy is always considered fundamental. What is perhaps most significant of all in Tillich's philosophy of life, however, is the view that all dimensions of life are subject in one way or another to the basic functions of life. Tillich explicitly refuses to make any claims of differing degrees of valuation or validation as to the experience of finitude under existential estrangement (*i.e.*, of suffering, disintegration, death) among the various dimensions of life. What he recognizes is that all forms of life – from the most primitive inorganic realms to the most complex dimensions of human community – share in the elementary transition from essence to existence. As such, all dimensions of life are related one to the other in an essential and in an existential or estranged manner. What this means is that even the most formidable and sophisticated creations of human culture cannot escape the processes of disintegration, destruction, and profanization. In all dimensions of life, "[i]n push and counterpush, life effects a preliminary balance..., but there is no a priori certainty about the outcome of these conflicts. The balance achieved in one moment is destroyed in the next."[48] The ambiguity of life is such that while it seeks to integrate, create, and transcend itself, it is at every opportunity thwarted with seeming indifference from realizing that for which it most deeply thirsts. Tillich recognizes this when he observes that

[l]ife lives on life, but it also lives through life, being defended, strengthened, and driven beyond itself by struggle. The survival of the strongest is the means by which life in the process of self-creation reaches its preliminary balance, a balance which is continuously threatened by the dynamics of being and the growth of life. It is only by the waste of innumerable seeds of generative power and actual individuals that a preliminary balance in nature is maintained. Without such waste a whole complex of natural life would be destroyed, as happens when climatic conditions or human activities interfere. The conditions of death are also the conditions of life.[49]

What Tillich's philosophy of life demonstrates is that the fundamental drive or *eros* which motivates every created thing to be reunited with the source of its existence is evident in all realms of life, including that of the spirit. This is why Tillich can affirm, on the one hand, the liberating and healing effects of human technical and cultural developments and creations while, on the other hand, he can condemn those which otherwise contribute to the frustration, disruption, or destruction of life. "For man, the technical is something natural, and enslavement to natural primitivism would be unnatural."[50] The ambiguous character of human creativity (as in all realms of life) does not therefore allow for a "romantic, that is, pre-technical, return to the so-called natural."[51] However, when the realm of spirit – in its drive to attain on its own terms an unambiguous validation of its own technical and cultural progress – forgets or ignores its interrelatedness and interdependency with other dimensions of life, it threatens to "thingify" not only those less complex dimensions of life but to make of itself an object:

[T]his means that the subjection of nature and man by man is a telos that negates a telos. The dominant view of man in the present period is characterized by an inner contradiction of an end that is the endless production of means without an end.[52]

What is lacking in such a phenomenon is a certain humility before reality, that is, an acknowledgment that in subjecting nature to the process of objectification we are diminishing ourselves. We are part of nature and nature is part of us. The term "humility" of course is from the Latin *humus*, meaning "of the earth." It is impossible for Tillich to distinguish in any type of Cartesian or Kantian dualistic fashion between the human and non-human dimensions of life, since they interpenetrate one another, from the simplest inorganic dimensions to the most complex, abstract, theoretical ones. To deny this is to deny life itself. Indeed, this denial in many ways forms the root of the estrangement between humanity and nature, for it is in our unrestricted pursuit of the technical control of nature that we seek, in misguided fashion, to express human creativity and transcendence. But we cannot create out of nothing nor are we ever able to fully transcend that which remains as a constant reminder of our failure to escape the limitations of finitude. For Tillich, we are the one species in whom all dimensions of life are encountered and yet we refuse to acknowledge precisely that. The fact of our colossal failure to transform and liberate the earth for our own purposes has now risen up, threatening to destroy the planet and us along with it. The awareness of such failure leads us to the quest for the unambiguous fulfilment of the essential possibilities that are present in every dimension of life, for

> [i]n every life process within every dimension, from the inorganic to the spiritual, self-integration and disintegration, self-production and destruction, self-manifestation and concealment are inseparably together. This is the ambiguous character which life presents in every moment, and is the basis of the quest for unambiguous or eternal life.[53]

The significance for the non-human world of this quest for ultimate fulfillment will be discussed later in this chapter. Next, however, I will consider the question of nature in its existential or estranged form and its role in the great cosmic drama of redemption.

The Fall and Redemption of Nature

Tillich understands the mythological symbol of "the Fall" to signify in philosophical terms the "transition from essence to existence."[54] He sees this interpretation of the symbol as a "half-way demythologization" in that, while it removes the "once upon a time" element from the myth, it still retains a temporal element.[55] The myth of the Fall itself cannot be completely demythologized since "sin is not created, and the transition from essence to existence is a fact, a story to be told and not a derived dialectical step."[56] In this way, Tillich's Christian existentialism attempts to avoid the errors of idealism (in which the Fall is interpreted not as a break but as an imperfect fulfilment) and pure naturalism (in which such ideas as "estrangement" from nature are rejected).[57]

The question for Tillich arises, however, concerning the relationship of humanity with the universe in its essential and existential forms. If, as both the biblical and non-biblical myths suggest, it is humanity which is solely responsible for the estranged character of existence, how is the non-human universe affected by this, if at all? Of course, in the biblical account it is Adam who, through his own decision, brings a curse upon both humanity and nature.[58] This is expressive for Tillich of the fact that, in some way, "man is responsible for the transition from essence to existence because he has finite freedom and because all dimensions of reality are united in him."[59] At the same time, however, it is clear that human freedom is

> imbedded in universal destiny and that therefore the transition from essence to existence has both moral and tragic character. This makes it necessary to ask how universal existence is related to man's existence. In respect to the Fall, how is man related to nature? And if the universe participates in the Fall in the same way, what is the relation between creation and the Fall?[60]

Tillich asks if the term "fallen world" can be used intelligibly when a literalist interpretation of the biblical understanding of the Fall is properly rejected as absurd (*i.e.*, that the divine curse upon Adam and Eve involved a change of nature in and outside of them).[61] Is it possible to speak of the participation of nature in the existential estrangement of humanity? In asking if "nature [has] been corrupted by man," Tillich wonders if such a "combination of words [has] any meaning at all...."[62]

His initial response to such questions concerns the temporal and spatial meaning of the transition from essence to existence. Understood ontologically, the symbol of the Fall points not to one event that occurred at some time in the primeval past but to

> the transhistorical quality of all events in time and space. This is equally true of man and of nature. "Adam before the Fall" and "nature before the curse" are states of potentiality. They are not actual states. *The actual state is that existence in which man finds himself along with the whole universe, and there is no time in which this was otherwise.*[63]

However, Tillich refuses on this basis to reject the concept of a fallen world and to speak in terms of a radical distinction between the human and non-human communities, since such a rejection does not take into account the "tragic element, the element of destiny, in man's predicament."[64] Here of course he is very much in line with Augustine, Luther, Calvin, and even his neo-orthodox contemporaries in trying to safeguard Christianity from the various forms of Pelagianism that continually threaten to undermine "its knowledge of the tragic universality of existential estrangement."[65] Accordingly, Tillich borrows from the insights provided by biological, sociological, and psychological theorists in rejecting any idealistic division between an innocent nature and a fallen humanity:

> First, it can be shown that in the development of man there is no absolute discontinuity between animal bondage and human freedom.... Second, one cannot decide at which points in the development of the human individual responsibility begins and ends.... Third, we must refer to the present rediscovery of the unconscious and its determining power in man's conscious decisions.... Fourth, the social dimension of unconscious strivings must be considered....
>   The universe works through us as part of the universe....
>   In this way the universe participates in every act of human freedom. It represents the side of destiny in the act of freedom.[66]

In defining freedom as "the possibility of a total and centered act of the personality,"[67] Tillich observes "analogies to freedom in all parts of the universe. From the atomic structures to the most highly developed animals, there are total and centered reactions which can be called 'spontaneous' in the dimension of organic life."[68] While such spontaneous reactions in the non-human realm cannot of course be considered those of responsible agents as such (and hence imputed with guilt), nevertheless for Tillich "it does not seem adequate, either, to apply the adjective 'innocent' to nature":

> Logically, it is not correct to speak of innocence where there is no possibility of becoming guilty. And, as there are analogies to human freedom in nature, so there are also analogies to human good and human evil in all parts of the universe. It is worthy of note that Isaiah prophesied peace in nature for the new eon, thereby showing that he would not call nature "innocent." Nor would the writer who, in Genesis, chapter 3, tells about the curse over the land declare nature innocent. Nor would Paul do so in Romans, chapter 8, when he speaks about the bondage to futility which is the fate of nature. Certainly, all these expressions are poetic-mythical. They could not be otherwise, since only poetic empathy opens the inner

life of nature. Nevertheless, they are realistic in substance and certainly more realistic than the moral utopianism which confronts immoral man with innocent nature. Just as, within man, nature participates in the good and evil he does, so nature, outside man, shows analogies to man's good and evil doing. *Man reaches into nature, as nature reaches into man. They participate in each other and cannot be separated from each other.*[69]

Because Tillich employs an *analogia entis* as the basis for his statements about reality, the anxiety that is experienced by human beings in the moral equivalent of non-being (*i.e.*, the feeling of guilt) is therefore also expressive, in analogous fashion, of the tragic estrangement of nature.[70] According to Tillich, "[a]nxiety about non-being is present in everything finite. It is consciously or unconsciously effective in the whole process of living. Like the beating of the heart, it is always present, although one is not always aware of it."[71] In this regard, Tillich refers to the inescapable quality of the "situation of universal estrangement" which transforms the otherwise neutral ontological categories of finitude into demonic "structures of destruction."[72] Death, guilt, time, space, suffering, loneliness, doubt, and meaninglessness are all structural symptoms of universal estrangement. However, Tillich distinguishes between such concrete manifestations and the underlying universal character of existence:

> Estrangement is a quality of the structure of existence, but the way in which estrangement is predominantly manifest is a matter of history. There are always structures of destruction in history, but they are possible only because there are structures of finitude which can be transformed into structures of estrangement.[73]

In this way, Tillich claims that one can "speak of 'sin' in the one context and of 'evil' in the other. It is a difference more of focus than of content."[74] The "groaning of creation" of which Paul speaks in Romans 8 expresses therefore both an historical and an *un*historical truth about the universal nature of existence. Creation, by virtue of its separation from the ground of being is, according to Paul, "subjected to futility" and "waits with eager longing...to be set free from its bondage to decay."[75] Because this "groaning" can be observed phenomenologically (*i.e.*, in the natural processes of life and decay), it possesses an historical character, the character of that which suffers under the historical conditions of estrangement. The story of the universe is that of its glory and of its tragedy, of the destiny it shares with humanity and of its longing to be reunited with the source of its existence. Why is nature tragic? Because, as we have seen, "[i]t is subjected to the laws of finitude and destruction. It is suffering and sighing with us."[76] Tillich points out that the Greek word which is used in Paul's letter to designate "'creation' is especially used for the non-animated section of nature":

> The sighing of the wind and the ever restless, futile breaking of the waves have often inspired poetic, melancholic verse about nature's subjection to vanity. But the words of Paul cover also, and in a more direct way, the sphere of living things. The melancholy of the leaves falling in autumn, the end of the jubilant life of spring and summer, the quiet death of innumerable beings in the cold air of the approaching winter – all this has grasped and always will grasp the hearts, not only of poets, but of every feeling man and woman.[77]

Tillich was concerned, however, that humanity in the industrial and post-industrial ages has "become incapable of perceiving the tragic as well as the harmonious sounds of nature...."[78] He wonders if, in the employment of our Cartesian-Kantian ways of understanding and interpreting reality, we have not perhaps "too much isolated ourselves in human superiority, in intellectual arrogance, and in a domineering attitude toward nature."[79] Our deafness to the cry of the non-human world for fulfilment with and through humanity has not only had devastating effects on that world but has diminished *humanity* as well. The answer to Paul's question concerning the cause of the tragedy of nature can be found, according to Tillich, in our anthropocentric attitude of attempting to master or control the universe:

> Who is responsible for the suffering of animals, for the ugliness of death and decay, for the universal dread of death?...Paul tries to penetrate the mystery of the question. And his surprising answer is: nature is subjected to vanity by the curse that God had uttered over nature because of the fall of Adam. The tragedy of nature is tied up with the tragedy of man, as the salvation of nature is dependent on the salvation of man.... As nature, represented by the "Serpent," leads man into temptation, so man, by his trespassing of the divine law, leads nature into tragedy. This did not happen once upon a time,...but at every time and within every space it happens, so long as there is time and space. Man...is determined to fulfill the longing of nature. In so far as he has failed and still

fails to come to his own fulfillment, he is unable to fulfill nature...his own bodily being and nature around him.[80]

The failure of humanity on its own to "save" itself and the universe, to bring itself and the non-human world to fulfilment, is the basis for the Christian doctrine of redemption. While it is "through a human being"[81] that salvation or fulfilment becomes possible, Tillich does not understand the meaning of such fulfilment in narrow, human-centered terms at all. Indeed, his entire theory of redemption rests on the conviction that "there is no salvation of man if there is no salvation of nature, because man is in nature and nature is in man."[82] The longing of all creation for liberation – both the human and the non-human aspects of it – realizes its hope, according to Tillich, in Jesus as the Christ. This is why "Jesus is called the Son of Man, the man from above, the true man, in whom the forces of separation and tragedy are overcome, not only in mankind but also in the universe."[83] As "the Christ," Jesus was the bearer of the New Being, whose

> function...is not only to save individuals and transform man's historical existence but to renew the universe. And the assumption is that mankind and individual men are so dependent on the powers of the universe that salvation of the one without the other is unthinkable.[84]

Tillich's interpretation of the doctrine of the Incarnation is equally expansive. According to Tillich, "[t]he doctrine of the Incarnation concerns an event which *has* happened, and is independent of any interpretation of it. The doctrine presupposes the event and tries to interpret it."[85] With this statement, Tillich rejects the strict Schleiermacherian view that "the Incarnation is a product of our religious experience," or the Bultmannian idea that it is "a present interpretation of our existence," or the Enlightenment understanding of the Incarnation as "a universal concept, a truth of reason," or, finally, the Hegelian interpretation of it as "an idea describing essential human nature."[86] Tillich perceives both the particular *and* the universal implications of the Incarnation, preferring to interpret it dialectically and thus preserving its paradoxical character:

> On the one hand, it is an event with all the characteristics of an "event in time and space": namely, occurring "but once", unrepeatable, possible only in a special situation and in a special, incomparable, individual form, a subject of report and not of analysis or deduction.

On the other hand, the Incarnation is an event of universal significance, concerning the whole of being, and transforming the conditions of existence generally. Therefore it must be interpreted in universal categories. Without such an interpretation it would be a stumbling-block, strange to our mind and alien to our spirit, and therefore without actual concern for us.[87]

The Incarnation, therefore, is one of those special "events" in history that possesses the genuine character of givenness (as does all of history) but which also discloses by its very nature a universal, transhistorical significance. Tillich's understanding of the Johannine statement that "the Word became flesh"[88] thus follows the same line of reasoning that his ontological interpretation of the Fall did. In other words, for Tillich *logos* represents

> the principle of the divine self-manifestation in God as well as in the universe, in nature as well as in history. "Flesh" does not mean a material substance but stands for historical existence. And "became" points to the paradox of God participating in that which did not receive him and in that which is estranged from him.[89]

Moreover, Tillich argues that while the manifestation of the New Being in Jesus as the Christ becomes the central event in *human* history, the universe is left "open for possible divine manifestations in other areas or periods of being.... Man cannot claim to occupy the only possible place for Incarnation."[90] In leaving the question of the "uniqueness" of the Christ event open, Tillich's ontology allows for a non-anthropocentric, expansive view of grace which rightfully relates the ultimate fate of the universe to an all-embracing divine love:

> The interdependence of everything with everything else in the totality of being includes a participation of nature in history and demands a participation of the universe in salvation. Therefore, if there are non-human "worlds" in which existential estrangement is not only real – as it is in the whole universe – but in which there is also a type of awareness of this estrangement, such worlds cannot be without the operation of saving power within them.... The manifestation of saving power in one place implies that saving power is operating in all places. The expectation of the Messiah as the bearer of the New Being presupposes that "God loves the universe," even though in the appearance of the Christ he actualizes this love for historical man alone.[91]

Tillich defines the symbol New Being as "essential being under the conditions of existence, conquering the gap between essence and existence."[92] He argues that the New Being could not have appeared in history in any other way than in a personal, *human* life although, as we have seen, such an appearance does not exclude the non-human world. In fact, because the human person "is a universe in himself...[,] [w]hat happens in him happens, therefore, by mutual universal participation.... This gives cosmic significance to the person and confirms that only in a personal life can the New Being manifest itself."[93]

According to Tillich, the two central symbols of the Christian faith (*i.e.*, the Cross and the Resurrection) contain the respective expressions of the subjection to, and conquest of, existence, thus pointing to the universal significance of the Christ event. The interdependent nature of the relationship between the "events" that correspond to the symbolic statements "Cross of the Christ" and "Resurrection of the Christ" indicates the attempt on the part of "the disciples and of the writers of the New Testament...[to] elevate the objective event indicated in the stories of the Crucifixion to universal symbolic significance."[94] In this way, according to Tillich, "[o]ne could say that...the Cross is both an event and a symbol and that the Resurrection is both a symbol and an event."[95] Both Cross and Resurrection thus contain within themselves those elements necessary to sustain their universal application as living religious symbols, *viz.,* the ability to meaningfully communicate the concrete content of an ultimate concern.[96] In particular, Tillich finds the satisfaction of the criteria essential for the truth of any symbol of faith in the symbol of the Cross of the Christ, in that it "expresses not only the ultimate but also its own lack of ultimacy."[97] The death of the Christ on the Cross has universal significance insofar as it is interpreted to signify that Jesus shared in the conditions and structures of estrangement with every created thing.[98] Both Incarnation and Cross suggest Jesus' creatureliness, his ontological solidarity with every creature that is subject to finitude.

When these two symbols are interpreted in light of the event and symbol of the Resurrection of the Christ, the ubiquitous manifoldness of the entire "Christ event" becomes apparent. Tillich proposes a theory of "restitution" to explain the meaning of the "event" of the Resurrection of the Christ.[99] This ontological interpretation of the Christ event – comprising the interrelated and interdependent symbols and events of Incarnation, Cross, and Resurrection – relates it to soteriology in terms of its cosmic, trans-historical, universal significance.

In accepting the original meaning of the term "salvation" (from the Latin *salvus*) as designating in the broadest sense the idea and reality of "healing," Tillich is able to apply the redemptive act of God in Jesus as the Christ to all of creation.[100] While it is true that the experience of healing as the manifestation of the power of New Being can only be known in a partial or fragmentary way by all creatures as long as they are subject to the conditions of existence, it is nevertheless "[o]n these healing forces [that] the life of [the universe] depends; they prevent the self-destructive structures of existence from plunging [creation] into complete annihilation."[101] Elsewhere, Tillich observes that "[s]alvation does not destroy creation; it transforms the old creation into a new one. Therefore, we can speak of the new in terms of a *re*-newal, threefold – *re*-conciliation, *re*-union, *re*-surrection."[102] Resurrection as thus understood is, according to Tillich,

> not an event that might happen in some remote future, but it is the power of the new being to create life out of death, here and now, today and to-morrow.... Resurrection happens *now,* or it does not happen at all. It happens in us and around us, in soul and history, in nature and universe.[103]

What the event of Resurrection therefore represents is the universal manifestation of the power of being conquering the threat of annihilation under the conditions of estranged existence. The Christ event is therefore "unique" not because it is the unparalleled and unsurpassable revelatory event in history (*i.e.*, that there is no saving power apart from it), but because of the fact that it "is the ultimate criterion of every healing and saving process."[104] That is, "wherever there is saving power in [the universe], it must be judged by the saving power in Jesus as the Christ."[105] If this were not true, the New Being would not have appeared in the Christ event; the universe would still be awaiting its manifestation. As it is, while the universe "remains in the state of relativity with respect to salvation[,] the New Being in the Christ transcends every relativity in its quality and power of healing."[106] Under the power of being overcoming the threat of non-being in every created thing, the universe is continuously repaired and healed, awaiting with "eager longing" the final restoration of all things reunited with the source of creation.

The notion of salvation as understood by Tillich consists then of a "cosmic healing"[107] and is by no means limited to that infinitesimal sector of the universe occupied by humanity. In asking us to "listen...to the words of the prophet about the salvation of nature," Tillich draws on the powerful images of the author of Revelation (specifically verses 21:1 and 22:1, 2) to describe the universal conquest of being over non-being:

[T]he last book of the Bible describes the salvation of man and nature from the bondage of corruption: the city of God is built with the most precious materials of non-animated nature.... The river is not polluted by any rot. The trees carry fruits without change and decay; the animals, together with the saints, adore the throne of glory. The daemonic forces are thrown into nothingness. There is no suffering nor death.[108]

According to Tillich, such a vision points

to something mysterious within our present world – namely, the forces of salvation. And one thing is made very clear by the vision of the prophet: salvation means salvation of the *world* and not of human beings alone.... The resurrection of the body – not an immortal soul – is the symbol of the victory over death. The bodiless spirit – and this is the meaning of all these images – is not the aim of creation: the purpose of salvation is not the abstract intellect of a natureless moral person.[109]

Salvation is therefore something that the universe experiences at every moment, otherwise it would fall into nothingness. Though it is experienced and known only in a fragmentary and inchoate fashion, it is nevertheless the foundational element present in everything that has existed, exists now, and will exist in the future. This is why such symbols as "resurrection" and "redemption" can make sense to us, because they are both derived from experience and, at the same time, have the character of that which lies outside our experience. By implication, our understanding of the experience by human beings of "redemption" – of being "made whole," of being "healed," of being "reconstituted" – can and should be extended to the entire created universe. With his usual characteristic prophetic wisdom and insight, Tillich observes that even within the human/non-human relationship itself, the experience of estrangement and of dissolution is disruptive and results in adverse consequences for both humanity and for the non-human universe:

Do we not experience every day how people who are estranged from nature, from their own natural forces and from the nature around them, become dry and uncreative in their mental life, hard and arrogant in their

moral attitude, suppressed and poisoned in their vitality? They certainly
are not the images of salvation....
    Therefore, have communion with nature! Become reconciled with
nature after your estrangement from it. Listen to nature in quietness, and
you will find its heart. It will sound the glory of its divine ground; it will
sigh with us in the bondage of tragedy; and it will speak of the inde-
structible hope of salvation.[110]

By understanding salvation in this way – as the healing and saving
power made manifest through the appearance of the New Being – the
relationship between history and the ultimate destiny of the universe is
placed on another level, that of eschatology. The partial and fragmentary character of salvation within time "drives us to the symbol of
cosmic healing and to the question of the relation of the eternal to the
temporal with respect to the future."[111] Tillich's treatment of this
question will now be examined.

God, World, and
the Meaning and End of History

Instead of conceiving of the natural world in Newtonian terms as a
fundamentally stable place in which the important drama of human
life unfolds, it became apparent during the twentieth century that such
a view was not only scientifically incorrect, but potentially hazardous
as well. The universe is not as stable as we once imagined; it is,
rather, despite its incomprehensible enormity, as precariously finite as
human life. What has therefore become profoundly and disturbingly
obvious is that *the fate of humanity is linked with the fate of the universe.* Paul Tillich witnessed the gradual coming to awareness of this
reality in the world about him and attempted to provide a theological
understanding of it. In maintaining that God is spirit, he nevertheless
affirmed that the "divine self-love includes all creatures"[112] and, in the
words of Ötinger, that "corporality is the end of the ways of God."[113]
    Accordingly, his efforts to recover and to reinterpret the meaning of
the word "God" for a modern audience includes this important aspect.
He seeks to reclaim the term "God" by demonstrating that what is
meant by the use of that term is that which is beyond, and yet can embrace, all apparent dualisms, conflicts, tensions, and ambiguities.[114]
Not surprisingly, he finds in the trinitarian monotheism of Christianity

the answer to the problem of ultimacy and concreteness in every idea of God. In affirming the living God, trinitarian monotheism endeavours to preserve the divine "unity between ultimacy and concreteness."[115] As we observed earlier, in the symbol of Jesus as the Christ the ultimate has become concretized under the conditions of existence and yet has not been overcome by the threat of non-being and the forces of estrangement.[116] Such an event has far-reaching implications for all of creation and of history, including the purpose and destiny of the non-human world.

Any notion, therefore, of divinity that emphasizes either divine transcendence or divine immanence to the exclusion of the other generates an inadequate conception of God.[117] For Tillich, the term "God" points to a living reality which is neither wholly identified with the world nor completely independent of it:

> God is being-itself, not *a* being.... As the power of being, God transcends every being and also the totality of beings – the world. Being-itself is beyond finitude and infinity; otherwise it would be conditioned by something other than itself, and the real power of being would lie beyond both it and that which conditioned it. Being-itself infinitely transcends every finite being. There is an absolute break, an infinite "jump." On the other hand, everything finite participates in being-itself and in its infinity. Otherwise it would not have the power of being. It would be swallowed by nonbeing, or it never would have emerged out of nonbeing. This double relation of all beings to being-itself gives being-itself a double characteristic. In calling it creative, we point to the fact that everything participates in the infinite power of being. In calling it abysmal, we point to the fact that everything participates in the power of being in a finite way, that all beings are infinitely transcended by their creative ground.[118]

God is therefore variously understood by Tillich as the creative and abysmal ground, power, and depth of being.[119] And "[s]ince God is the ground of being, he is the ground of the structure of being.... He *is* this structure, and it is impossible to speak about him except in terms of this structure."[120] In his treatment of the doctrine of creation, Tillich observes that in the "doctrine of *creatio ex nihilo* [lies] Christianity's protection against any type of ultimate dualism."[121] The universe, while not identified with God, nevertheless proceeds from God. It participates in the being of God, else it would not have being at all. In the doctrine of divine creativity, then, Tillich includes not only the preservation of the world but also providence as well: "God *has* cre-

ated the world, he *is* creative in the present moment, and he *will* creatively fulfil his *telos*."[122]

According to Tillich, insofar as the fulfilment of creation is the actualization of finite freedom, the *telos* of creation is the human person,
for "no other being is aware of finitude on the basis of an awareness of
potential infinity."[123] However, as we have seen, Tillich's ontological
interpretation of the fall raises the question of human solidarity with
the non-human world in terms of the traditional Protestant treatment
of the doctrine of grace. Tillich follows the Reformers in rejecting the
Roman Catholic position that grace is a supranatural substance, but
questions the Protestant understanding which restricts the sphere of
grace to an interior form of forgiveness received in the center of the
human personality. While the doctrine of grace, for Tillich, is not
dependent on the doctrine of the fall, it is nevertheless related to it.
Hence, the question of grace and of redemption for Tillich begins with
the question of the mutual participation between human beings and the
non-human world:

A last question must be asked, namely, how does man participate in the
subhuman creature and vice versa? The classical answer is that man is
the microcosmos because in him all levels of reality are present. In the
myths of the "original man," the "man from above," "The Man" (cf. especially the Persian tradition and I Corinthians, chap. 15) and in similar
philosophical ideas (cf. Paracelsus, Böhme, Schelling) the mutual participation of man and nature is symbolically expressed. The myth of the
curse over nature and its potential participation in salvation points in the
same direction. *All this is hard to understand in a culture which is de-
termined by nominalism and individuals. But it belongs to a heritage
which the Western mind is about to reconquer.* The problem is most ur-
gent when Christian theology deals with the fall and the salvation of the
world. Does "world" refer to the human race alone? And, if so, can the
human race be separated from other beings? Where is the boundary line
in the general biological development; where is the boundary line in the
development of the individual man? Is it possible to separate the nature
which belongs to him through his body from universal nature? Does the
unconscious realm of man's personality belong to nature or to man?
Does the collective unconscious admit of the isolation of the individual
from the other individuals and from the whole of the living substance?
These questions show that the elements of participation in the polarity of
individualization and participation must be considered much more seriously with respect to the mutual participation of nature and man. Here
theology should learn from modern naturalism, which at this point can

serve as an introduction to a half-forgotten theological truth. *What happens in the microcosm happens by mutual participation in the macrocosmos, for being itself is one.*[124]

Here Tillich demonstrates theologically that it is not just humanity which is dependent on divine grace in order to sustain it and bring it to fulfilment. By extending the ontological principle of mutual participation to include the entire created universe, Tillich successfully preserves a doctrine of creation that complements, rather than contradicts, the doctrine of redemption. This is accomplished by interpreting the traditional doctrine of God in light of what the science of his time taught him about the universe, including the insights of psychology, biology, and quantum physics.[125] The Newtonian world-view had fostered an attitude that

completely excluded the awareness of God's sustaining creativity. Nature was considered a system of measurable and calculable laws resting in themselves without beginning or end. The "well-founded earth" was a safe place within a safe universe. Although no one would deny that every special thing was threatened by nonbeing, the structure of the whole seemed beyond such a threat. Consequently, one could speak of *deus sive natura,* a phrase which indicates that the name "God" does not add anything to what is already involved in the name "nature." One may call such ideas "pantheistic"; but, if one does, one must realize that they are not much different from a deism which consigns God to the fringe of reality and relegates to the world the same independence which it has in naturalistic pantheism. The symbol of God's sustaining creativity has disappeared in both cases. *Today the main trend of the modern world view has been reversed. The foundations of the self-sufficient universe have been shaken. The questions of its beginning and end have become theoretically significant, pointing to the element of nonbeing in the universe as a whole.*[126]

In addressing the question of the "end" of the universe, that is, of ultimate (or of unambiguous) fulfilment throughout all dimensions of life, Tillich finds it "adequate to discuss, first, history in its full and proper sense, *i.e.*, human history, then to strive to understand the historical dimension in all realms of life, and finally, to relate human history to the 'history of the universe.'"[127] He argues further that "only the valuation of the creation as good makes an eschatology of fulfilment possible...[,] and only the idea of fulfilment makes the creation meaningful."[128] In this way, Tillich seeks to unite being and meaning in his eschatological understanding of the fulfilment of universal history. And for Tillich, an ontological interpretation of eschatology as such deals not so much with the "last things" as with the relation of the temporal to the eternal.

According to Tillich, "history remains an anticipated, but unactualized, dimension in all realms [of life] except that of human history."[129] This is because in every dimension of life, including the inorganic, there exists a quasi-historical *telos* which, while it may not be part of history proper, analogously accounts for the spontaneous manifestation of the "new" in the genesis of species and the development of the universe. The dimension of spirit is only actualized in anticipation in such phenomena, however, and it cannot therefore be claimed of them that the elements of freedom and absolute meaning are operative in the same way that they are in human history. However, while the historical dimension is present in unactualized form in all dimensions of life (except that of human history), it nevertheless points to a universal feature of the multidimensional unity of life where "the meaning of creation is revealed in its end."[130] Accordingly, Tillich argues that

> historical existence is embedded in universal existence and cannot be separated from it. "Nature participates in history" and in the fulfilment of the universe. With respect to historical time, this means that the fulfilment toward which historical time runs is the fulfilment toward which time under all dimensions runs....
>
> Since history is the all-embracing dimension of life, and since historical time is the time in which all other dimensions of time are presupposed, the answer to the meaning of history implies an answer to the universal meaning of being. The historical dimension is present in all realms of life, though only as a subordinated dimension. But after it has come into its own, it draws into itself the ambiguities and problems under the other dimensions.[131]

In this regard, Tillich prefers to use the symbol "Kingdom of God" as the most adequate and positive answer to the question of the meaning of history. This is because it possesses both an inner-historical/transhistorical and an immanental/transcendental character. Moreover, despite the sometimes narrow connotations associated with its emergence as a symbol out of the fabric of political life, it is in its universality able to embrace life in all realms, not just that of the human:

It is a kingdom not only of men; it involves the fulfilment of life under all dimensions. This agrees with the multidimensional unity of life: fulfilment under one dimension implies fulfilment in all dimensions.... Paul expresses this in the symbols "God being all in all" and "the Christ surrendering the rule over history to God" when the dynamics of history have reached their end.[132]

Tillich's ontological interpretation of the "end of history" rests, as was mentioned before, on a paradoxical understanding of the relation of the temporal to the eternal. His dynamic-creative interpretation of the symbol "Kingdom of God" therefore regards history in its relation to eternity in terms, once again, of *ontological transition, that is*, of the transition from the temporal to the eternal. Just as the creation is not a temporal event, neither is the "end" of time or history a temporal event. Time and space are forms of the created finite, while eternity is its *telos*. According to Tillich, then, the "end" of history in terms of its ultimate aim or fulfilment consists in its elevation into the eternal at every moment of created time. And this elevation of the temporal into the eternal life is not restricted to human beings alone, else it would not be a genuine elevation but only a partial and, therefore, false one. The basic assertion of the symbol "Kingdom of God" therefore "is that the ever present end of history elevates the positive content of history into eternity at the same time that it excludes the negative from participation in it."[133] And since the historical dimension is present in either actualized or potential form in all realms of life, this movement and elevation into the eternal life is universal:

In fully symbolic language one could say that life in the whole of creation...contributes in every moment of time to the Kingdom of God and its eternal life. What happens in time and space, in the smallest particle of matter as well as in the greatest personality, is significant for the eternal life. And since eternal life is participation in the divine life, every finite happening is significant for God.[134]

Participation of all things in the divine life is participation in the eternal conquest of the negative. In the relation of the symbol of Eternal Life to being and non-being, Tillich asserts that this "negation of the negative" is what gives the idea of "eternal blessedness" its paradoxical character.[135] The symbol "eternal blessedness" therefore refers to the state of fulfilment in which only the positive or essential aspects of universal life are expressly made unambiguously manifest. It represents the eternally present process of the overcoming of non-being in every created reality, an overcoming that does not simply take place within the Divine Life of the Godhead but is achieved through genuine conflict and victory throughout the entire universe.

The process of what Tillich refers to as "essentialization" involves the assurance that *in spite of* the negative elements of existence that drive toward death and destruction, the promise cf the unambiguous fulfilment of life is always present. God is deeply concerned for God's creation and will bring it to fulfilment. This is particularly true of the non-human universe which labors in agony to give birth, with humanity, to the new creation. Hence, while hardly denying the negativity that makes possible participation in the life of eternal blessedness, Tillich nonetheless affirms the sustaining and directing creativity of God for both humanity and the universe. He therefore asks the question: "What does the symbol of eternal blessedness mean for the universe besides man?"

> There are indications in biblical literature of the idea that nature participates in showing and praising the divine glory; but there are other passages in which the animals are excluded from the divine care (Paul) and man's misery is seen in the fact that he is not better off than flowers and animals (Job). In the first group of expressions, nature somehow participates (symbolically expressed in the visions of the Apocalypse) in the divine blessedness, whereas in the second group, nature *and* man are excluded from eternity (most parts of the Old Testament).... [A] possible solution would be that all things – since they are good by creation – participate in the Divine Life according to their essence.... The conflicts and sufferings of nature under the conditions of existence and its longing for salvation, of which Paul speaks..., serve the enrichment of essential being after the negation of the negative in everything that has being.[136]

The non-human universe, in other words, is a vital element in the comprehensive essentialization of history. It is God who initiates and activates the saving power throughout all of creation. The world as such is not left behind in Tillich's eschatological vision while human souls are restored and reunited with God. *All* things are reunited with God or *nothing* is. God is not who God is without the world, and the world is not what it is without God.

Tillich therefore offers the symbol of "eschatological pan-en-theism" to describe the relation of the living God to the inner aim of all creation.[137] God's relationship to the world is such that the ground and depth of being which sustains the living character of all creation is the very power which also drives it to seek fulfilment in that which is both within and yet beyond itself. That is, all things have their creative origin in the divine ground of being, they possess an ontological dependence on that ground, and they find their unambiguous fulfilment as well in that same ground. As Divine Life, God is neither an endless process of becoming nor an absolute identity characterized by a sort of timeless detachment. Rather, as "living," God possesses in Godself "the unity of identity and alteration which characterizes life and which is fulfilled in Eternal Life."[138] Tillich's symbol of "eschatological pan-en-theism" therefore expresses the simultaneous reality that the universe is created for fulfilment in God and that God's most profound concern is that all of creation share fully in the Divine Life.

For Tillich, nothing could be more obvious than this assertion, that is, that God cares deeply and actively for creation. That is why he can maintain, according to this view, that "the world process means something for God. He is not a separated self-sufficient entity who, driven by a whim, creates what he wants and saves whom he wants.... God...drives toward the actualization and essentialization of everything that has being."[139] At the same time, however, Tillich is aware that such formulations concerning God and God's relation to the life of the universe may serve to undermine the legitimate notion of God as ultimate mystery. For this reason, he points out that his language is symbolic and therefore is able to transcend the subject-object scheme, thus preserving the abysmal character of the divine "otherness." Additionally,

in the all-embracing symbolism, a genuine religious interest is preserved, that is, the affirmation of the ultimate seriousness of life in the light of the eternal; for a world which is only external to God and not also internal to Him, in the last consideration, is a divine play of no essential concern for God. This is certainly not the biblical view which emphasizes in many ways God's infinite concern for his creation.... And there may be a third answer to the criticism of the universal theology that embraces both God and the world, the answer that it sharply transcends a merely anthropocentric as well as a merely cosmocentric theology and expresses a theocentric vision of the meaning of existence.[140]

Tillich's theocentric model of reality incorporates elements of both contemporary science and the Judeo-Christian theological tradition. As such, it stands as a legitimate theological response to the peril posed by our global environmental crisis. It offers an expansive understanding of the God-world relationship that seeks to overcome the inadequate interpretations of more human-centered and naturalistic models. The integrity and inviolability of the non-human world are not compromised in such a vision; on the contrary, they are accentuated and even given favored status. The next chapter will accordingly consider the significance of Paul Tillich's theology of nature in the Protestant theological tradition and its usefulness for contemporary theologians.

Notes

1.   J. Philip Newell, *Celtic Prayers from Iona* (New York and Mahwah, NJ: Paulist Press, 1997), 39.
2.   In this way, I would argue that Tillich fulfills what one of his contemporaries (and one of the earliest genuine "theologians of nature") suggested for systematic theology when confronted with the environmental crisis: "That means that theological categories may no longer be only historical categories. They have got to deal with man as history and as nature; and, therefore, categories of creation, redemption, and sanctification have got to operate with the same scope as the fundamental categories of man and God. And this requires not only that Christian and Jewish *morality* shall be offended by pollution but that *theology* must do more; it must be reconceived, under the shock of filth, into fresh scope and profundity" (Joseph Sittler, "Ecological Commitment as Theological Responsibility," *Zygon* 5 [June 1970]: 177-178).
3.   Paul Tillich, "Nature and Sacrament," in *PRE,* 99-101. Cf. *GW* 7 (1962), 108-110 and *RW,* 152-154.
4.   Tillich, "Nature and Sacrament," 101.
5.   Kenan B. Osborne, *New Being: A Study on the Relationship Between Conditioned and Unconditioned Being According to Paul Tillich* (The Hague: Martinus Nijhoff, 1969), 103-104.
6.   Paul Tillich, *ST* 3, 159, 274.
7.   See Paul Tillich, "Protestantische Gestaltung," in *GW* 7, 59. Cf. Tillich, *RV,* 49.
8.   Cf. in this regard Tillich's discussion of the ambiguity between the dignity and violation of life: "The holiness of a living being, its greatness and dignity, is ambiguously united with its profanization, its smallness, and its violability. The general rule that all organisms live through the assimilation

of other organisms implies that they become 'things' for each other, 'food-things,' so to speak, to be digested, absorbed as nourishment, and thrown out as debris. This is radical profanization in terms of their independent life.... But in the relation of man to all other living beings a change took place only where the relation of man to some animals (or, as in India to animals in general) became analogous to the relation of man to man. This shows most clearly the ambiguity between the dignity or inviolability of life and the actual violation of life by life. The biblical vision of peace in nature envisages an unambiguous self-transcendence in the realm of the organic which would change the actual conditions of organic life (Isaiah 11:6-9)." *ST* 3, 91.

9. Tillich, "Nature and Sacrament," 110.
10. Ibid.
11. That is, "eschatological pan-en-theism" (Tillich, *ST* 3, 421). This notion is discussed further on pp. 101-102.
12. Tillich, "Nature and Sacrament," 110-111. Cf. Tillich, *ST* 3, 121: "The largest sense of the term [*i.e.*, 'sacramental'] denotes everything in which the Spiritual Presence has been experienced; in a narrower sense, it denotes particular objects and acts in which a Spiritual community experiences the Spiritual Presence; and in the narrowest sense, it merely refers to some 'great' sacraments in the performance of which the Spiritual Community actualizes itself. If the meaning of 'sacramental' in the largest sense is disregarded, sacramental activities in the narrower sense (sacramentalia) lose their religious significance – as happened in the Reformation – and the great sacraments become insignificant – as happened in several Protestant denominations.... Sacraments, if retained, become obsolete rudiments of the past."
13. Tillich, *ST* 3, 123.
14. Tillich, "Nature and Sacrament," 111.
15. Ibid., 111-112: "In the revival of Reformation theology in our day, the word plays an immense role, whereas the sacraments play no role whatsoever. It is fairly evident that the Protestant sacraments are disappearing.... [T]he one thing needful is that the whole Protestant attitude toward the sacraments be changed."
16. Tillich, *ST* 3, 120.
17. Tillich, "Nature and Sacrament," 112.
18. Tillich, "The Redemption of Nature," *Christendom* 10 (Summer 1945): 305.
19. Tillich, "Nature and Sacrament," 112.
20. Ibid.
21. Tillich, "Redemption," 305.
22. Tillich, *ST* 3, 122.
23. Tillich, *ST* 3, 5.
24. In this respect, Tillich's interpretation of evolutionary theory may have been more consistent with current views than that of Teilhard. See, for exam-

ple, Stephen J. Gould, *Wonderful Life: The Burgess Shale and the Nature of History* (New York: Norton, 1989).
25. Tillich, *ST* 3, 5.
26. Ibid.
27. Ibid., 4.
28. Ibid., 5.
29. Ibid., 12-17. See also Paul Tillich, "Dimensions, Levels, and the Unity of Life," *Kenyon Alumni Bulletin* 17 (1959): 5, where he defines "levels" as "'self-contained and mutually exclusive sections of reality.'"
30. Tillich, "Dimensions," 5.
31. Tillich, *ST* 3, 12.
32. Ibid.
33. Ibid., 1.
34. Ibid., 18.
35. Ibid., 19.
36. Ibid.
37. In this regard, see Paul Tillich, "Thing and Self," in *SSTS,* 114: "In man, all dimensions of life are actual. In the atom all dimensions of life are potential. And in the levels between atom and man they are partially potential, partially actual."
38. Tillich, *ST* 3, 20.
39. Ibid., 20-21.
40. Ibid., 21.
41. Ibid., 24-25.
42. Ibid., 25-26.
43. Ibid., 25.
44. Ibid., 32.
45. Ibid.
46. Ibid., 34, 52, 98-106.
47. Ibid., 89-91.
48. Ibid., 53.
49. Ibid., 54.
50. Ibid., 74.
51. Ibid.
52. Paul Tillich, "How Has Science in the Last Century Changed Man's View of Himself?" in *SSTS,* 80. Cf. Tillich, "Thing and Self," 112-116.
53. Tillich, "Dimensions," 8.
54. Tillich, *ST* 2, 29.
55. Ibid.
56. Ibid.
57. Ibid., 30.
58. Genesis 3:17.
59. Tillich, *ST* 2, 40.

60. Ibid.
61. See Ibid., 67: "The idea that the "Fall" has physically changed the cellular or psychological structure of man (and nature?) is absurd and unbiblical."
62. Ibid., 40.
63. Ibid. Emphasis mine.
64. Ibid., 41.
65. Ibid.
66. Ibid., 41-43.
67. Ibid., 42.
68. Ibid., 43.
69. Ibid. Emphasis mine.
70. See Tillich, *CB,* 51-54.
71. Tillich, *ST* 2, 67.
72. Ibid., 66-75.
73. Ibid., 74.
74. Ibid.
75. Romans 8:19-21.
76. Tillich, "Redemption," 302.
77. Ibid. To illustrate this point of Tillich concerning the poetic sensibility aroused by the bond that is formed by the shared tragedy and destiny of the human and non-human communities, the poignancy that is evoked by the loss of even one bird is eloquently described by a contemporary naturalist:

"I've been needing a beach for a month and a half. I needed the quiet. I yearned for the scented wind, the ceaseless motion and the endless horizon. I needed the perspective. Friends were too busy to make the drive with me; my family too engaged in their own social lives. I kept putting off the beach, waiting for a companion.

"Last week, I stood alone in the wind, facing gray waves. As the rising sun tinted a cloudy sky silver, I realized I had a companion after all. Twenty feet down the beach a dark form lay on the sand. Gradually the sky brightened, and I could see it was a common loon in winter plumage. Together in silence, we faced the dawn....

"...Why was this wildest of birds here, so still next to a possible predator? Could it be injured? There was no oil apparent on its feathers. Sometimes birds are lucky enough to simply grow old and die, instead of dying violently. I hoped this one was only resting....

"Watching the loon and imagining its timelessness, I thought I had uncovered the perspective I'd been driven to the sea to find. The sun was up and the sky was clearing. I was chilled. As I stood to go, the loon turned and looked at me, its eyes flat, scarlet and wild. It was visibly weak. It opened its heavy beak and uttered the typical loon cry, incredibly mournful, low and for my ears only. I backed away. As much as I wanted to, there was nothing I could do for this bird....

"An hour later, I went down to the sea again. The loon lay twisted in a sandy tangle, its feathers sodden, its eyes dull. Waves had tumbled its body over and over, and the tide had left it behind. I sat down, closer to it this time, looking at the lonely sea and the sky, thinking. It was a lovely place; the right place for both of us. As timeless as loons are, this particular bird only had a few hours left. I still have half my life, and a fresh perspective" (Kathleen Kudlinski, "A Loon Encounter at the Water's Edge," *New Haven* [CT] *Register,* 22 February 1998).

78. Tillich, "Redemption," 303.
79. Ibid.
80. Ibid., 303-304.
81. 1 Corinthians 15:21.
82. Tillich, "Redemption," 304.
83. Ibid.
84. Tillich, *ST* 2, 95.
85. Paul Tillich, "A Reinterpretation of the Doctrine of the Incarnation," *Church Quarterly Review* 148 (January-March 1949): 133.
86. Ibid.
87. Ibid.
88. John 1:14.
89. Tillich, *ST* 2, 95.
90. Ibid., 96.
91. Ibid.
92. Ibid., 118.
93. Ibid., 120-121. Cf. Ibid., 100: "But God is not only for us, he is for everything created."
94. Ibid., 153.
95. Ibid.
96. See on this point Tillich, *DF,* 44-48.
97. Ibid., 97.
98. Tillich expresses this rather eloquently in one of his sermons: "In the stories of the Crucifixion the agony and the death of Jesus are connected with a group of events in nature: Darkness covers the land; the curtain of the temple is torn in two; the earth is shaken and the bodies of saints rise out of their graves. Nature, with trembling, participates in the decisive event of history.... Nature is in an uproar because something is happening which concerns the universe" ("Universal Salvation," in *NB,* 175-176).
99. Tillich, *ST* 2, 157.
100. Ibid., 166-167.
101. Ibid., 167.

102. Paul J. Tillich, "The New Being," *Religion in Life* 19 (Autumn 1950): 514. Cf. his understanding of the "threefold character of salvation" in the system as participation (regeneration), acceptance (justification), and transformation (sanctification) (*ST* 2, 177-180).
103. Ibid., 516-517.
104. Tillich, *ST* 2, 168.
105. Ibid.
106. Ibid.
107. Paul Tillich, "The Relation of Religion and Health," in *The Meaning of Health*, ed. Paul Lee (Richmond, CA: North Atlantic Books, 1981), 14.
108. Tillich, "Redemption," 304.
109. Ibid.
110. Ibid., 304-305.
111. Tillich, *ST* 2, 167.
112. Paul Tillich, *ST* 1, 282.
113. Ibid., 278.
114. Cf. Tillich, *CB*, 182-190, where he develops his notion of the "God above God."
115. Tillich, *ST* 1, 228.
116. Tillich, *ST* 2, 97-180.
117. For example, the characteristic of divine immanence is compromised and in danger of relapsing into "monarchic monotheism" when, according to Tillich, "[a] theology...does not dare to identify God and the power of being as the first step toward a doctrine of God..., for if God is not being-itself, he is subordinate to it, just as Zeus is subordinate to fate in Greek religion" (Ibid., 236), albeit the "highest being" in the "The Great Chain of Being" (Ibid., 233). On the other hand, those conceptions of divinity which stress divine immanence, such as pantheism and mystical monotheism, are in danger of collapsing the divine creative power into a complete identification with the world, thus abrogating the distinctive transcendent character of God (Ibid., 233- 234). Cf. Tillich, "The Nature of Religious Language," in *TC*, 61-65.
118. Tillich, *ST* 1, 237.
119. In addition to the numerous instances throughout his system where Tillich utilizes the terms "ground of being," "power of being," and "being-itself" in virtual synonymous fashion (*e.g.*, *ST* 1, 270-273, 283-284; *ST* 2, 10-11; and *ST* 3, 293-294), Tillich elsewhere employs the terms "ground of being" and "power of being" interchangeably with the terms "ultimate reality" and "being itself" in their collective reference to the "non-symbolic element in our image of God," and uses the term "Being Itself" as the symbolic referent "for that which is not symbolic in God" ("Religious Language," 61). The term "depth of being" is found in the system in two places (*ST* 1, 113, 124). In the first instance, it refers to the unifying character of revelation and the ecstatic experience in which it is received. In the second, it is used in connection with the

transparent nature of "Word of God" language, that is, the depth of being and meaning can manifest itself through otherwise ordinary language because the "Word of God" is able to transmit the "sound" of ultimacy. For hermeneutical reasons, however, Richard Grigg distinguishes between the terms "depth of being" and what he refers to as the "depth of the structure of being" (*i.e.*, "being-itself"), understanding the former as being "inconceivable, possessing no positive and nonrelational attributes," while the latter term is to be used for purposes of conceptualization (*Symbol and Empowerment: Paul Tillich's Post-Theistic System* [Macon, GA: Mercer University Press, 1985], 62-63). In the present study, the terms ground of being, power of being, and depth of being will be considered synonymous symbolic correlates to the non-symbolic philosophical statement that "God is being-itself" (Tillich, *ST* 1, 238).
120. Tillich, *ST* 1, 238.
121. Ibid., 253.
122. Ibid.
123. Ibid., 258.
124. Ibid., 261. Emphasis mine.
125. See, for example, two of the essays by Tillich in *TC*, "The Theological Significance of Existentialism and Psychoanalysis," 112-126, and "Science and Theology: A Discussion with Einstein," 127-132. Cf. Paul Tillich, "The Relationship Today Between Science and Religion," in *The Student Seeks an Answer*, ed. John A. Clark (Waterville, ME: Colby College Press, 1960), 297-306.
126. Tillich, *ST* 1, 262-263. Emphasis mine.
127. Tillich, *ST* 3, 298.
128. Ibid., 299.
129. Ibid., 306.
130. Ibid., 299.
131. Ibid., 320, 350.
132. Ibid., 359.
133. Ibid., 397.
134. Ibid., 398.
135. Ibid., 403.
136. Ibid., 405-406.
137. Ibid., 421.
138. Ibid., 420.
139. Ibid., 422.
140. Ibid.

The world is not God, but it is God's.[1]

Chapter 4

An Analysis and Evaluation of Tillich's Theology of Nature

The foregoing critical retrieval of Paul Tillich's theology of nature has yielded a vision rich with nature-affirming images and full of prophetic warnings addressed to humankind concerning the abuse and degradation of the non-human universe. It is now time to examine the most distinctive features of Tillich's theology of nature and to assess its importance in the history of Protestant thought and its value for us today.

Recapitulation and Analysis

A number of observations can now be made concerning Tillich's theology of nature. First, as we have seen, Tillich was aware that the mechanistic, Cartesian world-view which came to prominence during the rise of the Protestant influence in the West (*i.e.*, from the sixteenth to the eighteenth centuries) suffered from an erroneous dualism in its understanding of the material universe. This particular world-view, according to Tillich, proved neither benign nor neutral – it had disastrous consequences for both humanity and the environment. For Tillich, such a dualistic world-view denied the fundamental reality that, though infinitely varied, "being itself is one."[2] It had fostered a somewhat uncritical deism wherein God remained rather unconcerned about earthly affairs, including the fate of the non-human universe, leaving human beings in the position not so much of stewards and caretakers of the earth but of abusive landlords. Ultimately, it had encouraged the increasing separation of science and technology from religion, allowing the former to occupy autonomous spheres of knowledge virtually unconstrained by questions of morality or meaning.

Moreover, in criticizing certain aspects of his own theological tradition concerning the severe dualism influencing its doctrine of the relationship between nature and grace, Tillich demonstrated that he was equally concerned with the retreat of an authentic religious voice from the public domain. In many respects, the radical "interiorization" of grace was responsible for an attitude among scientists and theologians alike that the non-human world was of little value. If the realm of religion was limited largely to questions of human justification and salvation, science and technology could proceed apace with their respective agendas, giving little thought to their often cumulative deleterious consequences for the environment. With his notion of the "multidimensional unity of life" and his understanding of grace as the healing element within all of creation, Tillich challenged this approach to reality, seeking instead to establish a genuine correlation between the findings of science and the truths of revelation.

Tillich found great merit in those mytho-poetic passages from Scripture that point to the mystery within reality of the mutual participation of the human and the non-human realms in the process of universal redemption. His dynamic-creative interpretation of such passages and their application to the question of the human/non-human relationship constituted a new paradigm within which new images could be constructed, images that would prove far more favorable to a biocentric understanding of the universe. For example, in positing an understanding of the God-world relationship in terms of "eschatological pan-en-theism," Tillich avoids making a transcendent object of

God while, at the same time, he asserts the integrity of all creation. Such an image is consistent with the God of both biblical testaments whose providential concern for creation extends from the vaults of the heavens to the smallest of sparrows. His interpretation of Revelation as describing "the salvation of man and nature from the bondage of corruption"[3] is significant for its appropriation of a biblical text that is often misunderstood in the service of a more theologically expansive context, one that of necessity must include the question of the redemption of the non-human universe. Despite the claim of some critics to the contrary, Tillich's Lutheran heritage never allowed him to stray so far from the biblical witnesses as to completely abandon his distinctively Christian vision.

Unlike the early Schelling, therefore, whose primary task was the shaping of a *philosophy* of nature, Tillich's treatment of the question of nature was an integral part of his philosophical *theology.* His theocentric understanding of reality – a product both of his reading of the Bible and of his philosophical approach to the question of being – has thus proven to be an effective basis for a biocentric model of the universe. For Tillich, at the center of life *is* life. It is characterized first and foremost by the quality of givenness, of gratuitousness. Grace, according to Tillich, is the manifestation of healing power throughout the entire universe, not just in human beings. Because of this gracious character inherent in all of creation, Tillich was able to claim that nothing created stands very far removed from its Creator. Plants, animals, water, rocks, trees, human culture – all are intrinsically worthy of respect and wonder since all share in the fountain of being. Despite the threat of non-being in the forms of sin and disintegration, the fact that all things are essentially related to one another can never be entirely repudiated.

The importance, then, of Tillich's approach to the non-human world cannot be underestimated. During his early years, as we have seen, Tillich regarded Protestant theology as having become dominated largely by a ruthless contempt for the non-human elements within creation. This tendency he traced primarily to Ritschl and his followers, such as Wilhelm Herrmann and Adolph von Harnack, who had tried to create a new synthesis "on the level of Kant's division of the world of knowledge from the world of values."[4] There was, of course, the significant romantic movement within Protestant thought that had fostered a more affirmative view toward nature. But this had over-

come neither the dominant trend in Protestantism nor its own ambiguities regarding the non-human world (*i.e.*, its alternating identification of God with world [pantheism] or of human beings with nature).

Tillich himself, of course, was influenced by many of the movements of his theological predecessors and contemporaries, but sought
to position himself both between and beyond them. This is why one
finds strong elements of such influences in his thought while he remains critical of them as well. For example, in his attempt to preserve
the "otherness" of God, Tillich has imbibed one of the main tenets of
the neo-orthodox position. At the same time, however, he rejects, as
we have seen, the neo-Kantian attitude toward nature prevalent among
the Ritschlian school. In like manner, one often finds in Tillich a
certain "immediacy" with the non-human world that is reflective of his
romantic ancestors such as Schelling and Schleiermacher. Yet his
"new realism," while influenced by such figures, soberly acknowledges
the sinfulness of human beings with respect to the non-human world
and seeks corrective measures which are neither sentimental nor im-
practical. Hence, the neo-orthodox, romantic, and liberal Protestant
positions with regard to the non-human world all played a role in the
shaping of Tillich's own views, sometimes favorably, sometimes critically.

Tillich's particular dismay at the way in which the non-human
world was considered and treated by the neo-Kantian element within
Protestantism (*i.e.*, Ritschl *et al.*) was as much a function of his fundamentally ontological approach to reality as was his innate love of
nature. As theologian, he was concerned that the negative Calvinist
assessment of the world and human-as-nature had become so solidified
as to have begotten complete freedom of action toward the world of the
Creation. And this freedom of action, unrestrained by any care for the
Creation, had even been sanctified theologically as humanity's proper
service of God – to control and subdue the earth in the course of one's
work in the world. The whole emphasis had gradually come to rest on
human agency and productiveness. The Calvinist tradition, from Calvin himself up to Ritschl and Barth, had often left out of account the
positive role of the non-human world in the theological categories.
Tillich not only saw the theological danger in this but had, during
World War I, witnessed first-hand humanity's senseless destruction of
the earth.

He emerged from that devastating experience with an awareness of
sharing in the guilt for ravaging the land. And, as we have seen, Til-

lich would later identify in his theological system what one writer has described elsewhere as "the ecological Fall."[5] His non-anthropocentric treatment of the fall and redemption of nature allows for an understanding of grace that is best supported by the ontological approach to reality. That is, the principle of the "interdependence of everything with everything else in the totality of being"[6] is logically extended to include all non-human realms in the event of salvation. Humanity is neither the centerpiece of creation, according to Tillich, nor the axis upon which redemption occurs. Rather, there exists a mutuality between the human and non-human spheres in which both share in the tragic aspects of existence as well as in the New Being manifest in the operation of saving power throughout the universe. In such a scheme, the integrity of the non-human dimension in its essential character can never be lost since its participation in the universal redemptive work of Jesus as the Christ is able to overcome its subjection to existential estrangement. This is the theological counterpart to the philosophical statement that the power of being is the negation of the negation of non-being. While Tillich's christology has been criticized by some as being too "symbolic" (*i.e.*, more concerned with explaining the Christ event in terms of philosophical categories and myth than in its historical and intellectually "offensive" significance[7]), it would appear that his very deliberate inclusion of nature in the universal process of fall and redemption is, ironically, more dependent on the historicity of the Christ event than are some of the more "existentialist" christological interpretations, such as those of Kierkegaard and Bultmann. In fact, as we observed in Chapter Three, it could be argued that Tillich's christology, precisely *because* of its inclusive and symbolic character, is more in line with Chalcedon than that of Karl Barth.

Because one of the "boundaries" upon which Tillich's theology operated was formed by science and religion, he was well acquainted with the developments in twentieth-century science which had begun to displace the Newtonian world-view. One effect of scientific developments in the post-modern world has been that of undermining "our feeling of living in an ultimately secure world."[8] In this respect, Tillich's existential analysis of reality appears dramatically accurate, especially when it is understood to include not just the "human situation" but the entire universe as well. In acknowledging the validity of the scientific data regarding evolution and the beginning and end of the universe, Tillich was able to anticipate the gravity of humanity's neglect of the natural world, that is, of the environmental crisis. For Tillich, there was little question that such disregard and, at times, outright hostility toward the non-human world had deep religious roots, although the forms it assumed were often technological or scientific ones.

Hence, far from "ontologizing away"[9] the ecological problem, Tillich's attack on the radical split between the supernatural and the natural in much of Protestant theology was the very thing needed to bring the issue of the non-human world back into the theological discussion. His bold attempt to develop a "theology of the inorganic" is an example of this. Tillich's insistence on the primacy of the inorganic among all the dimensions of life would have been inconceivable to someone like Karl Barth; indeed, it would have been considered odious. For Tillich, the dismissal of those inanimate dimensions of the non-human world as inaccessible, opaque forms of some Kantian noumenal realm ignores the traditional Christian doctrine which emphasizes the goodness of *all* creation, not just those aspects of it which involve human beings. Tillich's critique of the neo-Kantian stress on human agency at the expense of the non-human world, therefore, is an effort to steer contemporary Protestant theology in a direction that is appreciative of the interdependency existing between the human and non-human dimensions. In this, he implicitly raises the question of humanity's moral obligation towards the non-human universe, a subject that will be taken up in detail at the beginning of Chapter Five.

Another example of his efforts to creatively re-introduce the matter of the human/non-human relationship into the theological conversation is Tillich's life-long effort to "sacramentalize" the universe for Protestant theology. While he realized in this that humanity's estrangement from nature had led to a decidedly sterile form of Protestantism, Tillich's principal goal was to foster a defensible concern toward the non-human world. He knew that the fate of the planet was a question of far more significance than whether or not a particular form of religious expression survived. As it was, the final eclipse of the "Protestant Era" of which Tillich writes occurred almost simultaneously with the incipient awareness of what has proven to be an ecological crisis of global proportions.[10]

Finally, such callous disregard for nature as that exhibited by the Ritschlian school constituted for Tillich a theological issue insofar as it raised concrete questions of ultimacy, that is, of being and nonbeing. In this latter respect, Tillich saw that the traditional answers given by

Protestant theology concerning the ultimate fate of creation (apart from human beings) had been found to be inadequate from the point of view of modern science. Popular theological notions of God's relationship with the world often drifted unintelligibly between a virtual deism and a naturalistic pantheism, leaving out of account divine involvement and human responsibility. Indeed, "the structure of the whole"[11] *had* come under attack and needed to be reconceived in a radically different way. Tillich's recovery of the symbol of God's sustaining creativity (as including within it the entire created universe) is an example of his effort to "re-mythologize" one of the classic symbols of Christian faith in light of his contemporary cultural situation. In this case, it was the questions raised by the destruction and neglect of the natural world that led Tillich to attempt a response utilizing his distinctive theological interpretation of "new realism."

For the foregoing reasons, it would seem that Tillich's vast theological enterprise contains within it what was earlier referred to as the "ecological motif."[12] Tillich's theology of nature, in "existentializing" and endorsing the integrity of the non-human universe, successfully combines the two themes that have been observed in the Judeo-Christian tradition known as "the metaphor of fecundity" and "the metaphor of migration to a good land."[13] Tillich's notion of the "multidimensional unity of life" accords well with the metaphor of fecundity, while his comprehensive eschatological vision points to a similar conclusion with respect to the latter metaphor. In both instances, the entire universe is regarded as more or less "charged with the glory of God."[14] The goodness that characterizes every created thing is never wholly lost since it would not exist if it were not good. In Tillich's case, he argues that because we are able to experience the goodness of creation *now* (albeit in an ambiguous and inchoate fashion), we can genuinely hope for the unequivocal fulfilment of that goodness as anticipated in the Christ event. This is the story of the essentialization of the universe, according to Tillich, as told through the Christian theological tradition.[15] As such, it takes into account the very real forces that oppose this process while, at the same time, affirming the ever-victorious character of the triumph of being over non-being as symbolized in the event of the Resurrection.[16]

Moreover, in delineating a Kierkegaardian "infinite qualitative difference" among God, humanity, and the non-human universe, Tillich avoids identifying this process with the Godhead itself.[17] The divine alterity is preserved, thus making the question of redemption a genuine one. By asking the question of the redemption of nature as he does in terms of ontology rather than of moral agency, Tillich enlarges the stage upon which the great drama of redemption is performed to include not only human beings but the whole of creation.[18]

Tillich's concomitant refusal to pit nature against grace accordingly earns him a rather unique place in the pantheon of Protestant theologians.[19] As we saw in his sacramental theology, if the non-human universe can be not only a bearer of grace but a *beneficiary* as well, then the traditional Protestant understanding of an adversarial relationship obtaining between nature and grace needs to be re-examined. It is to Tillich's credit that he has provided us with a working basis upon which to undertake this re-examination in light of the current ecological crisis. His insistence that "[b]oth the Protestant and democratic principles negate the mutually independent and hierarchically organized levels of the power of being"[20] constitutes a genuine attempt to recover one of the original insights or charisms of the early Reformers. In this sense, Tillich can be understood historically as a transitional or "bridge" figure of the twentieth century, one who stands in many ways at the end of an era characterized by the breakdown and undermining of modernity, yet who was able to anticipate the concerns of the twenty-first century. In his efforts near the end of his life to enter into constructive dialogue with the world's religions, Tillich's interpretation of Christianity attempted to retain the distinctive historical character of Christianity while emphasizing its universal appeal and significance. In suggesting the idea of the Protestant principle, Tillich found in Christianity a potentially "self-critical spirit" which, when properly invoked, is able to overcome at all times and places the various ideologies that form out of the elevation of preliminary concerns into ultimate concerns, including those having to do with the relationship between humanity and nature:

> In a secular form the conflict is alive even today as the conflict between a romantic philosophy of nature and its religious-artistic expressions, on the one hand, and the total profanization of nature and its moral and technical subjection to man's purposes, on the other.[21]

One of Tillich's earliest writings in English was an article entitled "History as *the* Problem of Our Period."[22] There he argues that, with the rise of historical consciousness in the West, the question of the meaning and purpose of human history has become of paramount significance. In terms of the emergence of National Socialism in his native Germany, Tillich maintains that only a sort of historical amnesia could have allowed such an event to have ever occurred. In light of the Nazi tragedy, he concludes, theology will now have to take into account as well the ambiguous character of human historicity, especially in its eschatological dimensions.

However, as we have seen, Tillich elsewhere suggests that history alone is *not* the most important problem with which we are confronted. In a number of places throughout his work, Tillich reminds us that the question of history can never be separated from the fact of nature. History is imbedded in nature just as nature itself participates in history.[23] Such a view was extremely important since it countered both those who claimed that human history and culture were of little or no significance and those who believed that human history alone provided the key to understanding the divine purpose at work in the universe.[24] In Tillich's case, however, the dialectic that moves history toward fulfilment is neither exclusively a negative one (the definitive "Nein!" of Barth's methodology), nor that of an Absolute Spirit coming to completion (Hegel), nor one defined by class conflicts and struggles (the materialist Marxist version of the Hegelian dialectic). In some sense Tillich's understanding of the question of the meaning of history includes some aspects of all of these interpretations of history and culture. However, in the end his use of the symbol "Kingdom of God" to describe history in its relation to eternity reveals his fundamentally *theocentric* understanding of reality, since it involves "the fulfilment of life under all dimensions,"[25] including that of the non-human universe. The scope of Tillich's trinitarian theocentrism is therefore comprehensive enough to consider the importance of *both* history and nature in their relation to eternal fulfilment. Such a conception of the meaning of history *within* nature is a clear departure from some of the major figures in the Christian tradition, from Augustine's interpretation of history in the *City of God* to the Barthian rejection of an intrinsically meaningful history. For Tillich, then, we cannot simply look to history alone as somehow pointing to the fulfilment of human beings and human culture. We must also seek in "the answer to the meaning of history...an answer to the universal meaning of being,"[26] including the meaning of that immense sector of creation uninhabited by human beings.

Critique and Evaluation

It is probably at this point that Tillich runs into the most trouble with
many of his more recent critics, especially those who claim that any
talk of a "universal" meaning of history or of being is unintelligible,
biased, and even quite dangerous.[27] Against Tillich's ontological approach it is argued in this first critique that assertion of some underlying metaphysical principle of reality such as "being" is intellectually
dishonest in that it ignores the inherent relativism of human experience. While it would be impossible to claim (with Tillich) that theology can be done from a more or less neutral perspective, I would suggest that the various positions from which such ideology criticism
emanates – while generally valid – often suffer from a certain type of
nominalism, one which tends to lack a sense of history and has little
interest in social change.[28] Tillich was always wary of such nominalistic impulses in Western thought, arguing that existence itself,
consisting of both vitalistic and destructive principles, could not be
sustained for one moment without being grounded in some reality
which both transcends and permeates it. For purposes of the present
work, it can be argued further that an ontological approach to reality is
much more favorable to the non-human world for precisely this reason, namely, that such nominalistic impulses, with their emphasis on
linguistic analysis and philosophical positivism, are in no way capable
of adequately addressing the dire ecological problems with which we
are faced. In fact, such recent movements as deconstructionism and
post-structuralism, while unquestionably shaping the intellectual climate and providing a needful criticism of the "Modern Age," have
(with some notable exceptions) continued to harbor a peculiar unwill-
ingness to take on the question of the human/non-human relationship.
In this sense, then, Tillich's philosophical theology, while certainly
contextual and limited, is nonetheless of great value when discussing
the theological importance of the non-human world.

Somewhat related to the "postmodernist" critique of Tillich's use of
metaphysics and "being" language is a second critique which argues
that "[t]he Christian tradition out of which Tillich worked had a
strongly anthropocentric slant to it...and [his] theology does not adequately overcome that deep Christian bias."[29] For such critics, despite
the strong favorable elements in Tillich's treatment of nature in his
systematic thought, he never completely broke away from his de-

liberate emphasis on things human. As Protestant existentialist his starting and ending points were always the same: the human person. For someone like Gordon Kaufman,

[o]ur most fundamental human problems today have to do with what we might call the *objective* conditions that make human life possible on planet Earth.... [This is a] very different focus than the existentialist concern with human subjectivity evinced in traditional Christian concepts like sin, guilt, anxiety, meaninglessness, etc., concepts that were central in Tillich's anthropological thinking.[30]

According to this view little, if any, of Tillich's theology can be realistically mined for anything of value to contemporary ecological theologians. In fact, for such critics, Tillich can be considered a contributor to, rather than an opponent of, the global ecological crisis.

I would agree with Kaufman that Tillich's Protestant existentialism presents us with limitations when looking to his theological project as a resource for a contemporary ecological theology. But they are just that – *limitations*. These particular limitations and even biases should be duly noted when examining Tillich's theology through an ecological lens, as one should similarly acknowledge the larger intellectual climate within which Tillich operated (*i.e.*, a male Euro-American one). As Langdon Gilkey has commented, however, Tillich should not be taken to task too hard for not developing a full-fledged theology of nature since such issues were not generally being addressed during his lifetime.[31] Of course, a critic of Tillich would counter by saying that that is precisely the point: his failure to so address the ecological problem constituted his contribution to it. While there is some validity to this view, it ignores the constraints that are placed on all of us by virtue of our existence as historical beings. Moreover, according to Tillich himself, his decidedly "theocentric" view of reality *specifically* and "sharply transcends a merely anthropocentric...theology."[32] What is so amazing about Tillich is that, *given the time in which he lived,* we are able to discern so much in his work that *is* favorable concerning the relationship among God, human beings, and the non-human world.

I would argue, therefore, that such anthropocentric elements should not thereby become the reason for rejecting Tillich outright as an important and valuable resource in this regard. In fact, it was Tillich's unique ability to combine existentialism with his "new realism" that

proved so favorable to the non-human world in the considerable cor-
pus of his work. In addition, as we saw in Chapter One, Tillich was
acutely aware of how much damage the Calvinist tradition had
wreaked on the non-human world with its radically anthropocentric
understanding of grace. As we also saw in Chapter One, Tillich's
rallying cry that "[u]nderstanding Kant means transcending Kant" is
further evidence that he wanted to avoid the philosophical pitfalls associated with the radical Kantian emphasis on human subjectivity, one
of which was the neglect and devaluation of the non-human world.
Finally, it could be argued that it was precisely the fact that Tillich
saw himself as operating out of the ontological *Christian* tradition (as
opposed to merely the *Protestant* tradition) that his theology (1) possesses the character of sacramentality (and, hence, respect for the non-
human elements of the universe) and (2) *was* able to effectively interpret the traditional categories of Christian 'heology in a broad rather
than a narrow sense.

   Hence, while it is true that Tillich cannot fully escape the charge of
anthropocentrism, it hardly overshadows his work to the point of ren-
dering it unfit as a resource for contemporary eco-theologians. It is
my hope that this study, at least up to this point, has in fact demonstrated that Tillich's theology is richly deserving of further consideration on this basis.

   The remaining two critiques that could be applied to Tillich's theology of nature are also somewhat related to each other by virtue of their
respective bases in the Christian scriptural tradition. The third critique we might label the "biblicist" critique, the fourth that of the critique from the "biblical tradition."

   What I am referring to here as the "biblicist" critique was mentioned in passing earlier in this chapter. Kenneth Hamilton argues
from a basically Kierkegaardian standpoint that Tillich's use of a
"system" to explicate the fundamental concepts of the Christian tradition are, in his words, "incompatible with the Christian gospel."[33]
More specifically for purposes of this book, Hamilton contends that
"Tillich's claim that his system does not conflict with the biblical concept of the personal God is irreconcilable with the biblical insistance
[*sic*] that God is known through his mighty acts."[34] Hamilton goes on
to say that the relationship into which God enters with God's creatures
is impossible if one conceives of God in impersonal terms as the creative and abysmal Ground of Being. For Hamilton this relationship,
not surprisingly, consists solely in God revealing God's self "to

men."[35] He accuses Tillich of advocating a pantheistic conception of the God-world relationship because of his "denial of a true relationship between God and creation, where individuals are real because God made them and not simply because they participate essentially in being."[36] According to Hamilton, Tillich's "nature mysticism" clouds over the fact that God can be known only indirectly, as one who "addresses us as individuals through grace."[37] In such a scheme, anything that smacks of divine immanence or of some type of "natural theology" must be vehemently repudiated.

In light of the second critique discussed earlier, that of Tillich's anthropocentrism, this third critique appears rather ironic, coming from what would seem to be the opposite direction than that of Kaufman. In this sense, then, what is attacked by Hamilton is not Tillich's existentialism but his philosophical *Idealism*. He sees Tillich very much in the tradition of Hegel and Schleiermacher, theologians whose attempts to create speculative systems out of the fabric of human history and universal human religiosity ultimately proved to be failures. However, Tillich's understanding of God as the Unconditioned or as the Ground of Being is not the same as Hegel's concept of the Absolute Spirit. Nor, for that matter, is Tillich's idea of religion as "ultimate concern" identical with Schleiermacher's notion of religion as the "feeling of absolute dependence." There are marked differences among the three figures, not least of which is Tillich's deliberate inclusion of the non-human realm throughout his work as an integral part of his system, something that neither Hegel nor Schleiermacher really take seriously. Moreover, Tillich's correlational method in which, for example, science and theology are allowed a critical dialogue, neither ignores nor violates the integrity of the genuinely religious voice. That is, Tillich's *Christian* existentialism recognizes the legitimacy of a God personal to all *as well as* the God who has created, and continues to create, a non-human universe every bit as rich and as wonderful as the experience of faith. For Tillich, however, faith in God could not be divorced from the fate of the rest of the universe. Tillich could not conceive of a God that would "save" human beings alone while allowing the rest of the universe to fend for itself.

If nothing else, then, Tillich's doctrines of creation, redemption, and eschatology are consistent for this reason.[38] Of course, Hamilton is not interested in the "consistency" of the system but in its failure to adequately come to terms with those very Kierkegaardian "inconsistencies" which form, in many respects, the basis of the individual's relationship with his or her God. Tillich, however, as we have seen was hardly unaware of the estranged nature obtaining between the essential and existential elements of the universe. This is one facet of his system that allowed him to develop the notion of "eschatological pan-entheism" (a fact which Hamilton did not address since it did not appear until the third volume of the system was published, the same year as Hamilton's critique). Nevertheless, it would seem that for Hamilton the non-human elements of the universe are of little value when interpreted in light of the "gospel." For him, the Christian gospel's message of salvation is communicated directly from God's self to the human person alone – it cannot be acquired in any other fashion. Hamilton in this respect stands well within that form of the Protestant tradition which regards nature and grace as being at odds with each other. And, as we have seen often throughout this book, this was precisely one of the major problems of traditional Protestant theology that Tillich sought to address and to change. In so doing, Tillich shows himself to be a defender of the non-human world, as both theologian and concerned individual.

The question of what "gospel" meant for Tillich leads us to our fourth and final critique, that arising from the biblical tradition itself. Basically, this critique consists in recognizing the idea that the biblical treatment of creation contains not only the theme of stewardship but also that of human domination over the earth. In other words, we must acknowledge the relatively recent scholarship which has shown that interpretations of biblical doctrines can never be totally one-sided.[39] The Bible, it is argued, is made up of so many diverse traditions, many of which appear to contradict each other theologically. One can always find biblical proof texts for one's position as easily as one's opponent can. For instance, there are numerous images of God to be found among the biblical writings that defy easy classification. In this sense, to seek theological consistency in the normative scriptures of the Judeo-Christian tradition is to court absurdity.

So, for example, the argument could be made in some quarters that Tillich's ontological interpretation of creation, fall, and redemption supports only the biblical idea of stewardship while ignoring the equally valid claim of Genesis 1:28 that humanity is the crown of creation.[40] But Tillich does something interesting. He recognizes that in the human person "all levels of reality are present."[41] This idea that humanity as "microcosmos" may lead one to conclude that Tillich, in this case, favors the idea of humanity as crown of creation. However, he goes on to speak about the "mutual participation of man and nature" and questions whether the term "world," in a soteriological sense, must refer to the human race alone.[42] This would seem to recommend the stewardship model. His notion developed later in the third volume of the *Systematic Theology* of the multidimensional unity of life and his eschewing of a hierarchical model of reality would also suggest affinity with the biblical model of stewardship. In this way, he is able to do justice to both themes of the biblical tradition without radically rejecting either.

What Tillich *does* oppose is a fundamentalist-literalist approach to biblical interpretation which ignores the complexities involved in such an enterprise.[43] This applies to the question of the relationship among God, humanity, and the non-human universe as much as it does to any other question posed to the biblical sources. We must also remember that Tillich himself was not a biblical scholar but a systematic theologian. His work consisted of doing creative, constructive theology. And while he clearly wished to remain within the Christian theological tradition (and, hence, stay rooted in the Christian scriptures), he did not utilize the Bible as his sole methodological criterion.

For Paul Tillich, then, there is little doubt that the formulation of the question of being in light of the present environmental crisis would clearly have been worthy of theological consideration, that is, it would have been regarded as a matter of ultimate concern. It is evident, for example, in his notion of the "God above the God of theism" that a theocentric understanding of reality need not stand in the way of religious and political dialogue among those seeking constructive ways of dealing with the environmental crisis.[44] In fact, he would argue, such an understanding of the universe is essential to grasp the breadth of the problem itself and to come to terms with humanity's role in the various solutions that may be proposed. But in order for a religious approach to be viable, Tillich would maintain that it must not be afraid to ask the question of being with courage and conviction. As one observer comments:

> Anxiety about the future today even more than in Tillich's time discloses elements of alienation from self, others and the environment that seem unsurmountable [*sic*]. While such anxiety cannot be relieved simply by intellectual exercise, by explanation, it is at the same time not relieved

without one. A leap into a bizarre mythology without consonance with a cogent view of the universe is more a disclosure of anxiety than a cure. The affirmation of meaning will require our total involvement, nothing less than the "centered act of faith" foundational for "the courage to be."[45]

Hence, while Tillich did not specifically address what has come to be known in our own day as the "environmental" or "ecological" crisis, I believe that in his correlational approach to theology and philosophy he has offered us a constructive interpretive framework within which to do "ecological theology." I have called this framework an "ecology of being." Such an approach recognizes, as Tillich did, that the evolutionary process (*i.e.*, the story of the universe) and the work of redemption (what has been understood in traditional Christian doctrinal theology as "salvation history") are correlates of the same reality. In other words, what science tells us about the incomprehensibly complex way in which the universe has evolved, and what revelation tells us about God's inscrutable purposes in history, are not inconsistent interpretations of reality. Indeed, they dovetail with each other when seen in the light of an ecological ontology. What our anxiety about our current planetary crisis discloses is that the crisis is both an existential or religious one *and* a scientific or technological one.

Notes

1. Joseph Sittler, "Ecological Commitment as Theological Responsibility," *Zygon* 5 (June 1970): 178.
2. Paul Tillich, *ST* 1, 261.
3. Paul Tillich, "The Redemption of Nature," *Christendom* 10 (Summer 1945): 304.
4. Paul Tillich, *HCT*, 292.
5. Peter Heinegg, "Ecology and the Fall," *Christian Century* 93 (May 12, 1976): 465.
6. Paul Tillich, *ST* 2, 96.

7.   Among the fiercest of these critics in this regard is Kenneth Hamilton, *The System and the Gospel: A Critique of Paul Tillich* (London: SCM Press Ltd., 1963), 158-173.
8.   Tillich, *ST* 1, 263.
9.   This criticism has been leveled against Tillich by a number of process thinkers primarily with respect to his doctrine of God. Certain aspects of the entire system, however, have come under attack as well, including his treatment of the doctrine of creation. See, for example, Lewis S. Ford, "Tillich's Tergiversations Toward the Power of Being," *Scottish Journal of Theology* 28 (1975): 323-340.
10.   Along similar lines, Paul Lee suggests that the first Earth Day, held in April 1970, signaled both the "birth" of environmentalism and the "death" of existentialism ("Ecotopia and Political Expectations" [paper presented at the annual meeting of the North American Paul Tillich Society, San Francisco, CA, 21 November 1997]). However, in that same presentation, Lee argues that the environmental movement could never have emerged without the type of Christian existentialism practiced by Tillich, that is, one which consists of an "outcry against...inhumanity, a protest against industrial society, substituting machines for human beings and turning them into cogs in the wheels of production and consumption, on daylight saving time, on the assembly line, or worse yet, turning them out into homelessness."
11.   Tillich, *ST* 1, 262.
12.   This phrase, borrowed from Santmire, is introduced on page 5. According to Santmire, the "ecological motif" is distinguished from the "spiritual motif" (a motif that is less favorably disposed toward nature) by the latter's almost exclusive employment of the "metaphor of ascent," that is, of the individual soul's attempt to become liberated from the prison of its earthly body (H. Paul Santmire, *The Travail of Nature: The Ambiguous Ecological Promise of Christian Theology* [Minneapolis: Fortress Press, 1985], 16-21). Examples of the "metaphor of ascent," according to Santmire, are the account of Moses at Sinai (Exodus 24:15-18) and Dante's *Divine Comedy*. Santmire also argues that such a "metaphor of ascent" gives rise to such hierarchical metaphysical models as the "Great Chain of Being," which emerged as the predominant model of reality in the Christian West during the Middle Ages.
13.   Ibid., 18-29. Santmire argues in this regard that "[t]he metaphor of fecundity and the metaphor of migration...will as a matter of course tend to cluster with each other, if they are given in the same imaginative environment, since both lead the mind into an experience of solidarity with the earth and both envision that solidarity...in terms of goodness" (27).
14.   Gerard Manley Hopkins, "God's Grandeur," *A Hopkins Reader,* ed. John Pick (Garden City, NY: Doubleday, 1966), 47-48.

15. In similar fashion, Sallie McFague observes that "[i]n space versus time, the old dichotomy of nature versus history is played out. The dichotomy is certainly not absolute, for history takes place in nature and nature itself has a history, as the common creation story clearly demonstrates, but for the past several hundred years at least, the focus and preference for Western thought has been on history to the detriment of nature" (*The Body of God: An Ecological Theology* [Minneapolis: Fortress Press, 1993], 100).

16. Cf. Colossians 1:15-20.

17. Tillich, *ST* 3, 18.

18. In his notion of a "cruciform creation," Holmes Rolston, III understands the role of nature in this drama in comparable terms: "Whatever is in travail needs redemption, whether or not there is any sin to be dealt with. If we take the moral component out of redemption…, and ask whether the biodiverse amoral values present in nature need to be saved, then the answer is most certainly that they do. 'Conserved' is the biological word; life is the unrelenting conservation of biological identity above all else, an identity that is threatened every moment, every hour, every generation. But that threatened life has prevailed for several billion years. If we make the correct translation into theology, we will not say that nature does not need to be redeemed, nor that it has never been redeemed; to the contrary it is ever redeemed" ("Does Nature Need to be Redeemed?" *Horizons in Biblical Theology* 14/2 [December 1992]): 158-159).

19. This point is particularly emphasized by James A. Carpenter, *Nature and Grace: Toward an Integral Perspective* (New York: Crossroad, 1988), 55.

20. Tillich, *ST* 3, 13.

21. Paul Tillich, *CEWR*, 86-87. Cf. Claude Geffré, "Paul Tillich and the Future of Interreligious Ecumenism," in *Paul Tillich: A New Catholic Assessment*, ed. Raymond F. Bulman and Frederick J. Parrella (Collegeville, MN: Liturgical Press, 1994), 268-288.

22. Paul Tillich, "History as *the* Problem of Our Period," *Review of Religion* 3 (March, 1939): 255-264.

23. Tillich, *ST* 3, 320.

24. This describes one of the fundamental differences between the Schleiermacher-Troeltsch line of thinking concerning the relationship of culture and religion and that emanating from Kierkegaard and Barth. Tillich, *ST* 3, 359.

26. Ibid., 350.

27. The growing literature on the phenomenon known as "postmodernism" in all fields of intellectual scholarship is immense, and I have no intention in this study of taking on such an unwieldy creature. However, it is important to at least note that Tillich's use of such terms as "universal meaning" and "absolute reality" presents problems to a number of scholars, among them Paul Van Buren, "The Dissolution of the Absolute," *Religion in Life* (Summer 1965):

334-342; Lonnie Kliever, *The Shattered Spectrum* (Atlanta: John Knox Press, 1981), 188-203; and John Carey, "Are There Any Absolutes Left? Post Modernism and the Crisis for Tillich Scholars," *The North American Paul Tillich Society Newsletter* 24/4 (Fall 1998): 3-9. Carey argues, however, that while it can be difficult to defend Tillich against such criticisms, "Tillich...does provide a corrective to the power of post-modernist thought. He recognized that human beings live by faith, trust, passions, and symbols. Even if these are not empirically provable, they have power to shape life and destiny.... Even within a more modest conceptual framework, we can affirm the reality of grace and of a healing Spirit" (Ibid., 8-9). And, of course, there are those who also maintain that Tillich himself can be considered an early "postmodernist" in terms of his openness to change and the future, his appreciation of the natural world, and his development of a "post-theistic" system. See especially Richard Grigg, *Symbol and Empowerment: Paul Tillich's Post-Theistic System* (Macon, GA: Mercer University Press, 1985) and David Griffin, *God and Religion in the Postmodern World* (New York: State University of New York Press, 1989).

28. I am thinking here of such postmodernist figures as Mark C. Taylor, *Erring: A Postmodern A/Theology* (Chicago: University of Chicago Press, 1984) and Walter Lowe, *Theology and Difference: The Wound of Reason* (Bloomington, IN and Indianapolis: Indiana University Press, 1993). In commenting on both Taylor's and Lowe's deconstructionist positions, however, Susan E. Wennemyr recommends "that any postmodern theology be defended explicitly as a plausible interpreter of the Christ-event. Otherwise – if postmodernism can be said to represent our 'culture' while the tradition of contending theologies represents 'Christianity' – our theology of culture will have failed by the standard of dialogue between theology and Christianity [*sic*]; 'culture' will have been granted the upper hand in the conversation between theology and culture, a methodological crime no less spurious than the fundamentalist demand that culture yield altogether to alleged values of Christian theology" ("Dancing in the Dark," *Journal of the American Academy of Religion* 66/3 (Fall 1998): 584-585. Wennemyr mentions both Tillich and David Tracy as two of the primary shapers of this "standard of dialogue." Cf. also the article by Joseph A. Bracken in which he argues for the continued validity of metaphysics as a logical foundation for systematic theology ("Toward a New Philosophical Theology Based on Intersubjectivity," *Theological Studies* 59/4 [December 1998]: 703-719).

29. E-mail letter from Gordon Kaufman to Paul H. Carr, 28 September 1998, a copy of which was kindly provided to the author by Professor Carr. Kaufman further elaborates on the anthropocentric character of the dominant categorial scheme in Christian theology (including Tillich) concerning male im-

ages of God in his *In Face of Mystery: A Constructive Theology* (Cambridge, MA and London: Harvard University Press, 1993), 75-77. Other ecologically-minded critics, while not singling Tillich out, have remarked on the radically anthropocentric features of traditional Christian thought and twentieth-century existentialism, of which Tillich was most certainly a practitioner on both accounts. See, for example, Lynn White, Jr., "The Historical Roots of Our Ecologic Crisis," *Science* 155 (March 10, 1967): 1205-1206; Santmire, *Travail,* 121-144; Jürgen Moltmann, *God in Creation: A New Theology of Creation and the Spirit of God* (San Francisco: HarperSanFrancisco, 1985), 27; Harold H. Oliver, "The Neglect and Recovery of Nature in Twentieth-Century Protestant Thought," *Journal of the American Academy of Religion* 60/3 (Autumn 1992): 379-388; Sallie McFague, *The Body of God: An Ecological Theology* (Minneapolis: Fortress Press, 1993), 185; and John B. Cobb, Jr., *Is it Too Late? A Theology of Ecology,* rev. ed. (Denton, TX: Environmental Ethics Books, 1995), 56-57.
30. Kaufman, letter to Carr.
31. Langdon Gilkey, *Gilkey on Tillich* (New York: Crossroad, 1990), 184.
32. Tillich, *ST* 3, 422.
33. Hamilton, *System,* 227.
34. Ibid., 188.
35. Ibid., 189.
36. Ibid., 192.
37. Ibid., 193.
38. Tillich himself, somewhat in reply to Hamilton, remarks in the Introduction to the third volume of the *Systematic Theology* that "the systematic-constructive form...forced me to be consistent" (*ST* 3, 3).
39. Among these would include Rosemary Radford Ruether, *To Change the World: Christology and Cultural Criticism* (New York: Crossroad Publishing Co., 1981), 59-60; Santmire, *Travail,* 189; and William Dyrness, "Stewardship of the Earth in the Old Testament," in *Tending the Garden: Essays on the Gospel and the Earth,* ed. Wesley Granberg-Michaelson (Grand Rapids, MI: William B. Eerdmans, 1987), 50-65.
40. In this regard, it is important to remember, once again, that Genesis 1:28 became the proof text of the "industrial age's attitude toward the resources of creation. Adam Smith and Karl Marx alike have regarded nature as nothing more than the warehouse supplying the raw materials for the transformation of society and history" (Wesley Granberg-Michaelson, "At the Dawn of the New Creation," *Sojourners* [November 1981]: 15).
41. Tillich, *ST* 1, 260.
42. Ibid., 261.
43. Tillich, *ST* 1, 3-4.

44. For a discussion of the relation of various religious and social attitudes toward the ecological crisis, see Leonardo Boff, *Ecology & Liberation: A New Paradigm,* tr. John Cumming (Maryknoll, NY: Orbis, 1995), 9-90. Cf. also Paul Albrecht, "The Future as a 'Religious' Problem," *Ecumenical Review* 24 (April 1972): 176-189 and J. Ronald Engel, "Liberal Democracy and the Fate of the Earth," in *Spirit and Nature: Why the Environment is a Religious Issue,* ed. Steven C. Rockefeller and John C. Elder (Boston: Beacon Press, 1992), 61-81.

45. A. Arnold Wettstein, "Tillich's Cosmology and Chaos Theory," in *Natürliche Theologie versus Theologie der Natur? Tillichs Denken als Anstoss zum Gespräch zwischen Theologie, Philosophie und Naturwissenschaft,* ed. Gert Hummel (Berlin and New York: Walter de Gruyter, 1994), 40.

Then I heard the voices of every creature in heaven and on earth and
under the earth and in the sea; everything in the universe cried aloud:
"To the one seated on the throne and to the Lamb,
be praise and honor, glory and might,
forever and ever!"[1]

Chapter 5

Being and Earth:
The Divine Symphony of Love

This concluding chapter consists of three parts: (1) a discussion of
Tillich's ontology of love and its application to the global environmental crisis, (2) the proposal of a Tillichean ecological ontology
or an "ecology of being," and (3) a brief concluding section. The
chapter is constructed in this manner since the first section logically
leads into the second. That is, it will become evident that, without a
discussion of Tillich's ethics in general, an essential and important aspect of the ecology of being would be missing. In the process, and in
an effort to address the existential dimensions of the current crisis, I
will utilize those elements of Tillich's theology of nature as critically
retrieved in the previous chapters as a foundation from which to move
beyond him. This chapter is intended to serve, therefore, as a creative
summary of Tillich's thought with respect to the question of the hu-
man/non-human relationship while developing my own theological re-

sponse to the environmental problems with which we are presently confronted.

Love, Kairos, and the Environment

Paul Tillich recognized over fifty years ago that there would be "innumerable ethical consequences [if]...Christian theology should interpret the meaning of salvation in nature."[2] It could be argued with equal legitimacy that in the years since those words were written it has become evident that the failure of Christian theology to so interpret the meaning of salvation in nature has resulted in dire *environmental* consequences as well as, by default, the afore-mentioned ethical ones. Tillich himself largely left the task of assessing such ethical consequences to others. However, as has been shown, he *did* provide a theological interpretation of the meaning of salvation in nature. Hence, although Tillich's writings on ethics deal almost exclusively with person-to-person encounters, it will be shown that his ontology of love, when applied to the non-human world, can be productive for an environmental ethic. The next section of this chapter will outline specifically what shape such an environmental ethic might assume.

Perhaps one of the reasons Tillich never developed a theological ethic toward nature was his attitude toward ethics in general. Tillich had become convinced with the breakdown of the great synthesis of German Idealism that human thought can never be understood in terms of a complete system. This was particularly the case with Christian ethics. As a disciple in this area of Troeltsch, Tillich had observed that Christian ethical judgments were subject to change over time and from culture to culture. Accordingly, even as early as 1923 in his *System of the Sciences,* Tillich understood ethics as "the science of ethos: that is, it is the science of the *active realization of the Unconditioned.*"[3] He therefore sought to protect the relative autonomy of ethics while, at the same time, placing it in a larger scheme of meaning. The relationship of ethics was such that it maintained its own sphere apart from the other social sciences but, as science of the ethos, it was understood by Tillich to act as the unconditioned vector in all those other sciences. In other words, the goals of the social sciences should come from ethics as their "direction of practical activity toward the unconditional."[4]

For this reason, Tillich rejects an understanding of theological ethics as an independent theological discipline in favor of a theonomous ethics "in which the ethical principles and processes are described in the light of the Spiritual Presence."[5] Tillich locates a "theonomous element" in all ethical approaches, however hidden, distorted, or secularized, because what is universally operative in every ethic is "the experience of an ultimate concern."[6] In Christian ethics, the one overriding concern that exerts an unconditioned moral demand, according to Tillich, is that expressed in the New Testament commandment to love one another.[7] In his ontology of love, Tillich sees all forms of love as manifestations of the different qualities of the one nature of love, of "the drive towards the reunion of the separated."[8] Such a drive, for Tillich, is not unique to human beings, but is characteristic "of all living beings."[9]

In his various discussions of the relationship among the different forms of love,[10] Tillich makes it clear that in their essential character they express different qualities of the unity of love. *Libido,* for example, is not simply the desire for pleasure but is an expression of the normal drive for vital self-fulfilment. Its shortcoming lies in its intrinsic lack of measure or form, in the limitlessness of a Dionysian love that is unrestrained by the Divine love.[11] This is known in traditional terms as *concupiscentia,* or as the "infinite desire to draw the universe into one's particular existence."[12] The *eros* form of love "strives for a union with that which is a bearer of values because of the values it embodies."[13] The passionate pursuit of truth and beauty is the embodiment of this type of love, finding its ultimate fulfilment in cultural creativity and mystical union. The supreme danger here is not that of losing oneself in a sea of sensuality but of disappearing into the void or of developing an uninvolved aestheticism. In confusing it with the *libido* type of love, the self can be swallowed up by a formless chaos. Its ambiguity rests in "its detachment from the realities which it expresses and consequently the disappearing of existential participation and ultimate responsibility."[14] The *philia* type of love is dependent on *eros* in that it represents the personal pole of love, while *eros* represents the transpersonal.[15] *Philia* love has to do with friendship, participation, and community, hence its reliance on *eros.* But the ecstatic element of *philia* love "is the participation in the self-realization of the friend in his changes and negativities"[16] and, hence, goes beyond *eros* in seeking its fulfilment not in the value the other represents but in the embracing unity afforded by equal participants in the same act. The liability of *philia,* however, is two-fold: (1) in its seeking of a unity of equals it cannot attain union with that which is unequal, that is, the risks of prejudice and jingoism become viable; and (2) conversely, one can lose oneself in the great mass of humanity in one's desperate search for acceptance as an equal.

All these forms of love possess a divine character since they are forms of participation in the whole process of self-realization and re-union, which process rests on the one truth of revelation and of on-tology:

> The answer to the question: what does it mean that God is Love, is this: The Ground of Being from which every being takes its power of being has the character of self-separating and self-returning life. Self-separating is the abbreviation for complete individualization. Self-returning is the abbreviation of the return of life to itself in the power of reuniting love....
> ...God is Love and Being is Love....[17]

However, as we have just seen, despite their divine character these forms of love also hold within themselves "the tragic perversion and frustration, the self-centeredness which contradicts the return to the unity. Only *agape* can overcome it."[18] For Tillich, that form of love known as *caritas* or *agape* is "the depth of love or love in relation to the ground of life.... *Agape* is love cutting into love...."[19] *Agape* seeks the other in the other's center. It is, unlike *philia* love, an un-conditional love. In this respect, *agape* "is an ecstatic anticipation which is creative in the anticipated direction."[20] It prevents the pow-erful *eros* form of love from remaining a detached aesthetic by making "the cultural *eros* responsible and the mystical *eros* personal."[21] The *libido* form of love (*i.e.,* eating, drinking, and sex) is transformed by *agape* into a sacramental act.[22]

Accordingly, God's love toward creation is essentially *agape* love. The clearest expression of this is the charity character of *agape* love which sees in each existing thing its potential fulfilment and makes union dependent not on a judging wrath or the lack of *philia.*[23] This is most evident, of course, in the Christian tradition in the symbol of God sending God's Son to the Cross, that is, in the symbol of the suffering God. The God who loves in *agapeic* fashion is the One who suffers with creation: "[T]he suffering of God, universally and in the Christ, is the power which overcomes creaturely self-destruction by participa-tion and transformation."[24] The symbol also functions, according to

Tillich, as "the foundation and corrective of the other types."[25] This is the element of "divine justice" that appears whenever genuine *agape* love is actualized.

As that form of love which overcomes the negative or ambiguous elements in the other forms of love, thereby directing them toward the ground of being and providing them with unconditional validity, *agape* love "offers a principle of ethics which maintains an eternal, unchangeable element but makes its realization dependent on continuous acts of a creative intuition."[26] In rejecting what he refers to as the "three great types of life and thought representing...different solutions of the problem of ethics"[27] (*i.e.*, the static supra-naturalistic solution of Aquinas; the dynamic-naturalistic solution of, among others, Nietzsche; and the rationalistic-progressive solution represented by British and American positivism and pragmatism), Tillich offers instead an ethic that combines the *agape* principle of the unconditional seriousness of the moral demand with the idea of *kairos*. He argues that the solution to the age-old ethical problem of the relationship between the absoluteness of the moral imperative and its application to the always shifting concrete personal and political realities is found in the linking of two very important New Testament ideas with each other. In the sense that Tillich understands the term, *kairos*

> is the historical moment in which something new, eternally important, manifests itself in temporal forms, in the potentialities and tasks of a special period.... All great changes in history are accompanied by a strong consciousness of a kairos at hand.[28]

Tillich thus distinguishes between the "great *kairos*" (*i.e.*, the appearance of the center of history) and "relative *kairoi*" throughout history (*i.e.*, *kairos*-experiences in which the Kingdom of God manifests itself in a particular breakthrough).[29] The ability to discern kairotic moments is a function of grace at work in the holy or Spiritual Community and "is a matter of vision.... It is not a matter of detached observation but of involved experience."[30] In other words, it combines an awareness of living under the order of historical destiny with a keen sense of genuine anticipation that, at any moment, the power of the Kingdom of God can – and *will* – break through. Tillich therefore concludes that

> ethics in a changing world must be understood as ethics of the kairos.... [B]ut only love is able to appear in every kairos.... Love, realizing itself

from kairos to kairos, creates an ethics which is beyond the alternative of absolute and relative ethics.[31]

The Tillichean ethic consists therefore in the bringing forth into history the "innermost center of Being-Itself"[32] through the manifestation of *agape* love. It is the establishment of and participation in the Kingdom of God. This is possible because *agape* "[l]ove alone can transform itself according to the concrete demands of every individual and social situation without losing its eternity and dignity and unconditional validity."[33]

With regard to the ecological crisis, the question is raised whether this type of love can embrace, if not the entire universe, at least the planet upon which we have co-evolved with an estimated 100 million other species. In other words, must the practice of an ethic of *agape* love – of unconditional love for one's neighbor – be confined to the "community of persons"?[34] Tillich acknowledges that, unlike the limits that *agape* love places on the I-thou relation,

> [i]n the...case [of]...man's encounter with nature outside him,...there is no limit in dealing with it. Man can make it into an object, dissect it, analyze it, or construct something new, a technical product, out of its parts or elements. Man can subject nature, progressively and almost limitlessly in all directions, to his knowledge and his action. The only limit is man's own finitude. But no one can actually establish this limit. Before it is reached nothing can resist man's cognitive and technical attack on nonpersonal reality. Nothing can resist man's will to transform it into an object and to use it for his purpose.[35]

At the same time, Tillich hints at an answer to the question concerning the possibility of an unconditional love for "nonpersonal reality" when he states that *"[a]gape* conquers the ambiguities of love, Spiritual power conquers the ambiguities of power, grace conquers the ambiguities of justice. This is true not only of the encounters of man with man...."[36]

The real concern, then, for purposes of the present study, is the viability of including the "I-Ens" relationship within the *agape* form of unconditional love. The question of whether or not there is something unique about the human/non-human relationship has been developed with great skill and originality by Paul Santmire[37] in the context of the Buberian vocabulary of I-Thou and I-It. There he suggests that a human being "properly can and occasionally does exist in a relation to his [or her] material-vital world which is neither an I-Thou relation as such nor an I-It relation."[38] In other words, the experience of the "Ens" lies somewhere between the two conceptually polar opposite experiences of the I-Thou (absolute subjectivity characterized by complete mutual participation) and the I-It (absolute objectivity characterized by complete detachment). While human beings are certainly capable of reducing any relationship to the level of an I-It (*i.e.*, by, as it were, "thingifying" the other, be it person, plant, creature, artifact, or idea), for Santmire, the experience, for example, of the human encounter with a tree or an animal potentially involves something other than that suggested by the terms "I-Thou" or "I-It". He therefore wishes to "call attention to an aspect of human *ad extra* relatedness" which he finds is not exhausted merely by characterizing human/non-human relations by the I-Thou, I-It distinction, as Buber and others have done:

> Perhaps the fundamental idea before us can be summarized as follows. In encountering the Ens, I am captivated by the Ens's openness to the Infinite, by its openness to a dimension which lies behind and permeates its givenness, its mysterious activity, and its beauty.... This could also be called, in Tillich's terminology, an awareness of a "dimension of depth" in the I-Ens relation.[39]

In light of this insight, the question I would like to ask is, according to Tillich's ethical model, are human beings capable of sustaining and participating in an *agape* type of relationship with other species and even with the earth itself? Can this "dimension of depth", which can potentially be revealed in every human/non-human encounter, be supportive of an environmental ethic of unconditional love?

While it would seem at times that Tillich might lean toward an affirmative response to this question, in actuality he never provided a definitive answer since, as was noted earlier, it was not an issue that was given serious attention during his life time. In other words, the *kairotic* elements and moments toward which Tillich turned his attention and in which he created his theological vision did not include the ecological crisis. Its time, so to speak, had not yet arrived in its fullness. Nonetheless, it is my position that Tillich's ethical model as related to his entire theological system does provide a basis for an effective and meaningful Protestant environmental ethic.

For Tillich, the responsibility to interpret the *kairotic* elements that fosters the type of anxiety described at the end of Chapter Four by

Arnold Wettstein falls on the shoulders of the Spiritual Community, that is, the church. It is the church's obligation to ask how the une- quivocal biblical mandate to love one another should be applied in this particular moment of history, or even if it *can* be applied. In other words, what is God asking of God's people in this time in which the environment continues to be degraded and, in Tillich's own words, "profanized"? How does the realization of the Kingdom of God ex- press itself on a planet that has been laid to waste by its human inhabi- tants? I believe that a Tillichean ecology of being, or ecological ontol- ogy, can meaningfully embrace such questions, since it begins with the assertion that

> a symbolically-expressed, faith-centered understanding of the *telos* of humanity within the *telos* of interactive life-systems is not only conso- nant with scientific thinking but foundational for the kind of courage all of us seek in an anxious world.[40]

Hence, the *tele* of humanity and other threatened ecosystems intersect with the *kairos* of the Kingdom of God at that point where being and human responsibility meet. In my estimation, it is the task of an ecol- ogy of being to disclose that point.

Beyond Tillich: Toward an Ecology of Being

In his essay "The Question Concerning Technology," Martin Heideg- ger undertakes a transcendental phenomenological inquiry to discover what, if anything, could be revealed to us about our relationship with the "essence" of technology.[41] According to Heidegger, what he refers to as "technological enframing" is characterized by a ubiquitous "challenging-forth" that, paradoxically, conceals that which it seeks to reveal, namely, human mastery over nature.[42] In other words, in our efforts to subdue the earth in accordance with our fundamental inclina- tion to order our world, we lose not only our respect for the material world as a means whereby truth can be revealed, but *we are in danger of losing ourselves as well:*

> As soon as what is concealed no longer concerns man even as object, but exclusively as standing-reserve [*Bestand*], and man in the midst of ob- jectlessness is nothing but the orderer of the standing-reserve, then he

comes to the very brink of a precipitous fall, that is, he comes to the point where he himself will have to be taken as standing-reserve. Meanwhile, man, precisely as the one so threatened, exalts himself to the posture of the lord of the earth....

Thus where enframing reigns, there is *danger* in the highest sense.[43]

Drawing on a quote from the poet Hölderlin, Heidegger construes this danger as concealing within itself the very possibility of what he terms "saving power": "Thus the coming to presence of technology harbors in itself what we least suspect, the possible upsurgence of the saving power.... We look into the danger and see the growth of the saving power."[44] This danger remains at all times potential given the character of human technical curiosity. However, Heidegger nonetheless concludes that *"human reflection can ponder the fact that all saving power must be of a higher essence than what is endangered, though at the same time kindred to it."*[45] For Heidegger, then, the technological crisis, when understood from the point of view of ontology, contains within itself the possibility of encountering a power capable of overcoming the essential "gathering together" or ordering which threatens to "reveal the real...as standing-reserve."[46] Most importantly, this "saving power" appears at the moment when human beings become aware of their unique role as stewards of Being:

On the other hand, enframing comes to pass for its part in the granting that lets man endure – as yet inexperienced, but perhaps more experienced in the future – that he may be the one who is needed and used for the safekeeping of the essence of truth. Thus does the arising of the saving power appear....

The closer we come to the danger, the more brightly do the ways into the saving power begin to shine and the more questioning we become. For questioning is the piety of thought.[47]

Similarly, Paul Tillich recognized in the sacraments – "all the great elements of nature" – a "saving power" as well.[48] The emergence of such saving power is particularly noticeable at the moment when the natural world appears most threatened. In other words, the greater the danger, the more aware do we become that nature, left bleeding and broken by humanity's open disregard, contains nevertheless the very seeds whereby humanity can assume a position of responsible and creative stewardship. Theologically, of course, the emergence of such awareness would be interpreted as the moment of conversion or of *metanoia,* that is, of literally "turning around" and becoming aware of right and wrong ways of being in relationship with the non-human universe.[49] In the case of the environmental crisis, we must seize on this moment now, lest it pass us by and with it the health and future of the planet.

In applying therefore an approach similar to that of Tillich and Heidegger to the environmental crisis, several observations can be made. First, the reality that ecological disasters (both the sudden and the gradual) have enjoyed wide-ranging and long-term effects outside of their own immediate environments, suggests a *fundamental interrelatedness* among all elements of the created order. In other words, the contemporary environmental crisis, for all of its obvious negative effects, has nevertheless made us acutely aware of the reality of interdependency. We have certainly observed the occurrence of such phenomena in smaller ecosystems in recent years and, on a global scale, the devastating effects of the loss of the South American rain forests ("the lungs of the earth") is well documented.[50] Truly, then, we can agree with John Cobb, Jr. when he declares that in our world today "[t]he smog of Tokyo is breathed in California."[51]

Therefore, every entity found either on the earth or within its atmosphere – from the smallest inorganic particle, to the complex creature known as *homo sapiens*, to the massive oceans and seas which nourish and support an inconceivable abundance of life – is an essential part of the whole. Indeed, this is what the discipline of "ecology" itself implies, when it is defined as

> the biological science of natural environmental communities...[which] examines how these natural communities function to sustain a healthy web of life and how they become disrupted, causing death to plant and animal life. *Human intervention is the major cause of such disruption.*[52]

The second, and related, observation one can make is that the disruption which threatens this fundamental interrelatedness also points to a deeper awareness of the *fundamental givenness* of all things created. What the global ecological crisis has in effect brought to consciousness can be understood as an extended application of the principle of metaphysical or existential shock. It has become increasingly and dramatically apparent in the last generation or so that the earth, like the individual human being, could just as easily *not* exist as exist. In our collective realization that we cannot take the planet for granted, many have come to view the earth itself as a living organism which, like any living organism, depends upon many other life-giving factors to sustain it. The fragile character of the web that unites all life has been revealed to us out of profound anxiety about the future of the planet as a vital, living entity.

Whereas the existentialist philosophers of the past concerned themselves largely with the question of *human* being as a way into the discussion of *being at all*,[53] today that question can be raised concerning the fate of the earth itself.[54] Leibniz' famous query "Why something rather than nothing?" is no longer an idle speculative concern of metaphysicians, but can now often be a legitimate starting point for serious scientific study of our global environmental problems and our response to them.[55] What has therefore amounted to a "planetary ontological shock" has, in the last thirty years, produced a growing movement among scientists, philosophers, politicians, and ordinary citizens, a movement that is at once profoundly concerned with the earth and with our relationship to it.[56]

Thirdly, what does the ecological crisis reveal to us about ourselves and our relationship to the non-human universe? In other words, when we are able to really penetrate to the heart of the matter, to courageously look at the utter neglect and devastation of the natural world for which we are largely responsible, how then do we understand our relationship with the "essence" of the modern assault on the non-human universe? Tillich himself in a number of places offers the *notion of "forwardism"* as a characteristically modern problem that is responsible for and indicative of the "estrangement between man and earth."[57] He defines "forwardism" as the "triumph of the horizontal line over the vertical,"[58] of a constant pressing forward into an apparent limitlessness that is neither tempered nor restricted in any way by the concrete demands of finitude, death, or the moral conscience. Since "[t]he aim [here] is to go forward for the sake of going forward, endlessly without a concrete focus," this "*exclusive* surrender to the horizontal line...leads to the loss of any meaningful content and to complete emptiness."[59] In ignoring the demands of the vertical, we have succeeded in "objectifying" the earth and, consequently, ourselves, by creating a spiritual vacuum that now determines "our inner and outer existence."[60]

Closely related to the notion of forwardism is the *category of concupiscence* employed by Tillich to describe the "unlimited desire to draw the whole of reality into one's self. It refers to all aspects of man's relation to himself and to his world."[61] Unlike Augustine and

Luther, however, in refusing to narrowly associate the meaning of the term "concupiscence" with inordinate sexual desire, Tillich applies this category to modern humanity's relationship with the entire world. It consists of an attempt to "swallow up", as it were, the whole universe. According to Langdon Gilkey, in this regard

> [h]uman being...manifests itself as infinitely greedy, as seeking to use and to use up everything there is.... As Tillich would put it, this demonic use and using up of nature bespeaks a deep alienation of human being from itself, from nature, and from its own infinite ground; consequently, it seeks that infinity of meaning, and so seeks itself and its unity, through taking the infinite into itself, by possessing and using the finite *infinitely*.... Tillich has, in reinterpreting [the category of concupiscence], given it a much wider meaning as the prime symptom of estrangement of human being from the whole world of goods and so of nature – and as the key "sin" of our technical, commercial culture.[62]

What we have here, then, are related demonic impulses, which result, in the ecological crisis, in the complete loss of the "ontological and...religious understanding of the unity of the natural and the human world."[63] The one question raised most poignantly by the twin phenomena of "forwardism" and "concupiscence" yet which, not surprisingly, they cannot answer, is that of "For what?"[64] That is, for what purpose do we allow ourselves to participate in this mad headlong rush toward no apparent goal and this attempt to take into ourselves the whole world? What is the inner *telos* of such phenomena? To what, if anything, is such a driving intensity and an insatiable appetite ultimately ordered?

It is precisely from an analysis of the present ecological situation and its devastating effects that the answer to these questions might be provided. Tillich hints at it in one of his last lectures when he states that our resistance to the meaningless forwardism of our time "may lead to the rediscovery of the depth dimension, the vertical depth in everything encountered."[65] It is therefore in the notion of "taking care of" or of safeguarding our natural environment that we may encounter the dimension of depth to which Tillich refers or the "saving power" of which both Tillich and Heidegger speak. Unlike Heidegger, however, the term "saving power" for Tillich constitutes in this context the theological correlate to the philosophical expression "dimension of depth." What Tillich is suggesting is that, when viewed sacramentally and respectfully, the non-human world is not merely a means of orienting us toward God; it actually participates *in* God in a unique and distinct fashion. Hence, for Tillich the world is not created for the sake of helping to bring about in human beings some sort of "salvation" in terms of a personal, acosmic deliverance from sin. Rather, in its intrinsic and dynamic integrity, the whole universe radiates the glory of its Creator. The *real* sin for human beings consists in not recognizing this or in ignoring it altogether. By allowing our attitude and "feeling" toward nature to change,[66] in other words, in opening ourselves up to the possibility of a genuine, active, and sober concern for the non-human community, we may begin to recover a sense of reverence for the universe. And in so doing, Tillich argues, we recover our deepest selves.

In this respect, the fourth observation that can be made is that a Tillichean ecology of being suggests an environmental ethic governing humanity's relationship with the non-human world that can best be described as *"creative stewardship."* The medical scientist René Dubos first articulated this model in 1972.[67] Basically, such a model offers the notion of "creative stewardship" as the expression of a genuine, practical concern for creation.[68] It is in "the Benedictine and Cistercian work ethic" that we witness "the living out of belief in creation."[69] This medieval prototype blends human scientific curiosity and technical ability with a deep reverence for God's creation. In contrast to Francis of Assisi's "romantic and unworldly attitude" resulting from his "absolute identification with nature,"[70] we find in the vision of Benedict of Nursia an ecologically sensitive model "where work is religiously sanctified and nature is transformed while maintaining environmental quality."[71] In recommending the Benedictine model as a more appropriate and viable one for our present period, Dubos acknowledges that the Judeo-Christian tradition and technological civilization go hand-in-glove. A retreat from either or both, however, is not the answer:

> Francis of Assisi's loving and contemplative reverence in the face of nature survives today in the awareness of our kinship to all other living things and in the conservation movement. But reverence is not enough, because man has never been a passive witness of nature. He changes the environment by his very presence and his only options in his dealings with the earth are to be destructive or constructive. To be creative, man must relate to nature with his senses as much as with his common sense, with his heart as much as with knowledge....

I have chosen to illustrate this creativeness by the Benedictine way of
life – its wisdom in managing the land, in fitting architecture to worship
and landscape, in adapting rituals and work to the cosmic rhythms....
Human life implies choices as to the best way to govern natural systems
and to create new environments out of wilderness. Reverence for nature
is compatible with willingness to accept responsibility for a creative
stewardship.[72]

It may appear ironic that a Tillichean (and, in this sense, Protestant)
vision of environmental administration would accord so well with a
medieval model. However, given what we have seen of Tillich's theology of nature, this should come as no surprise. In adamantly refusing to share the callous Ritschlian disregard for the natural world
(whose theological and philosophical roots were in early Calvinism
and Fichte, respectively), Tillich's theology of nature is able to temper
a mystical communing with nature with a realistic assessment of our
ethical responsibilities toward one another and toward the non-human
universe. The idea of creative stewardship as a viable Tillichean
model of environmental ethic is expressive of Tillich's understanding
of "ultimate concern" as a fundamentally religious basis from which
arises, and toward which are directed, all of one's energies. To claim,
therefore, that "the environment is, or can be, a matter of legitimate
ultimate concern" means that the manifestation of the environmental
crisis should be interpreted and understood as a religious claim in the
broadest sense possible, that is, as a manifestation of the question of
being and non-being. In this sense, a Christian could equate the reck-
less clear-cutting of an old-growth forest in the Pacific Northwest with
the tossing into the ocean of the Gospel of John. In light of a Tillichean ecology of being, these acts are, christologically, comparable to
each other.[73]

Finally, the idea raised earlier by Dubos of a "kinship" existing
among all living beings is one that is often suggested by scientists and
theologians alike. The term "biophilia" has been coined by one scientist to designate the "innate [human] tendency to focus on life and life-
like processes."[74] A Tillichean ecology of being would, I believe, feel
right at home with such an idea, that "[w]oven into our lives is the
very fire from the stars and the genes from the sea creatures, and everyone, utterly everyone, is kin in the radiant tapestry of being."[75] For
many, this idea of kinship among all living things forms the foundation for a non-anthropocentric, biocentric environmental ethic. I
would argue, however, that, using a Tillichean ecology of being, one

can go beyond mere "kinship" or "fellow-feeling" among all living things as a basis for an environmental ethic to that of true mutuality. By this I mean that, instead of using the term "biophilia" to define the relationship between humanity and the rest of the universe, one could use the term *"bio-agape."* This distinctively Christian notion of unconditional love, when wedded to the prefix "bio-", implies that there exists – or at the very least there *should* exist – a mutuality among all creatures that is reflective of God's love for God's creation. Such a notion of course includes within it all other forms of love (*i.e.*, *libido, eros, philia*), but allows them to express themselves in an unambiguously positive fashion. To place this type of love at the heart of our relationship with all living things liberates it from strictly anthropocentric usage and situates it in a biocentric context. Understanding our obligation to love the earth as the earth loves us – with long-suffering solicitude and patient tenderness, regardless of the abuse and neglect we give back in return – draws out of us the most noble Christian attribute, that of loving the other as God loves them.[76] The tree and plant that naturally furnish us with oxygen are provided in turn by us with the material that allows them to live. Similarly, in a pet's devotion to its owner there can be observed a blessed, almost gratuitous excess that is virtually impossible to duplicate, one which clearly surpasses simple companionship.[77] The act of existence itself is, in these cases, an act of love.

The notion of bio-*agape* therefore recognizes that at the deepest dimensions of being there is a fundamental unity which cannot be disturbed without placing oneself in peril. And yet while *agape* love may be the criteria by which our relationship with the non-human world should be judged, it is the discernment of the presence of a *kairos* that determines how one shall act in any specific circumstance. With *agape* love as our guide, we seek to actualize the Kingdom of God in our creative stewardship of the earth. By enlarging the field of *agape* love to include all living things, we place upon ourselves the responsibility of caring for creation in terms of justice. This means that, in the last analysis, every decision made and every attitude fostered toward the non-human world will have to contain within it the most fundamental conviction of all: that all life is sacred and, hence, possesses an inviolable and intrinsic dignity.[78]

Conclusion

This attempt at a Tillichean ecology of being has led to a number of conclusions: 1) there exists a *fundamental interrelatedness* among all the elements of the created order that are equally characterized by a *fundamental givenness;* 2) the *notion of "forwardism"* and the *category of concupiscence* are expressive of the "essence" of our broken relationship with the material universe; 3) in our efforts to exercise a *creative stewardship* of the earth, the "vertical" or "depth" dimension of reality is potentially revealed as "saving power"; and 4) the Christian attitude of justice toward the non-human universe that should be encouraged is best described by the term *"bio-*agape. *"*

It is therefore apparent that Paul Tillich's theological vision would be particularly favorable to the views of many contemporary eco-theologians. Tillich's unique ontological approach to reality is able to overcome the dualism inherent in much of Western thought which, in many ways, has contributed greatly to the crisis we now face. What we have discovered in this modest attempt at an "ecology of being" is that such an approach, while certainly consistent with Paul Tillich's own correlational model, succeeds in taking him one step further into the twenty-first century. I am convinced that had Tillich lived into the present day he would be offering, in his own inimitable style, a similar sobering diagnosis of our age accompanied, of course, by his usual realistic hopefulness.

Throughout his life, Paul Tillich possessed a deep, prophetic, enduring concern for his world, including the vast non-human part of it. He can therefore be considered a warm and welcome companion for those on the journey toward the healing of a wounded earth, one who also mourned the loss of reverence for creation and yet who, in the name of justice and compassion, fearlessly and tirelessly spoke out on its behalf.

Notes

1. Revelation 5:10.
2. Paul Tillich, "Redemption in Cosmic and Social History," *Journal of Religious Thought* 3 (Autumn-Winter 1946): 23.
3. Paul Tillich, *The System of the Sciences According to Objects and Methods,* tr. Paul Wiebe (Lewisburg, PA: Bucknell University Press; London and Toronto: Associated University Presses, 1981), 201.
4. Ronald H. Stone, *Paul Tillich's Radical Social Thought* (Atlanta: John Knox Press, 1980), 116.
5. Paul Tillich, *ST* 3, 266.
6. Ibid., 267-268.
7. John 15:12.
8. Paul Tillich, *LPJ,* 28.
9. Ibid., 29.
10. For example, "Being and Love," in *Moral Principles of Action: Man's Ethical Imperative,* ed. Ruth Nanda Anshen (New York: Harper and Row, 1952), 666-672; *LPJ,* 24-34; *ST* 2, 53-55; *MB,* 40-42.
11. Tillich, "Being and Love," 667.
12. Tillich, *ST* 2, 54.
13. Tillich, *LPJ,* 30.
14. Ibid., 118.
15. Ibid., 30.
16. Tillich, "Being and Love," 668.
17. Ibid., 671-672.
18. Ibid., 672.
19. Tillich, *LPJ,* 33.
20. Tillich, "Being and Love," 668.
21. Tillich, *LPJ,* 118.
22. Tillich, "Being and Love," 672.
23. Ibid., 668.
24. Tillich, *ST* 2, 176.
25. Tillich, "Being and Love," 672. Cf. Tillich, *LPJ,* 115; Tillich, *ST* 2, 173-176.
26. Paul Tillich, "Ethics in a Changing World," in *PRE,* 154-155.
27. Ibid., 151.

28. Ibid., 155.
29. Tillich, *ST* 3, 370.
30. Ibid., 370-371.
31. Tillich, "Ethics," 155-156.
32. Tillich, "Being and Love," 672.
33. Tillich, "Ethics," 155.
34. Tillich, *MB*, 36.
35. Ibid.
36. Tillich, *LPJ*, 121.
37. H. Paul Santmire, "I-Thou, I-It, I-Ens," *The Journal of Religion* 48 (July 1968): 260-273. Cf. as well the very interesting discussions on this same theme by Jay B. McDaniel, *With Roots and Wings: Christianity in an Age of Ecology and Dialogue* (Maryknoll, NY: Orbis Books, 1995), 155-159, and Stephanie Kaza, *The Attentive Heart: Conversations with Trees* (New York: Fawcett Columbine, 1993).
38. Ibid., 270.
39. Ibid., 272-273.
40. A. Arnold Wettstein, "Tillich's Cosmology and Chaos Theory," in *Natürliche Theologie versus Theologie der Natur? Tillichs Denken als Anstoss zum Gespräch zwischen Theologie, Philosophie und Naturwissenschaft,* ed. Gert Hummel (Berlin and New York: Walter de Gruyter, 1994), 41.
41. Martin Heidegger, "The Question Concerning Technology," in *Basic Writings,* ed. David Farrell Krell (New York: Harper and Row, 1977), 283-317.
42. Ibid., 308.
43. Ibid., 308-309.
44. Ibid., 314-315.
45. Ibid, 315. Emphasis mine.
46. Ibid., 305.
47. Ibid., 314, 317.
48. Paul Tillich, "The Redemption of Nature," *Christendom* 10 (Summer 1945): 305.
49. Cf. Rosemary Radford Ruether's suggestion that, insofar as the environmental crisis is concerned, the idea of conversion is preferable to a view that holds to a strictly extra-historical eschatology (*To Change the World: Christology and Cultural Criticism* [New York: Crossroad, 1981]), 68.
50. Concerning the matter of interdependency on the microcosmic level see, for example, Stephen Jay Gould, *Wonderful Life: The Burgess Shale and the Nature of History* (New York: Norton Press, 1989), 218-229; Richard Dawkins, "Worlds in Microcosm," in *Humanity, Environment and God,* ed. Neil Spurway (Cambridge, MA and Oxford: Blackwell Publishers, 1993), 106-125; and the conclusion of microbiologist Lynn Margulis regarding the principle of symbiosis on the microbial level as discussed in Loren Wilkinson,

"Gaia Spirituality: A Christian Critique," *Evangelical Review of Theology* 17 (April 1993): 178.

51. John B. Cobb, Jr., *Is It Too Late? A Theology of Ecology,* rev. ed. (Denton, TX: Environmental Ethics Books, 1995), 6.

52. Rosemary Radford Ruether, *Gaia and God: An Ecofeminist Theology of Earth Healing* (San Francisco: HarperSanFrancisco, 1992), 1. Emphasis mine.

53. Most notably, Søren Kierkegaard, *The Concept of Dread,* 2d ed., trans. Walter Lowrie (Princeton, NJ: Princeton University Press, 1957); Martin Heidegger, *Being and Time,* trans. John Macquarrie and Edward Robinson (New York: Harper and Row, 1962); Martin Buber, *I and Thou,* 2d ed., trans. Ronald G. Smith (New York: Charles Scribner's Sons, 1958); and Jean-Paul Sartre, *Being and Nothingness: An Essay on Phenomenological Ontology,* trans. Hazel E. Barnes (New York: Philosophical Library, 1956).

54. On this point, see Michael J. Himes and Kenneth R. Himes, "The Sacrament of Creation: Toward an Environmental Theology," *Commonweal* 117 (January 26, 1990): 45: "The doctrine of *creatio ex nihilo* insists on the fundamental poverty of the universe: the universe has no intrinsic ground for existence."

55. See, for example, Ian Barbour, *Ethics in an Age of Technology,* Gifford Lectures 1989-1991, vol. 2 (New York: Harper Collins, 1993); John Barrow, "Inner Space and Outer Space: The Quest for Ultimate Explanation," in *Humanity, Environment and God,* 48-103; Frederick Ferré, *Shaping the Future: Resources for the Post-Modern World* (New York: Harper and Row, 1976); Dieter T. Hessel, "Now That Animals Can Be Genetically Engineered: Biotechnology in Theological-Ethical Perspective," in *Ecotheology: Voices from South and North,* ed. David G. Hallman (Geneva: WCC Publications; Maryknoll, NY: Orbis Books, 1994), 284-99; Roger L. Shinn, *Forced Options: Social Decisions for the Twenty-First Century,* 3d ed. (Cleveland: Pilgrim Press, 1991); and Charles C. West, "God–Woman/Man–Creation: Some Comments on the Ethics of the Relationship," *Ecumenical Review* 33 (January 1981): 13-28.

56. Some have suggested that the relatively recent development in our appreciation of the global environmental crisis implies the emergence of a new paradigm that will characterize our age. In the case of the global-ecological area, such a paradigm centers around the organic features of interdependent systems. See, for example, Kenneth Cauthen, "Imaging the Future: New Visions and New Responsibilities," *Zygon* 20 (September 1985): 321-339. On the general question of scientific paradigm shifts throughout history, see Thomas S. Kuhn, *The Structure of Scientific Revolutions,* 2nd ed. (Chicago: University of Chicago Press, 1970).

57. Paul Tillich, "The Effects of Space Exploration on Man's Condition and Stature," in *FR,* 45.

58. Ibid.
59. Ibid., 46.
60. Paul Tillich, *IRCM*, 61.
61. Tillich, *ST* 2, 52.
62. Langdon Gilkey, *Gilkey on Tillich* (New York: Crossroad, 1990), 184-185.
63. Ibid., 184.
64. Tillich, "Effects," 45.
65. Tillich, *IRCM*, 61.
66. Ibid.
67. René Dubos, "Franciscan Conservation vs. Benedictine Stewardship," in *The World of René Dubos: A Collection from his Writings*, Gerard Piel and Osborn Segerberg, Jr., eds. (New York: Henry Holt and Co., 1990), 378-381.
68. Ibid., 392.
69. Alexandre Ganoczy, "Ecological Perspectives in the Christian Doctrine of Creation," *Concilium* 4 (April 1991): 48.
70. Dubos, "Franciscan Conservation," 390.
71. Thomas Sieger Derr, "Religion's Responsibility for the Ecological Crisis: An Argument Run Amok," *Worldview* 15 (January 1975): 44.
72. Dubos, "Franciscan Conservation," 392.
73. I would like to thank the Rev. Rickey Edwards for this image and insight.
74. Edward O. Wilson, *Biophilia: The Human Bond with Other Species* (Cambridge, MA and London: Harvard University Press, 1984), 1.
75. Elizabeth A. Johnson, *Women, Earth, and Creator Spirit* (New York: Paulist Press, 1993), 39.
76. I am aware of the very legitimate questions raised concerning the difficulty in reconciling the idea of a "good" Creator with naturally-occurring "evils" and the suffering entailed thereby (*e.g.* Hume, Voltaire, and, in more recent times, such thinkers as Daniel Dennett). While I am not here advocating a naïve position with respect to the apparent cruelty of the non-human world, it must not be forgotten that such events transpire in an *evolving* universe, one in which natural selection is the governing principle. The real question then becomes one not necessarily of classical theodicy (*i.e.*, trying to justify a "good" God in the face of inscrutable evil), but rather one of trying to reconcile the notion of divine creativity with the theory of evolution. On this point see, for example, John F. Haught, *Science and Religion: From Conflict to Conversation* (Mahwah, NJ: Paulist Press, 1995), 60; Arthur Peacocke, *Theology for a Scientific Age: Being and Becoming – Natural, Divine, and Human* (Minneapolis: Fortress Press, 1993), 68, 80; Holmes Rolston III, *Science and Religion: A Critical Survey* (New York: Random House, 1987), 287-289; and Ian G. Barbour, *Religion and Science: Historical and Contemporary Issues* (San Francisco: HarperSanFrancisco, 1997), 300-303.

77. In attempting to define the *raison d'être* of pets, for example, Stephen H. Webb offers the following insight: "Pets give us a sacrifice that is antie-conomical, based on a surplus of emotions and affection in which we give up something for the other in order to let the other become more than it otherwise would be rather than asking the other to give up its life so that we can benefit from it. What pets are for is, decisively, the end of the reign of animal sacrifice – the sacrifice of sacrifice – and the beginning of a different kind of laying on of hands" (*On God and Dogs: A Christian Theology of Compassion for Animals* [New York and Oxford: Oxford University Press, 1998], 154). Cf. the idea of "The Dog as Living Saint" in J. Moussaieff Masson, *Dogs Never Lie About Love: Reflections on the Emotional World of Dogs* (New York: Crown Publishers, 1997), 203-207. See also Charles Darwin's observations on the relationship of dogs to humans (*The Descent of Man* [Chicago: Encyclopaedia Britannica, 1952], 295, 303, 305, 307).

78. Some critics of an "ethics of intrinsic value" would maintain that such an ethics cannot be applied to human beings, let alone to the non-human world. Others may claim that such a position might possibly include sentient beings, but certainly not plants or inorganic matter. However, I would agree with Denis Edwards who argues from a trinitarian/ontological/sacramental perspective that "[t]he value of things comes not simply from their value to human beings. Things have value in themselves because they are the self-expression of God. They have intrinsic value.... Birds, plants, forests, mountains, and galaxies have value in themselves because they exist and are held in being by the divine Persons-in-Mutual-Communion, and because they are fruitful expressions of divine Wisdom. They are indeed the voice of the divine, and to destroy one of them irresponsibly is to destroy arbitrarily a mode of divine self-expression" (*The God of Evolution: A Trinitarian Theology* [Mahwah, NJ: Paulist Press, 1999]), 124.

Bibliography

Works by Tillich

Tillich, Paul. *Der Begriff des Übernatürlichen, sein dialektischer Charakter und das Prinzip der Identität, dargestellt an der supranaturalistischen Theologie vor Schleiermacher.* Königsberg: Madrasch, 1915.

———. "Being and Love." In *Moral Principles of Action: Man's Ethical Imperative,* ed. Ruth Nanda Anshen, 661-672. New York: Harper and Brothers, 1952.

———. *Biblical Religion and the Search for Ultimate Reality.* Chicago: University of Chicago Press, 1955.

———. *Christianity and the Encounter of the World Religions.* New York and London: Columbia University Press, 1963.

——. *The Construction of the History of Religion in Schelling's Positive Philosophy.* Translated by Victor Nuovo. Lewisburg, PA: Bucknell University Press, 1974.

——. *The Courage to Be.* New Haven: Yale University Press, 1952.

——. *Dogmatik: Marburger Vorlesung von 1925.* Edited by Werner Shüßler. Düsseldorf: Patmos, 1986.

——. "Depth." *Christendom* 9 (Summer 1944): 317-325.

——. "Dimensions, Levels, and the Unity of Life." *Kenyon Alumni Bulletin* 17 (1959): 4-8.

——. *Dynamics of Faith.* New York: Harper and Row, 1957.

——. "The Effects of Space Exploration on Man's Condition and Stature." In *The Future of Religions,* ed. Jerald C. Brauer, 39-51. New York: Harper and Row, 1966.

——. *The Eternal Now.* London: SCM Press, 1963.

——. "Environment and the Individual." *AIA: Journal of the American Institute of Architects* 28 (June 1957): 90-92.

——. "Das geistige Vakuum." *Das sozialistische Jahrhundert* 2 (September 15, 1948): 303-305.

——. *Gesammelte Werke.* 14 vols. Stuttgart: Evangelisches Verlagswerk, 1959-1974.

——. "The God of History." *Christianity and Crisis* 4 (May 15, 1944): 3-5.

——. "History as the Problem of Our Period." *Review of Religion* 3 (March, 1939): 255-264.

——. *A History of Christian Thought -- From Its Judaic and Hellenistic Origins to Existentialism.* Edited by Carl E. Braaten. New York: Simon and Schuster, 1968.

——. "Die Idee der Offenbarung." *Zeitschrift für Theologie und Kirche* 8 (1927): 403-412.

——. *The Interpretation of History.* Translated by N. A. Rasetzki and Elsa L. Talmey. New York: Scribner's, 1936.

——. *The Irrelevance and Relevance of the Christian Message.* Edited by Durwood Foster. Cleveland: Pilgrim Press, 1996.

——. "The Kingdom of God and History." In *The Kingdom of God and History,* 107-141. Chicago and New York: Willet, Clark and Co., 1938.

——. *Love, Power, and Justice.* New York: Oxford University Press, 1954.

——. "Man, the Earth, and the Universe." *Christianity and Crisis* 22 (1962): 108-112.

———. *Masse und Geist.* Studien zur Philosophie der Masse. Berlin: Verlag der Arbeitsgemeinschaft, 1922.

———. *The Meaning of Health.* Edited by Paul Lee. Richmond, CA: North Atlantic Books, 1981.

———. *Morality and Beyond.* New York: Harper and Row, 1963.

———. *My Search for Absolutes.* Edited by Ruth Nanda Anshen. New York: Simon and Schuster, 1969.

———. *Mystik und Schuldbewusstsein in Schellings philosophischer Entwicklung.* Beiträge zur Förderung christlicher Theologie, 16, No. 1. Gütersloh: Bertelsmann, 1912. Translated by Victor Nuovo as *Mysticism and Guilt-Consciousness in Schelling's Philosophical Development.* Lewisburg, PA: Bucknell University Press, 1974.

———. "Natural and Revealed Religion." *Christendom* 1 (Autumn, 1935): 159-170.

———. "The Nature of Man." *Journal of Philosophy* 43 (December 5, 1946): 675-677.

———. "The New Being." *Religion in Life* 19 (Autumn 1950): 511-517.

———. *The New Being.* New York: Charles Scribner's Sons, 1955.

———. *On the Boundary: An Autobiographical Sketch.* New York: Charles Scribner's Sons, 1966.

———. "On the Boundary Line." *The Christian Century* 77 (1960): 1435-1437.

———. *Political Expectation.* Edited by James Luther Adams. New York: Harper and Row, 1971. Reprint, Macon, GA: Mercer University Press, 1981.

———. *The Protestant Era.* Abridged edition. Translated by James Luther Adams. Chicago: University of Chicago Press, 1957.

———. "Redemption in Cosmic and Social History." *Journal of Religious Thought* 3 (Autumn-Winter 1946): 17-27.

———. "The Redemption of Nature." *Christendom* 10 (Summer 1945): 299-305.

———. "A Reinterpretation of the Doctrine of the Incarnation." *Church Quarterly Review* 148 (January-March 1949): 133-148.

———. "The Relationship Today between Science and Religion." In *The Student Seeks an Answer.* Waterville, ME: Colby College Press, 1960.

———. *Religiöse Verwirklichung.* Berlin: Furche, 1929.

———. *The Religious Situation.* Translated by H. Richard Niebuhr. Cleveland and New York: World Publishing, 1956.

——. "Reply to Interpretation and Criticism." In *The Theology of Paul Tillich,* ed. Charles W. Kegley, 74-94. Second edition. New York: Pilgrim Press, 1982.

——. "Schelling und die Anfänge des existentialistischen Protestes." *Zeitschrift für philosophische Forschung* 9 (1955): 197-208.

——. *The Shaking of the Foundations.* New York: Charles Scribner's Sons, 1948.

——. *The Spiritual Situation in Our Technical Society.* Edited by J. Mark Thomas. Macon, GA: Mercer University Press, 1988.

——. *Das System der Wissenschaften nach Gegenständen und Methoden. Ein Entwurf.* Göttingen: Vendenhoeck & Ruprecht, 1923. Translation by Paul Wiebe as *The System of the Sciences According to Objects and Methods.* Lewisburg, PA: Bucknell University Press, 1981.

——. *Systematic Theology.* 3 vols. Chicago: University of Chicago Press, 1951-1963.

——. *Theology of Culture.* Edited by Robert C. Kimball. New York: Oxford University Press, 1959.

——. "Über die Idee einer Theologie del Kultur." In *Religionsphilosophie der Kultur.* Berlin: Reuther and Reichard, 1919. Translated by Victor Nuovo as *Visionary Sciences: A Translation of Tillich's 'On the Idea of a Theology of Culture' with an Interpretive Essay.* Detroit: Wayne State University Press, 1987.

——. *Ultimate Concern: Tillich in Dialogue.* Edited by D. Mackenzie Brown. New York: Harper and Row, 1965.

——. "Um was es geht: Antwort an Emanuel Hirsch." *Theologische Blätter* 14 (May, 1935): 117-120.

——. *What is Religion?* Edited by James Luther Adams. New York: Harper and Row, 1969.

——. *The World Situation.* Philadelphia: Fortress Press, 1965.

Works on Tillich

Adams, James Luther. *Paul Tillich's Philosophy of Culture, Science and Religion.* New York: Harper and Row, 1965.
Armbruster, C. J. *The Vision of Paul Tillich.* New York: Sheed and Ward, 1967.

Carey, John. "Are There Any Absolutes Left? Post Modernism and the Crisis for Tillich Scholars." *The North American Paul Tillich Society Newsletter* 24/4 (Fall 1998): 3-9.

Dourley, John P. "Paul Tillich and Bonaventure: An Evaluation of Tillich's Claim to Stand in the Augustinian-Franciscan Tradition." Ph.D. diss., Fordham University, 1971.

Ford, Lewis S. "Tillich's Tergiversations Toward the Power of Being." *Scottish Journal of Theology* 28 (1975): 323-340.

Foster, Durwood. "Afterglows of Tillich." *Newsletter of the North American Paul Tillich Society* 23/1 (January 1997): 3-7.

Geffré, Claude. "Paul Tillich and the Future of Interreligious Ecumenism." In *Paul Tillich: A New Catholic Assessment*, ed. Raymond F. Bulman and Frederick J. Parrella, 268-288. Collegeville, MN: Liturgical Press, 1994.

Gilkey, Langdon. *Gilkey on Tillich.* New York: Crossroad, 1990.

Grean, Stanley. "Truth and Faith in Paul Tillich's Thought: The Criteria and Values of Ultimacy." *Ultimate Reality and Meaning* 16 (1993): 149-166.

Grigg, Richard. *Symbol and Empowerment: Paul Tillich's Post-Theistic System.* Macon, GA: Mercer University Press, 1985.

Hamilton, Kenneth. *The System and the Gospel: A Critique of Paul Tillich.* London: SCM Press Ltd., 1963.

Harrison, Peter. "Correlation and Theology: Barth and Tillich Reexamined." *Sciences Religieuses* 15/1 (Winter 1986): 65-76.

Hummel, Gert, ed. *Natürliche Theologie versus Theologie der Natur? Tillichs Denken als Anstoss zum Gespräch zwischen Theologie, Philosophie und Naturwissenschaft.* Berlin and New York: Walter de Gruyter, 1994.

Inbody, Tyron. "Paul Tillich and Process Theology." *Theological Studies* 36 (September 1975): 472-492.

Irwin, Alexander C. *Eros Toward the World: Paul Tillich and the Theology of the Erotic.* Minneapolis: Fortress Press, 1991.

Jahr, Hannelore. "Tillichs Theologie der Nature als Theologie der Versöhnung von Geist und Natur." In *Natürliche Theologie versus Theologie der Natur? Tillichs Denken als Anstoss zum Gespräch zwischen Theologie, Philosophie und Naturwissenschaft*, ed. Gert Hummel, 156-183. Berlin and New York: Walter de Gruyter, 1994.

Kelsey, D. *The Fabric of Paul Tillich's Theology.* New Haven and London: Yale University Press, 1967.

Lai, Pan-Chiu. "Paul Tillich and Ecological Theology." *The Journal of Religion* 79/2 (1999): 355-370.

Lamm, Julia A. "'Catholic Substance' Revisited: Reversals of Expectations in Tillich's Doctrine of God." In *Paul Tillich: A New Catholic Assessment,* ed. Raymond F. Bulman and Frederick J. Parrella, 48-72. Collegeville, MN: Liturgical Press, 1994.

Lee, Paul. Introduction to *The Meaning of Health,* by Paul Tillich. Richmond, CA: North Atlantic Books, 1981.

———. "Ecotopia and Political Expectations." Paper presented at the annual meeting of the North American Paul Tillich Society, San Francisco, CA, 21 November 1997.

Macleod, A. *Tillich: An Essay on the Role of Ontology in his Philosophical Theology.* London: Allen and Unwin, 1973.

Osborne, Kenan B. *New Being: A Study on the Relationship Between Conditioned and Unconditioned Being According to Paul Tillich.* The Hague: Martinus Nijhoff, 1969.

Otto, Randall E. "The Doctrine of God in the Theology of Paul Tillich." *Westminster Theological Journal* 52 (1990): 303-323.

Painadath, Sebastian. "Paul Tillich's Theology of Prayer: An Indian Perspective." In *Paul Tillich: A New Catholic Assessment,* ed. Raymond F. Bulman and Frederick J. Parrella, 218-240. Collegeville, MN: Liturgical Press, 1994.

Parrella, Frederick J. "Tillich and Contemporary Spirituality." In *Paul Tillich: A New Catholic Assessment,* ed. Raymond F. Bulman and Frederick J. Parrella, 241-267. Collegeville, MN: Liturgical Press, 1994.

Petit, Jean Claude. "Von den Schwierigkeiten und Grenzen einer Theologie der Natur heute. Einige Bemerkungen im Blick auf Paul Tillich." In *Natürliche Theologie versus Theologie der Natur? Tillichs Denken als Anstoss zum Gespräch zwischen Theologie, Philosophie und Naturwissenschaft,* ed. Gert Hummel, 3-14. Berlin and New York: Walter de Gruyter, 1994.

Plaskow, Judith. *Sex, Sin, and Grace: Women's Experience and the Theologies of Reinhold Niebuhr and Paul Tillich.* Washington, DC: University Press of America, 1980.

Randall, John Herman, Jr. "The Philosophical Legacy of Paul Tillich." In *The Intellectual Legacy of Paul Tillich,* ed. James R. Lyons, 19-54. Detroit: Wayne State University Press, 1969.

Reimer, James A. "Tillich, Hirsch and Barth: Three Different Paradigms of Theology and its Relation to the Sciences." In *Natürliche*

Theologie versus Theologie der Natur? Tillichs Denken als Anstoss zum Gespräch zwischen Theologie, Philosophie und Naturwissenschaft, ed. Gert Hummel, 101-124. Berlin and New York: Walter de Gruyter, 1994.

Richard, Jean. "La Révélation Finale D'Après Paul Tillich: Une Voie Théologique pour la Rencontre du Christianisme avec les Religions du Monde." *Etudes Théologique et Religieuses* 64/2 (1989): 211-224.

Ringleben, Joachim. "Die Macht des Negativen. Paul Tillichs Ontologie und Theologie des Lebendigen." In *Natürliche Theologie versus Theologie der Natur? Tillichs Denken als Anstoss zum Gespräch zwischen Theologie, Philosophie und Naturwissenschaft,* ed. Gert Hummel, 212-234. Berlin and New York: Walter de Gruyter, 1994.

Russell, John M. "Tillich's Implicit Ontological Argument." *Asia Journal of Theology* 2/2 (1988): 485-495.

Scharlemann, Robert P. "The No to Nothing and the Nothing to Know: Barth and Tillich and the Possibility of Theological Science." *Journal of the American Academy of Religion* 55/1 (1987): 57-72.

——. "Wie ist Gott göttlich und die Natur natürlich? Ansätze zu einer Naturtheologie im Sein und Nichtsein Gottes." In *Natürliche Theologie versus Theologie der Natur? Tillichs Denken als Anstoss zum Gespräch zwischen Theologie, Philosophie und Naturwissenschaft,* ed. Gert Hummel, 235-248. Berlin and New York: Walter de Gruyter, 1994.

Schlüßler, Werner. "Protestantisches Prinzip versus Natürliche Theologie? Zu Paul Tillichs Problemen mit einer natürlichen Theologie." In *Natürliche Theologie versus Theologie der Natur? Tillichs Denken als Anstoss zum Gespräch zwischen Theologie, Philosophie und Naturwissenschaft,* ed. Gert Hummel, 15-30. Berlin and New York: Walter de Gruyter, 1994.

Schwaarz, Hans. "The Potential for Dialogue with the Natural Sciences in Tillich's Method of Correlation." In *Natürliche Theologie versus Theologie der Natur? Tillichs Denken als Anstoss zum Gespräch zwischen Theologie, Philosophie und Naturwissenschaft,* ed. by Gert Hummel, 88-100. Berlin and New York: Walter de Gruyter, 1994.

Sommer, G. F. "The Significance of the Late Philosophy of Schelling for the Formation and Interpretation of the Thought of Paul Tillich." Ph.D. diss., Duke University, 1960.

Stenger, Mary Ann. "Tillich's Approach to Theology and Natural Sciences: Issues of Truth and Verification." In *Natürliche Theologie versus Theologie der Natur? Tillichs Denken als Anstoss zum Gespräch zwischen Theologie, Philosophie und Naturwissenschaft,* ed. Gert Hummel, 125-139. Berlin and New York: Walter de Gruyter, 1994.

———. "Paul Tillich and the Feminist Critique of Roman Catholic Theology." In *Paul Tillich: A New Catholic Assessment,* ed. Raymond F. Bulman and Frederick J. Parrella, 174-188. Collegeville, MN: Liturgical Press, 1994.

Thatcher, Adrian. *The Ontology of Paul Tillich.* Oxford: Oxford University Press, 1978.

Thomas, J. Heywood. *Paul Tillich: An Appraisal.* Philadelphia: Westminster Press, 1963.

Wettstein, A. Arnold. "Tillich's Cosmology and Chaos Theory." In *Natürliche Theologie versus Theologie der Natur? Tillichs Denken als Anstoss zum Gespräch zwischen Theologie, Philosophie und Naturwissenschaft,* ed. Gert Hummel, 31-41. Berlin and New York: Walter de Gruyter, 1994.

Works on Ecology and/or Religion

Abrecht, Paul. "The Future as a 'Religious' Problem." *Ecumenical Review* 24 (April 1972): 176-189.

———. "Humanity, Nature, and God." In *Faith and Science in an Unjust World: Report of the World Council of Churches' Conference on Faith, Science and the Future,* ed. Paul Abrecht, 28-38. Vol. 2, *Reports of Sections.* Geneva: World Council of Churches, 1980.

Albanese, Catherine L. "Having Nature All Ways: Liberal and Transcendental Perspectives on American Environmentalism." *The Journal of Religion* 77/1 (January 1997): 20-43.

Armstrong, Edward. *Saint Francis, Nature Mystic: The Derivation and Significance of the Nature Stories in the Franciscan Legend.*

Hermeneutics Studies in the History of Religions. Vol. 2. Berkeley, CA: University of California Press, 1973.

Attfield, Robin. *The Ethics of Environmental Concern.* Second edition. Athens, GA and London: The University of Georgia Press, 1991.

Ayers, Robert H. "Christian Realism and Environmental Ethics." In *Religion and Environmental Crisis,* ed. Eugene C. Hargrove, 154-171. Athens, GA: University of Georgia Press, 1986.

Baker, John Austin. "Biblical Views of Nature." In *Liberating Life: Contemporary Approaches to Ecological Theology,* ed. Charles Birch, William Eakin, and Jay B. McDaniel, 9-26. Maryknoll, NY: Orbis Books, 1990.

Bakken, Peter W. "The Ecology of Grace: Ultimacy and Environmental Ethics in Aldo Leopold and Joseph Sittler." Ph.D. diss., University of Chicago, 1991.

Bakken, Peter W., Joan Gibb Engel, and J. Ronald Engel, eds. *Ecology, Justice, and Christian Faith: A Critical Guide to the Literature.* Westport, CT and London: Greenwood Press, 1995.

Bamford, Christopher. "The Heritage of Celtic Christianity: Ecology and Holiness." In *The Celtic Consciousness,* ed. Robert O'Driscoll, 170-186. New York: George Braziller, 1982.

Barbour, Ian G. "An Ecological Ethic." *Christian Century* 87 (October 7, 1970): 1180-1184.

——. "Attitudes Toward Nature and Technology." In *Earth Might be Fair: Reflections on Ethics, Religion, and Ecology,* ed. idem., 146-168. Englewood Cliffs, NJ: Prentice Hall, 1972.

Barnette, Henlee H. *The Church and the Ecological Crisis.* Grand Rapids, MI: William B. Eerdmans Publishing Co., 1972.

Barrow, John. "Inner Space and Outer Space: The Quest for Ultimate Explanation." In *Humanity, Environment and God,* ed. Neil Spurway, 48-103. Cambridge, MA and Oxford: Blackwell Publishers, 1993.

Berry, Thomas F. "Economics is a Religious Issue." In *The Dream of the Earth,* 70-88. San Francisco: Sierra Club Books, 1988.

——. *The Great Work: Our Way Into the Future.* New York: Bell Tower, 1999.

Berry, Thomas F., and Thomas Clarke. *Befriending the Earth: A Theology of Reconciliation Between Humans and the Earth.* Edited by Stephen Dunn and Anne Lonergan. Mystic, CT: Twenty-Third Publications, 1991.

Berry, Wendell. "Christianity and the Survival of Creation." In *Sex, Economy, Freedom, and Community*, 93-116. New York: Pantheon Books, 1993.

Birch, Charles, and John B. Cobb, Jr. *The Liberation of Life: From the Cell to the Community*. Cambridge: Cambridge University Press, 1981.

Bloomquist, Karen. "Creation, Domination, and the Environment." *Lutheran Theological Seminary Bulletin* 69 (1989): 27-31.

Boff, Leonardo. *Ecology & Liberation: A New Paradigm*. Translated by John Cumming. Maryknoll, NY: Orbis Books, 1995.

Bonifazi, Conrad. *A Theology of Things: A Study of Man in His Physical Environment*. Philadelphia: J. B. Lippincott Co., 1967.

Bonsor, Jack A. "History, Dogma, and Nature: Further Reflections on Postmodernism and Theology." *Theological Studies* 55 (June 1994): 295-313.

Bouma-Prediger, Steven. *The Greening of Theology: The Ecological Models of Rosemary Radford Ruether, Joseph Sittler, and Jürgen Moltmann*. Atlanta: Scholars Press, 1995.

Bratton, Susan P. "Oaks, Wolves, and Love: Celtic Monks and Northern Forests." *Journal of Forest History* 33/1 (January 1989): 4-20.

———. "Loving Nature: Eros or Agape." *Environmental Ethics* 14 (Spring 1992): 3-25.

Brun, Tony. "Social Ecology: A Timely Paradigm for Reflection and Praxis for Life in Latin America." In *Ecotheology: Voices from South and North*, ed. David G. Hallman, 79-91. Geneva: WCC Publications; Maryknoll, NY: Orbis Books, 1994.

Caldecott, Stratford. "Cosmology, Eschatology, Ecology: Some Reflections on *Sollicitudo rei socialis.*" *Communio* 15 (Fall 1988): 305-18.

Carmody, John. *Ecology and Religion: Toward a New Christian Theology of Nature*. New York: Paulist Press, 1983.

Carpenter, James A. *Nature and Grace: Toward an Integral Perspective*. New York: Crossroad, 1988.

Cauthen, Kenneth. *Christian Biopolitics: A Credo and Strategy for the Future*. Nashville: Abingdon Press, 1971.

———. "Imagining the Future: New Visions and New Responsibilities." *Zygon* 20(September 1985): 321-339.

Christiansen, Drew. "Moral Theology, Ecology, Justice and Development." In *Covenant for a New Creation: Ethics, Religion, and*

Public Policy, ed. Carol S. Robb and Carl J. Casebolt, 251-271. Maryknoll, NY: Orbis Books, 1991.

Cobb, John B., Jr. *God and the World.* Philadelphia: Westminster Press, 1969.

——. "Ecological Disaster and the Church." *Christian Century* 87 (October 7, 1970): 1185-1187.

——. "Christian Theism and the Ecological Crisis." *Religious Education* 66 (January-February 1971): 31-35.

——. "Out of the Ashes of Disaster." *Resource* 12 (March 1971): 20-23.

——. "Ecology, Ethics and Theology." In *Toward a Steady-State Economy,* ed. Herman E. Daly, 303-320. San Francisco: W. H. Freeman and Company, 1973.

——. "The Christian Concern for the Non-Human World." *Anticipation* 16 (March 1974): 32-34.

——. "Sociological Theology or Ecological Theology." In *Process Theology as Political Theology,* 111-134. Philadelphia: Westminster Press; Manchester: Manchester University Press, 1982.

——. "Points of Contact Between Process Theology and Liberation Theology in Matters of Faith and Justice." *Process Studies* 14 (Summer 1985): 124-141.

——. "Afterword: The Role of Theology of Nature in the Church." In *Liberating Life: Contemporary Approaches to Ecological Theology,* ed. Charles Birch, William Eakin, and Jay B. McDaniel, 261-272. Maryknoll, NY: Orbis Books, 1990.

——. "Postmodern Christianity in Quest for Eco-Justice." In *After Nature's Revolt: Eco-Justice and Theology,* ed. Dieter T. Hessel, 21-39. Minneapolis: Fortress Press, 1992.

——. *Sustainability: Economics, Ecology, and Justice.* Maryknoll, NY: Orbis Books, 1992.

——. *Is It Too Late? A Theology of Ecology.* Revised edition. Denton, TX: Environmental Ethics Books, 1995.

Cobb, John and David Ray Griffin. *Process Theology: An Expository Introduction.* Philadelphia: Westminster Press, 1976.

Collingwood, R. G. *The Idea of Nature.* New York: Oxford University Press, 1972.

Compton, John J. "Science and God's Action in Nature." In *Earth Might be Fair: Reflections on Ethics, Religion, and Ecology,* ed. Ian G. Barbour, 33-47. Englewood Cliffs, NJ: Prentice-Hall, Inc., 1972.

Cooey, Paula M. *Jonathan Edwards on Nature and Destiny: A Systematic Analysis.* Studies in American Religion, Vol. 16. Lewiston, NY and Queenston, ON: Edwin Mellen Press, 1985.

Coward, Harold. "New Theology on Population, Consumption, and Ecology." *Journal of the American Academy of Religion* 65/2 (Summer 1997): 259-274.

Cupper, Don. "Nature and Culture." In *Humanity, Environment, and God,* ed. Neil Spurway, 33-45. Oxford and Cambridge, MA: Blackwell Publishers, 1993.

Daecke, Sigurd M. "Theologie der Natur als 'naturliche' Theologie? Interdisziplinäre und ökologische Überlegungen mit Tillichs Hilfe." In *Natürliche Theologie versus Theologie der Natur? Tillichs Denken als Anstoss zum Gespräch zwischen Theologie, Philosophie und Naturwissenschaft,* ed. Gert Hummel, 249-270. Berlin and New York: Walter de Gruyter, 1994.

de Bell, Garrett, ed. *The Environmental Handbook.* New York: Ballantine Books, 1970.

Derr, Thomas Sieger. "Religion's Responsibility for the Ecological Crisis: An Argument Run Amok." *Worldview* 18 (January 1975): 39-45.

———. *Ecology and Human Need.* Philadelphia: Westminster Press, 1975.

Derrick, Christopher. *The Delicate Creation: Towards a Theology of the Environment.* Old Greenwich, CT: Devin-Adair Co., 1972.

Dillenberger, John. *Protestant Thought and Natural Science: A Historical Interpretation.* Nashville: Abingdon Press, 1960.

Ditmanson, Harold H. "The Call for a Theology of Creation." *Dialog* 3 (August 1964): 264-273.

Dubos, René. *The World of René Dubos: A Collection from his Writings.* Edited by Gerard Piel and Osborn Segerberg, Jr. New York: Henry Holt and Co., 1990.

Dumas, André. "The Ecological Crisis and the Doctrine of Creation." *Ecumenical Review* 27 (January 1975): 24-35.

Dyrness, William. "Stewardship of the Earth in the Old Testament." In *Tending the Garden: Essays on the Gospel and the Earth,* ed. Wesley Granberg-Michaelson, 50-65. Grand Rapids, MI: William B. Eerdmans, 1987.

Edwards, Denis. *The God of Evolution: A Trinitarian Theology.* Mahwah, New Jersey: Paulist Press, 1999.

Elder, Frederick. *Crisis in Eden: A Religious Study of Man and Environment.* Nashville: Abingdon Press, 1970.

Falcke, Heino. "Deliverance and Renewal: The Integrity of Creation." *One World,* no. 124 (April 1987): 15-18.

Ferguson, Kitty. *The Fire in the Equations: Science, Religion and the Search for God.* Grand Rapids, MI: William B. Eerdmans Publishing Co., 1994.

Ferré, Frederick. *Shaping the Future: Resources for the Post-Modern World.* New York: Harper and Row, 1976.

Fowler, Robert Booth. *The Greening of Protestant Thought.* Chapel Hill, NC and London: The University of North Carolina Press, 1995.

Fox, Matthew. *The Coming of the Cosmic Christ: The Healing of Mother Earth and the Birth of a Global Renaissance.* San Francisco: Harper and Row, 1988.

Fritsch, Albert J. "Appropriate Technology and Healing the Earth." In *Embracing Earth: Catholic Approaches to Ecology,* ed. Albert J. LaChance and John E. Carroll, 96-114. Maryknoll, NY: Orbis, 1994.

Ganoczy, Alexandre. "Ecological Perspectives in the Christian Doctrine of Creation." *Concilium* 4 (April 1991): 43-53.

Gilkey, Langdon. *Maker of Heaven and Earth: A Study of the Christian Doctrine of Creation.* Garden City, NJ: Doubleday and Co., 1965.

———. "The Theological Understanding of Humanity and Nature in a Technological Era." *Anticipation* 19 (November 1974): 33-35.

———. *Nature, Reality and the Sacred.* Minneapolis: Fortress Press, 1993.

———. "Nature as the Image of God: Signs of the Sacred." *Theology Today* 51 (April 1994): 127-141.

Gottlieb, Roger S. *A Spirituality of Resistance: Finding a Peaceful Heart and Protecting the Earth.* New York: Crossroad, 1999.

Granberg-Michaelson, Wesley. "At the Dawn of the New Creation." *Sojourners* (November 1981): 13-18.

Gross, Rita M. "Toward a Buddhist Environmental Ethic." *Journal of the American Academy of Religion* 65/2 (Summer 1997): 333-354.

Halkes, Catharina J. M. *New Creation: Christian Feminism and the Renewal of the Earth.* Louisville, KY: Westminster/John Knox Press, 1991.

Hall, Douglas John. *Imaging God: Dominion as Stewardship.* Grand Rapids, MI: William B. Eerdmans Publishing Co.; New York: Friendship Press, 1986.

———. *Thinking the Faith: Christian Theology in a North American Context.* Minneapolis: Fortress Press, 1989.

———. *Professing the Faith: Christian Theology in a North American Context.* Minneapolis: Fortress Press, 1993.

Hallman, David G. *A Place in Creation: Ecological Visions in Science, Religion, and Economics.* Toronto: United Church Publishing House, 1992.

Harlow, Elizabeth M. "The Human Face of Nature: Environmental Values and the Limits of Nonanthropocentrism." *Environmental Ethics* 14 (Spring 1992): 27-42.

Haught, John A. "Religion and the Origins of the Environmental Crisis." In *An Ecology of the Spirit: Religious Reflection and Environmental Consciousness,* ed. Michael H. Barnes, 27-44. Lanham, MD: University Press of America, 1994.

Hefner, Philip J. "The Politics and Ontology of Nature and Grace." *Journal of Religion* 54 (April 1974): 138-153.

———. "Nature's History as Our History: A Proposal for Spirituality." In *After Nature's Revolt: Eco-Justice and Theology,* ed. Dieter T. Hessel, 171-183. Minneapolis: Fortress Press, 1992.

Hefner, Philip J., ed. *The Scope of Grace: Essays on Nature in Honor of Joseph Sittler.* Philadelphia: Fortress Press, 1964.

Heinegg, Peter. "Ecology and the Fall." *Christian Century* 93 (May 12, 1976): 464-466.

Hendry, George S. *Theology of Nature.* Philadelphia: Westminster Press, 1980.

Hessel, Dieter T. "Now That Animals Can Be Genetically Engineered: Biotechnology in Theological-Ethical Perspective." In *Ecotheology: Voices from South and North,* ed. David G. Hallman, 284-299. Geneva: WCC Publications; Maryknoll, NY: Orbis Books, 1994.

Hill, Brennan R. *Christian Faith and the Environment: Making Vital Connections.* Maryknoll, NY: Orbis Books, 1998.

Himes, Kenneth R., and Michael J. Himes. "The Sacrament of Creation: Toward an Environmental Theology." *Commonweal* 117 (January 26, 1990): 42-49.

Jantzen, Grace M. "Healing Our Brokenness: The Spirit and Creation." *Ecumenical Review* 42 (April 1990): 131-142.

Jaspers, Karl. "Nature and Ethics." In *Moral Principles of Action: Man's Ethical Imperative,* ed. Ruth Nanda Anshen, 48-61. New York: Harper and Brothers, 1952.
John Paul II. "Peace With All Creation." World Day of Peace Message, January 1, 1990. *Origins, CNS Documentary Service* 19 (December 14, 1989): 465-468.
Johnson, Elizabeth A. *Women, Earth, and Creator Spirit.* New York: Paulist Press, 1993.
Kaufman, Gordon D. "A Problem for Theology: The Concept of Nature." *The Harvard Theological Review* 65 (1972): 337-366.
———. *Theology for a Nuclear Age.* Philadelphia: Westminster Press; Manchester: Manchester University Press, 1985.
———. *In Face of Mystery: A Constructive Theology.* Cambridge, MA and London: Harvard University Press, 1993.
Kaza, Stephanie. *The Attentive Heart: Conversations with Trees.* New York: Fawcett Columbine, 1993.
Kehm, George H. "The New Story: Redemption as Fulfillment of Creation." In *After Nature's Revolt: Eco-Justice and Theology,* ed. Dieter T. Hessel, 89-106. Minneapolis: Fortress Press, 1992.
Keller, Catherine. "The Lost Fragrance: Protestantism and the Nature of What Matters." *Journal of the American Academy of Religion* 65/2 (Summer 1997): 355-370.
Kellert, Stephen R. and Edward O. Wilson, eds. *The Biophilia Hypothesis.* Washington, DC: Island Press, 1993.
Kenel, Sally. "Nature and Grace: An Ecological Metaphor." In *An Ecology of the Spirit: Religious Reflection and Environmental Consciousness,* ed. Michael H. Barnes, 231-240. Lanham, MD: University Press of America, 1994.
Kill, Donald and Nancy G. Wright. *Ecological Healing: A Christian Vision.* Maryknoll, NY: Orbis Books, 1993.
Kliever, Lonnie. *The Shattered Spectrum.* Atlanta: John Knox Press, 1981.
Kudlinski, Kathleen. "A Loon Encounter at the Water's Edge." *New Haven Register.* 22 February 1998.
Larsen, Dale, and Sandy Larsen. *While Creation Waits: A Christian Response to the Environmental Challenge.* Wheaton, IL: Harold Shaw Publishers, 1992.
Linzey, Andrew. *Animal Theology.* Urbana, IL and Chicago: University of Illinois Press, 1994.

Lovelock, James. *The Ages of Gaia: A Biography of Our Living Earth.* New York: Bantam Books, 1988.

Löwith, Karl. *Nature, History and Existentialism.* Edited by Arnold Levison. Evanston, IL: Northwestern University Press, 1966.

Luther, Martin. *The Book of Concord.* Translated and edited by Theodore G. Tappert. Philadelphia: Fortress Press, 1959.

———. *Selections.* Various translators. Edited by John Dillenberger. New York: Anchor, 1961.

Macquarrie, John. "The Idea of a Theology of Nature." *Union Seminary Quarterly Review* 30 (Winter-Summer 1975): 69-75.

Masson, J. Moussaieff. *Dogs Never Lie About Love: Reflections on the Emotional World of Dogs.* New York: Crown Publishers, 1997.

McDaniel, Jay B. *Of God and Pelicans: A Theology of Reverence for Life.* Louisville, KY: Westminster/John Knox Press, 1989.

———. "'Where is the Holy Spirit Anyway?' Response to a Skeptic Environmentalist." *Ecumenical Review* 42 (April 1990): 162-174.

———. *With Roots and Wings: Christianity in an Age of Ecology and Dialogue.* Maryknoll, NY: Orbis Books, 1995.

McFague, Sallie. *Models of God: Theology for an Ecological, Nuclear Age.* Philadelphia: Fortress Press, 1987.

———. "Imaging a Theology of Nature: The World as God's Body." In *Liberating Life: Contemporary Approaches to Ecological Theology,* ed. Charles Birch, William Eakin, and Jay B. McDaniel, 201-227. Maryknoll, NY: Orbis Books, 1990.

———. "A Square in the Quilt: One Theologian's Contribution to the Planetary Agenda." In *Spirit and Nature: Why the Environment is a Religious Issue,* ed. Steven C. Rockefeller and John C. Elder, 39-58. Boston: Beacon Press, 1992.

———. *The Body of God: An Ecological Theology.* Minneapolis: Fortress Press, 1993.

McPherson, James. "Ecumenical Discussion of the Environment, 1966-1987." *Modern Theology* 7 (July 1991): 363-371.

Meland, Bernard E. "New Perspectives on Nature and Grace." In *The Scope of Grace: Essays on Nature and Grace in Honor of Joseph Sittler,* ed. Philip Hefner, 141-161. Philadelphia: Fortress Press, 1964.

———. "Grace: A Dimension within Nature?" *Journal of Religion* 54 (April 1974): 119-137.

Merchant, Carolyn. *The Death of Nature: Women, Ecology, and the Scientific Revolution.* San Francisco: Harper and Row, 1980.

Moltmann, Jürgen. "Creation as an Open System." In *The Future of Creation,* 115-127. Philadelphia: Fortress Press, 1979.

——. *Creating a Just Future: The Politics of Peace and the Ethics of Creation in a Threatened World.* London: SCM Press; Philadelphia: Trinity Press International, 1989.

——. "The Scope of Renewal in the Spirit." *Ecumenical Review* 42 (April 1990): 98-106.

——. *God in Creation: A New Theology of Creation and the Spirit of God.* Translated by Margaret Kohl. San Francisco: HarperSanFrancisco, 1991.

——. *The Spirit of Life: A Universal Affirmation.* Translated by Margaret Kohl. Minneapolis: Fortress Press, 1992.

——. *The Way of Jesus Christ: Christology in Messianic Dimensions.* Translated by Margaret Kohl. Minneapolis: Fortress Press, 1993.

Moore, Robert J. "A New Christian Reformation." In *Ethics of Environment and Development: Global Challenge, International Response,* ed. J. Ronald Engel and Joan Gibb Engel, 104-113. Tucson: University of Arizona Press, 1990.

Murdy, W. H. "Anthropocentrism: A Modern Version." *Science* 187 (March 28, 1975): 1168-1172.

Narayanan, Vasudha. "'One Tree Is Equal to Ten Sons': Hindu Responses to the Problems of Ecology, Population, and Consumption." *Journal of the American Academy of Religion* 65/2 (Summer 1997): 291-332.

Ogden, Schubert M. "Subtler Forms of Bondage and Liberation." In *Faith and Freedom: Toward a Theology of Liberation,* 99-124. Nashville: Abingdon Press, 1979.

Oliver, Harold H. "The Neglect and Recovery of Nature in Twentieth-Century Protestant Thought." *Journal of the American Academy of Religion* 60/3 (Autumn 1992): 379-404.

Pannenberg, Wolfhart. *Toward a Theology of Nature: Essays on Science and Faith.* Edited by Ted Peters. Louisville, KY: Westminster/John Knox Press, 1993.

Peters, Ted F. *Futures–Human and Divine.* Atlanta: John Knox Press, 1978.

Petty, Michael W. *A Faith That Loves the Earth: The Ecological Theology of Karl Rahner.* Lanham, MD: University Press of America, 1996.

Preston, Ronald H. "Humanity, Nature, and the Integrity of Creation." *Ecumenical Review* 41 (October 1989): 552-563.

Primavesi, Anne. *From Apocalypse to Genesis: Ecology, Feminism, and Christianity.* Minneapolis: Fortress Press, 1991.

Ramphal, Shridath. *Our Country, The Planet: Forging a Partnership for Survival.* Washington, DC and Covelo, CA: Island Press, 1992.

Rasmussen, Larry L. "Honoring Creation's Integrity." *Christianity and Crisis* 52 (November 18, 1991): 354-358.

———. "Returning to Our Senses: The Theology of the Cross as a Theology for Eco-Justice." In *After Nature's Revolt: Eco-Justice and Theology,* ed. Dieter T. Hessel, 40-56. Minneapolis: Fortress Press, 1992.

———. "Theology of Life and Ecumenical Ethics." In *Ecotheology: Voices from South and North,* ed. David G. Hallman, 112-129. Geneva: WCC Publications; Maryknoll, NY: Orbis Books, 1994.

Rockefeller, Steven C. "Faith and Community in an Ecological Age." In *Spirit and Nature: Why the Environment is a Religious Issue,* ed. Steven C. Rockefeller and John C. Elder, 139-172. Boston: Beacon Press, 1992.

Rolston, Holmes, III. "Does Nature Need to Be Redeemed?" *Horizons in Biblical Theology* 14/2 (December 1992): 143-172.

Rowthorn, Anne. *Caring for Creation: Toward an Ethic of Responsibility.* Wilton, CT: Morehouse Publishing, 1989.

Ruether, Rosemary Radford. "Mother Earth and the Megamachine: A Theology of Liberation in a Feminine, Somatic, and Ecological Perspective." In *Liberation Theology: Human Hope Confronts Christian History and American Power,* 115-126. New York: Paulist Press, 1972.

———. "The Biblical Vision of the Ecological Crisis." *Christian Century* 95 (November 22, 1978): 1129-1132.

———. *To Change the World: Christology and Cultural Criticism.* New York: Crossroad Publishing Co., 1981.

———. *Sexism and God-Talk: Toward a Feminist Theology.* Boston: Beacon Press, 1983.

———. *Gaia and God: An Ecofeminist Theology of Earth Healing.* San Francisco: HarperSanFrancisco, 1992.

———. "Ecofeminism: Symbolic and Social Connections of the Oppression of Women and the Domination of Nature." In *An Ecology of the Spirit: Religious Reflections and Environmental Conscious-*

ness, ed. Michael H. Barnes, 45-56. Lanham, MD: University Press of America, 1994.

———. "Eco-feminism and Theology." In *Eco-Theology: Voices from South and North,* ed. David G. Hallman, 199-204. Geneva: WCC Publications; Maryknoll, NY: Orbis Books, 1994.

Santmire, H. Paul. "I-Thou, I-It, I-Ens." *The Journal of Religion* 48 (July 1968): 260-280.

———. "A New Theology of Nature?" *Lutheran Quarterly* 20 (August 1968): 290-308.

———. "The Reformation Problematic and the Ecological Crisis." *Metanoia* 2 (June 1970), Special Supplement.

———. *Brother Earth: Nature, God and Ecology in Time of Crisis.* New York: Thomas Nelson, 1970.

———. "Catastrophe and Ecstasy." In *Ecological Renewal,* ed. Paul Lutz and H. Paul Santmire, 75-153. Philadelphia: Fortress Press, 1972.

———. "Historical Dimensions of the American Crisis." In *Western Man and Environmental Ethics: Attitudes Toward Nature and Technology,* ed. Ian Barbour, 66-92. Reading, MA: Addison-Wesley Publishing Co., 1973.

———. "Reflections on the Alleged Ecological Bankruptcy of Western Theology." *Anglican Theological Review* 57 (April 1975): 131-152.

———. "Ecology, Justice, and Theology: Beyond the Preliminary Skirmishes." *Christian Century* 93 (May 12, 1976): 460-464.

———. "Ecology and Ethical Ecumenics." *Anglican Theological Review* 57 (January 1977): 98-102.

———. "The Liberation of Nature: Lynn White's Challenge Anew." *Christian Century* 102 (22 May 1985): 530-533.

———. *The Travail of Nature: The Ambiguous Ecological Promise of Christian Theology.* Minneapolis: Fortress Press, 1985.

———. "Healing the Protestant Mind: Beyond the Theology of Human Dominion." In *After Nature's Revolt: Eco-Justice and Theology,* ed. Dieter T. Hessel, 57-78. Minneapolis: Fortress Press, 1992.

———. "Is Christianity Ecologically Bankrupt? The View from Asylum Hill." In *An Ecology of the Spirit: Religious Reflection and Environmental Consciousness,* ed. Michael H. Barnes, 11-26. Lanham, MD: University Press of America, 1994.

Scharlemann, Robert P. "Models in a Theology of Nature." In *Philosophy of Religion and Theology: 1971,* ed. David Griffin, 150-165. Chambersburg, PA: American Academy of Religion, 1971.

Scheler, Max. *Man's Place in Nature*. Translated by Hans Meyer-hoff. New York: Noonday Press, 1961.

Schweitzer, Albert. *The Teaching of Reverence for Life*. New York: Holt, Rinehart and Winston, 1965.

Shinn, Roger L. *Forced Options: Social Decisions for the Twenty-First Century*. Third edition. Cleveland: Pilgrim Press, 1991.

Sittler, Joseph. *The Ecology of Faith*. Philadelphia: Muhlenberg Press, 1961.

——. "Called to Unity." *Ecumenical Review* 14 (January 1962): 177-87.

——. *The Care of the Earth and Other University Sermons*. Philadelphia: Fortress Press, 1964.

——. "Ecological Commitment as Theological Responsibility." *Zygon* 5 (June 1970): 172-181.

——. "An Aspect of American Religious Experience." In *Proceedings of the Twenty-Sixth Annual Convention of the Catholic Theological Society of America*, vol. 26, 1-17, 1971.

——. "Christian Theology and the Environment". In *Essays on Nature and Grace*, 112-122. Philadelphia: Fortress Press, 1972.

Spretnak, Charlene. *States of Grace: The Recovery of Meaning in the Post-modern Age*. San Francisco: HarperSanFrancisco, 1991.

Stevenson, W. Taylor. "Historical Consciousness and Ecological Crisis: A Theological Perspective." *Anglican Theological Review*, Supplementary Series (November 1976): 99-111.

Stewart, Claude Y., Jr. *Nature in Grace: A Study in the Theology of Nature*. Macon, GA: Mercer University Press, 1983.

——. "Factors Conditioning the Christian Creation Consciousness." In *Cry of the Environment: Rebuilding the Christian Creation Tradition*, ed. Philip N. Joranson and Ken Butigan, 107-131. Santa Fe, NM: Bear and Co., 1984.

Teilhard de Chardin, Pierre. *Hymns of the Universe*. Translated by Gerald Vann. New York: Harper and Row, 1972.

——. *Toward the Future*. Translated by René Hague. New York: Harcourt Brace Jovanovich, 1975.

Thomas, Lewis. *The Lives of a Cell: Notes of a Biology Watcher*. New York: Viking Press, 1974.

Tinker, George E. "The Integrity of Creation: Restoring Trinitarian Balance." *Ecumenical Review* 41 (October 1989): 527-536.

United States Conference of Catholic Bishops. "Renewing the Earth." *Origins, NCS Documentary Service* 21, 27 (December 12, 1991): 425-432.

Wallace, Mark I. *Fragments of the Spirit: Nature, Violence, and the Renewal of Creation.* New York: Continuum, 1996.

Webb, Steven H. *On God and Dogs: A Christian Theology of Compassion for Animals.* Oxford and New York: Oxford University Press, 1998.

West, Charles C. "God–Woman/Man–Creation: Some Comments on the Ethics of the Relationship." *Ecumenical Review* 33 (January 1981): 13-28.

White, Lynn, Jr. "The Historic Roots of the Ecologic Crisis." *Science* 155 (March 10, 1967): 1203-1207.

Whitney, Elspeth. "Lynn White, Ecotheology, and History." *Environmental Ethics* 15 (Summer 1993): 151-169.

Wilkinson, Loren. *Earthkeeping: Christian Stewardship of Natural Resources.* Grand Rapids, MI: William B. Eerdmans Publishing Co., 1980.

———. "Gaia Spirituality: A Christian Critique." *Evangelical Review of Theology* 17 (April 1993): 176-189.

Wilson, Edward O. *Biophilia.* Cambridge, MA: Harvard University Press, 1984.

Yonker, Nicholas. *God, Man, and the Planetary Age: Preface for a Theistic Humanism.* Corvallis, OR: Oregon State University Press, 1978.

General Works

Aquinas, Thomas. *Summa Theologica.* 3 vols. Translated by the Fathers of the English Dominican Province. New York: Benziger Brothers, 1947.

Aristotle. *Metaphysics.* Translated by H. Tredennick. London: Heinemann, 1933, 1935.

Augustine. *On the Grace of Christ, and On Original Sin.* Vol. 5, *Nicene and Post-Nicene Fathers, First Series,* ed. Philip Schaff, 217-256. Peabody, MA: Hendrickson Publishers, 1995.

——. *On Nature and Grace.* Vol. 5, *Nicene and Post-Nicene Fathers, First Series,* ed. Philip Schaff, 121-154. Peabody, MA: Hendrickson Publishers, 1995.

Barbour, Ian G. *Ethics in an Age of Technology.* The Gifford Lectures 1989-1991, Volume 2. New York: Harper Collins, 1993.

——. *Religion and Science: Historical and Contemporary Issues.* San Francisco: HarperSanFrancisco, 1997.

Barrow, John D. and F. J. Tiler. *The Anthropic Cosmological Principle.* New York: Oxford University Press, 1988.

Barth, Karl. *Church Dogmatics.* 4 vols. Translated by Geoffrey W. Bromiley and others. Edinburgh: T and T Clark, 1936-1969.

——. *The Epistle to the Romans.* Sixth edition. Translated by Edwyn C. Hoskins. London: Oxford, 1968.

——. *The Göttingen Dogmatics: Instruction in the Christian Religion: Volume One.* Edited by Hannelotte Reiffen. Translated by Geoffrey W. Bromiley. Grand Rapids, MI: William B. Eerdmans Publishing Co., 1991.

Bergson, Henri. *Creative Evolution.* Translated by Arthur Mitchell. New York: Modern Library, 1944.

Bolman, Frederick deWolfe, Jr. Introduction to *The Ages of the World,* by F. W. J. von Schelling. New York: AMS Press, 1967.

Bonaventure. *The Soul's Journey Into God, The Tree of Life, The Life of St. Francis.* Translated by Ewert Cousins. New York: Paulist Press, 1978.

Bracken, Joseph A. "Panentheism from a Trinitarian Perspective." *Horizons* 22/1 (1995): 7-28.

——. "Response to Elizabeth Johnson's 'Does God Play Dice?'" *Theological Studies* 57/4 (December 1996): 720-730.

——. "Toward a New Philosophical Theology Based on Intersubjectivity." *Theological Studies* 59/4 (December 1998): 703-719.

Brunner, Emil. *Die Mystik und das Wort: Der Gegensatz zwischen moderner Religionsfassung und christlichen Glauben dargestellt an der Theologie Schleiermachers.* Tübingen: Verlag von J. C. B. Mohr, 1924.

Brunner, Emil and Karl Barth. *Natural Theology: Comprising "Nature and Grace" by Emil Brunner and the Reply "No!" by Karl Barth.* Translated by Peter Fraenkel. London: Centenary Press, 1946.

Buber, Martin. *I and Thou.* Second edition. Translated by Ronald G. Smith. New York: Charles Scribner's Sons, 1958.

Bultmann, Rudolf. *Jesus and the Word*. New York: Charles Scribner's Sons, 1934.

Calvin, Jean. *Institutes of the Christian Religion*. Translated by F. L. Battles. Grand Rapids, MI: William B. Eerdmans Publishing Co., 1986.

Carmody, Denise Lardner. *Feminism and Christianity: A Two-Way Reflection*. Lanham, MD: University Press of America, 1982.

Copleston, Frederick C. *A History of Medieval Philosophy*. South Bend, IN and London: University of Notre Dame Press, 1972.

Daly, Mary. *Beyond God the Father: Toward a Philosophy of Women's Liberation*. Boston: Beacon Press, 1985.

Darwin, Charles. *The Descent of Man*. Chicago: Encyclopaedia Britannica, 1952.

Descartes, René. *The Method, Meditations and Selections from the Principles of Descartes*. Twelfth edition. Edited and translated by John Veitch. Edinburgh and London: W. Blackwood, 1899.

Dowey, Edward A., Jr. *The Knowledge of God in Calvin's Theology*. New York: Columbia University Press, 1952.

Drummy, Michael F. "God and Our View of the Universe: An Uneasy Compatibility." *Sciences Religieuses* 25/3 (1996): 253-272.

Esposito, Joseph L. *Schelling's Idealism and Philosophy of Nature*. Lewisburg, PA: Bucknell University Press, 1977.

Fiorenza, Francis Schüssler. "Systematic Theology: Task and Methods." In *Systematic Theology: Roman Catholic Perspectives* 1, ed. Francis Schüssler Fiorenza and John P. Galvin, 1-60. Minneapolis: Fortress Press, 1991.

Ford, Lewis S. *The Lure of God*. Philadelphia: Fortress Press, 1978.

Gay, John H. "Four Medieval Views of Creation." *The Harvard Theological Review* 56 (October 1963): 243-273.

Grant, Robert with David Tracy. *A Short History of the Interpretation of the Bible*. Revised edition. Philadelphia: Fortress Press, 1984.

Griffin, David. *God and Religion in the Postmodern World*. New York: State University of New York Press, 1989.

Harris, Errol E. *Cosmos and Theos: Ethical and Theological Implications of the Anthropic Cosmological Principle*. Atlantic Highlands, NJ: Humanities Press, 1992.

Hartshorne, Charles. *Omnipotence and Other Theological Mistakes*. Albany, NY: State University of New York Press, 1984.

Haught, John F. *Science and Religion: From Conflict to Conversation*. Mahwah, NJ: Paulist Press, 1995.

Hawking, Stephen W. *A Brief of History of Time: From the Big Bang to Black Holes.* New York: Bantam Press, 1988.

Hegel, G. W. F. *Phenomenology of Spirit.* Translated by A. V. Miller. Oxford: Clarendon Press, 1977.

——. *Philosophy of Nature.* Translated by A. V. Miller. Oxford: Clarendon Press, 1970.

Heidegger, Martin. *Basic Writings.* Edited by David Farrell Krell. New York: New York: Harper and Row, 1977.

——. *Being and Time.* Translated by John Macquarrie and Edward Robinson. New York: Harper and Row, 1962.

Heim, Karl. *Christian Faith and Natural Science.* London: SCM Press, 1953.

——. *The Transformation of the Scientific World View.* New York: Harper and Brothers, 1953.

Hook, Sidney. *The Quest for Being.* New York: St. Martin's Press, 1961.

Hopkins, Gerard Manley. *A Hopkins Reader.* Edited by John Pick. Garden City, NY: Doubleday, 1966.

Irenaeus. *Against Heresies.* Vol. 1, *Ante-Nicene Fathers,* ed. Alexander Roberts and James Donaldson, 315-567. Peabody, MA: Hendrickson Publishers, 1995.

Johnson, Elizabeth A. "Does God Play Dice? Divine Providence and Chance." *Theological Studies* 57 (March 1996): 3-18.

Kant, Immanuel. *Critique of Judgment.* Translated by Werner S. Pluhar. Indianapolis, IN: Hackett Publishing Co., 1987.

——. *Critique of Pure Reason.* Translated by J. M. D. Meiklejohn. London and Toronto: J. M. Dent and Sons, 1934.

Kenny, W. Henry. *A Path through Teilhard's* Phenomenon. Dayton, OH: Pflaum Press, 1970.

Kierkegaard, Søren. *Fear and Trembling* and *The Sickness Unto Death.* Translated by Walter Lowrie. Princeton, NJ: Princeton University Press, 1941, 1954.

——. *Concluding Unscientific Postscript.* Translated by David F. Swenson and Walter Lowrie. Princeton, NJ: Princeton University Press, 1941.

Kuhn, Thomas S. *The Structure of Scientific Revolutions.* Second edition. Chicago: University of Chicago Press, 1970.

Livingston, James C. *Anatomy of the Sacred: An Introduction to Religion.* Second edition. New York: Macmillan, 1993.

Lovejoy, Arthur O. *The Great Chain of Being: A Study of the History of an Idea.* Fifth edition. Cambridge: Harvard University Press, 1953.

Lowe, Walter. *Theology and Difference: The Wound of Reason.* Bloomington, IN and Indianapolis: Indiana University Press, 1993.

Niesel, Wilhelm. *The Theology of Calvin.* Translated by Harold Knight. Philadelphia: Westminster Press, 1956.

Nietzsche, Friedrich. *The Will to Power.* Translated by Walter Kaufmann and R. J. Hollingdale. Edited by Walter Kaufmann. New York: Random House, 1967.

Nygren, Anders. *Agape and Eros.* Philadelphia: Westminster Press, 1953.

Otto, Rudolf. *The Idea of the Holy.* Translated by J. Harvey. London: Penguin Books, 1959.

Peacocke, Arthur. *Theology for a Scientific Age: Being and Becoming – Natural, Divine, and Human.* Minneapolis: Fortress Press, 1993.

Rolston, Holmes, III. *Science and Religion: A Critical Survey.* New York: Random House, 1987.

——. *Genes, Genesis and God: Values and Their Origins in Natural and Human History.* New York and Cambridge: Cambridge University Press, 1999.

Schleiermacher, Friedrich. *The Christian Faith.* Second edition. Translated by D. M. Baillie and others. Edinburgh: T and T Clark, 1956.

——. *On Religion: Speeches to Its Cultured Despisers.* Translated by Richard Crouter. Cambridge and New York: Cambridge University Press, 1988.

Shelley, Percy Bysshe. "Love's Philosophy." In *A Reasonable Affliction: 1001 Love Poems to Read to Each Other,* ed. Sally Ann Berk and James Gordon Wakeman, 314. New York: Black Dog and Leventhal Publishers, 1996.

Stern, Robert. Introduction to *Ideas for a Philosophy of Nature as Introduction to the Study of This Science,* by F. W. J. von Schelling. Cambridge: Cambridge University Press, 1988.

Taylor, Mark C. *Erring: A Postmodern A/Theology.* Chicago: University of Chicago Press, 1984.

Teilhard de Chardin, Pierre. *The Phenomenon of Man.* Revised edition. Translated by Bernard Wall. London: Collins, 1965.

———. *Christianity and Evolution.* Translated by René Hague. New York: Harcourt Brace Jovanovich, 1971.

Tracy, David. *Blessed Rage for Order: The New Pluralism in Theology.* New York: Seabury, 1975.

Van Buren, Paul. "The Dissolution of the Absolute." *Religion in Life* (Summer 1965): 334-342.

Von Harnack, Adolf. *What is Christianity?* Translated by Thomas Bailey Saunders. Philadelphia: Fortress Press, 1986.

Von Schelling, F. W. J. *Sämmtliche Werke.* 14 vols. Edited by K. F. A. Schelling. Stuttgart and Augsburg: J. G. Cotta, 1856-1861.

———. *The Ages of the World.* Translated by Frederick deWolf Bolman, Jr. New York: AMS Press, Inc., 1967.

———. *Ideas for a Philosophy of Nature as Introduction to the Study of This Science.* Translated by Errol E. Harris and Peter Heath. Cambridge: Cambridge University Press, 1988.

———. *The Night Watches of Bonaventura.* Translated by Gerald Gillespie. Austin, TX: University of Texas Press, 1971.

———. *The Unconditional in Human Knowledge: Four Early Essays (1794-1796).* Translated by Fritz Marti. Lewisburg, PA: Bucknell University Press, 1980.

Weber, Max. *The Protestant Ethic and the Spirit of Capitalism.* Translated by Talcott Parsons. New York: Charles Scribner's Sons, 1930.

Webb, Steven H. *The Gifting God: A Trinitarian Ethics of Excess.* Oxford: Oxford University Press, 1996.

Wennemyr, Susan E. "Dancing in the Dark." *Journal of the American Academy of Religion* 66/3 (Fall 1998): 571-587.

Westerman, Claus. *The Genesis Accounts of Creation.* Translated by Norman E. Wagner. Philadelphia: Fortress Press, 1964.

———. *Creation.* Translated by John J. Scullion. Philadelphia: Fortress Press, 1974.

Whitehead, Alfred North. *Process and Reality.* Toronto: Collier Macmillan, 1969.

Zahrnt, Heinz. *The Question of God: Protestant Theology in the Twentieth Century.* Translated by R. A. Wilson. New York: Harcourt Brace Jovanovich, 1969.

Index

Absolute, 34, 61, 115; dialectic of, 35

Absolute Spirit, 115

agape (see also caritas, eros, libido, and philia), 132-135, 143

analogia entis, 62

anthropocentric dynamics of grace, 3, 26, 41, 48

anthropocentrism, 15, 63, 118-119

Apocalypse, 98

Aquinas, Thomas, 133

Aristotle, 61

Augustine of Hippo, 13-14, 19, 21, 24-26, 40, 61, 84, 115, 139; nature, 4; nature and grace, 14; ambiguity of, 48; Protestant theological tradition, 14; thought, 13, 59

autonomous reason, 27

autonomy: natural law, 26

Barth, Karl, 42, 46-48, 110-112, 115; confessionalism, 3; dualism in religion, 47-48; supernaturalism, 46

Bergson, Henri, 41, 43

Bible, 91, 109, 120-121

body of Christ, 17; omnipresence of, 17

Böhme, Jakob, 36, 94

136, 141, 143; and creation,
119; as Absolute Spirit, 119;
as Divine Life, 99; as judge,
16; as spirit and nature, 39;
as ultimate mystery, 99; as
Unconditioned, 119;
doctrine of, 14, 16, 45;
being all in all, 97; fear of,
20; glory of, 21-22, 113;
Ground of Being, 93; living,
93; love for historical man,
88; love of universe, 88;
manifestation of, 39; nature,
30; omnipresence of, 16;
redemptive act of, 90;
relation to life, 99;
revelation through nature,
47; the Fall, 21; saving
power of, 98; suffering, 132;
traditional doctrine of, 95
God and the world, 28, 31-32,
47, 99
God-human relationship, 42,
117, 121
God-non-human relationship,
121
Godself, 46, 99
God-world relationship, 7, 16,
22, 35, 43, 100, 108, 119
Gospel of John, 142
grace and nature: Augustine
ambiguity, 48;
Schleiermacher, 33
grace, 72; anthropocentric
dynamics of, 3, 33, 40, 41,
43, 48; as manifestation of
healing power, 109;
communion with God, 40;
doctrine of, 94; kairotic
moments, 133; Luther,
Martin, 15; influence on the

human person, 16; roots of
modern secularism, 15;
power of; Augustine, 14;
Protestant anthropocentric
dynamics of, 26; Roman
Catholic position, 94;
Spiritual Community, 133
Hegel, G.W.F., 34, 35, 41, 43,
61, 115, 119; history set
against nature, 42
Hermann, Wilhelm, 109
Hirsch, Emanuel, 48
Holy Spirit: presence of, 14
human culture, 34
human life: *Gestalt* notion of,
78
human-as-nature: Calvinist,
110
humanity, 7, 16, 35, 41, 44, 46,
62, 72, 76, 82-84, 86-87,
90-92, 95, 98, 108, 110-114,
120-121, 132, 136-137,
140-141, 143
humanity of Christ, 16
I-Ens, 134-135
I-It, 134
imago Dei, 46
Incarnation, 87-89
indirect immediacy, 18
integrity of nature, 39
I-Thou, 134
Jesus (*See Also* Christ), 47, 87,
89-90, 93, 111; as bearer of
the New Being, 87;
ontological solidarity, 89;
quest for historical; Rudolph
Bultmann, 46; saving power
of, 90; the Christ; bearer of
New Being, 87
Judeo-Christian theological
tradition, 5, 99